10th International Workshop on Finite State Methods and Natural Language Processing

(FSMNLP 2012)

Donostia, Spain
23-25 July 2012

ISBN: 978-1-62748-362-9

Printed from e-media with permission by:

Curran Associates, Inc.
57 Morehouse Lane
Red Hook, NY 12571

Some format issues inherent in the e-media version may also appear in this print version.

Printed by Curran Associates, Inc. (2013)

For permission requests, please contact the Association for Computational Linguistics
at the address below.

Association for Computational Linguistics
209 N. Eighth Street
Stroudsburg, Pennsylvania 18360

Phone: 1-570-476-8006
Fax: 1-570-476-0860

acl@aclweb.org

Additional copies of this publication are available from:

Curran Associates, Inc.
57 Morehouse Lane
Red Hook, NY 12571 USA
Phone: 845-758-0400
Fax: 845-758-2634
Email: curran@proceedings.com
Web: www.proceedings.com

Preface

These proceedings contain the papers presented at the 10th International Workshop on Finite State Methods and Natural Language Processing (FSMNLP 2012), held in Donostia-San Sebastián (Basque Country), July 23–25, 2012.

The workshop covers a wide range of topics from morphology to formal language theory. A special theme was chosen for FSMNLP 2012: "practical issues in finite-state technology," including:

- Practical implementations of linguistic descriptions with finite-state technology
- Software tools and utilities for finite-state NLP
- Finite-state models of linguistic theories
- Applications of finite-state-based NLP in closely related fields

This volume contains the 7 long and 12 short papers presented at the workshop. In total, 31 papers (13 long and 18 short papers) were submitted and double-blind refereed. Each paper was reviewed by 3 program committee members. The overall acceptance rate was 61 per cent.

The program committee was composed of internationally leading researchers and practitioners selected from academia, research labs, and companies.

The organizing committee would like to thank the program committee for their hard work, the referees for their valuable feedback, the invited speaker and the presenters of tutorials for their contributions and the local organizers for their tireless efforts. We are particularly indebted to the University of the Basque Country (UPV/EHU) and the Basque Government (Eusko Jaurlaritza) for significant financial support and to the Cursos de Verano/Uda Ikastaroak and the IXA research group for their support in organizing the event.

IÑAKI ALEGRIA
MANS HULDEN

Local Organizing Committee:

Iñaki Alegria (University of the Basque Country)
Koldo Gojenola (University of the Basque Country)
Izaskun Etxeberria (University of the Basque Country)
Nerea Ezeiza (University of the Basque Country)
Mans Hulden (University of the Basque Country / Ikerbasque, Basque Foundation for Science)
Amaia Lorenzo (University of the Basque Country)
Esther Miranda (University of the Basque Country)
Maite Oronoz (University of the Basque Country)

Invited Speaker:

Kimmo Koskenniemi (University of Helsinki)

Tutorials by:

Tommi Pirinen (University of Helsinki)
Iñaki Alegria (University of the Basque Country)
Mans Hulden (University of the Basque Country / Ikerbasque, Basque Foundation for Science)
Miikka Silfverberg (University of Helsinki)
Josef Novak (University of Tokyo)

Sponsors:

eman ta zabal zazu
Universidad del País Vasco Euskal Herriko Unibertsitatea

UPV / EHU

EUSKO JAURLARITZA
GOBIERNO VASCO

ixa
IXA Taldea
Euskal Herriko Unibertsitatea
Universidad del País Vasco

Program Committee:

Kenneth R. Beesley (SAP Business Objects, USA)
Francisco Casacuberta (Instituto Tecnológico De Informática, Spain)
Jan Daciuk (Gdańsk University of Technology, Poland)
Frank Drewes (Umea University, Sweden)
Dale Gerdemann (University of Tuebingen, Germany)
Mike Hammond (University of Arizona, USA)
Thomas Hanneforth (University of Potsdam, Germany)
Colin de la Higuera (University of Nantes, France)
Jan Holub (Czech Technical University in Prague, Czech Republic)
Mans Hulden (Ikerbasque, Basque Country)
André Kempe (CADEGE Technologies & Consulting, France)
Andras Kornai (Eotvos Lorand University, Hungary)
Andreas Maletti (University of Stuttgart, Germany)
Mark-Jan Nederhof (University of St Andrews, Scotland)
Kemal Oflazer (Carnegie Mellon University, Qatar)
Maite Oronoz (University of the Basque Country)
Laurette Pretorius (University of South Africa, South Africa)
Strahil Ristov (Ruder Boskovic Institute, Croatia)
Frederique Segond Frederique (ObjectDirect, France)
Max Silberztein (Université de Franche-Comte, France)
Richard Sproat (University of Illinois at Urbana-Champaign, USA)
Trond Trosterud (University of Tromsø, Norway)
Shuly Wintner (University of Haifa, Israel)
Anssi Yli-Jyra (University of Helsinki, Finland)
Menno van Zaanen (Tilburg University, Netherlands)
Lynette van Zijl (Stellenbosch University, South Africa)

Additional Reviewers:

Alicia Pérez (University of the Basque Country)
Suna Bensch (Umeå University, Sweden)
Emad Mohamed (Carnegie Mellon University, Qatar)
Johanna Björklund (Umeå University, Sweden)

Table of Contents

Conference Program

Monday, July 23rd, 2012

15:00–18:00 TUTORIALS

15:00–16:00 Tommi Pirinen and Mans Hulden: Spelling and Grammar Correction with FSTs

16:00–17:00 Miikka Silfverberg: Probabilistic Parsing with Weighted FSTs

17:00–18:00 Josef Novak: Grapheme-to-Phoneme Training and Conversion with Weighted FSTs

Tuesday, July 24th, 2012

9:00 Opening

9:30–10:30 Invited Speaker: Kimmo Koskenniemi: The Simplicity of Two-Level Morphology

10:30–11:00 Coffee Break

11:00–12:00 LONG PAPERS I

Effect of Language and Error Models on Efficiency of Finite-State Spell-Checking and Correction
Tommi A. Pirinen and Sam Hardwick

Practical Finite State Optimality Theory
Dale Gerdemann and Mans Hulden

12:00–13:00 SHORT PAPERS I

Handling Unknown Words in Arabic FST Morphology
Khaled Shaalan and Mohammed Attia

Urdu – Roman Transliteration via Finite State Transducers
Tina Bögel

Integrating Aspectually Relevant Properties of Verbs into a Morphological Analyzer for English
Katina Bontcheva

Finite-State Technology in a Verse-Making Tool
Manex Agirrezabal, Iñaki Alegria, Bertol Arrieta and Mans Hulden

13:00–14:30 Lunch

Tuesday, July 24th, 2012 (continued)

14:30–15:30 SHORT PAPERS II

DAGGER: A Toolkit for Automata on Directed Acyclic Graphs
Daniel Quernheim and Kevin Knight

WFST-based Grapheme-to-Phoneme conversion: Open Source Tools for Alignment, Model-Building and Decoding
Josef R. Novak, Nobuaki Minematsu and Keikichi Hirose

Kleene, a Free and Open-Source Language for Finite-State Programming
Kenneth R. Beesley

Implementation of Replace Rules Using Preference Operator
Senka Drobac, Miikka Silfverberg and Anssi Yli-Jyrä

15:30–16:30 SHORT PAPERS III

First Approaches on Spanish Medical Record Classification Using Diagnostic Term to Class Transduction
A. Casillas, A. Díaz de Ilarraza, K. Gojenola, M. Oronoz and A. Pérez

Developing an Open-Source FST Grammar for Verb Chain Transfer in a Spanish-Basque MT System
Aingeru Mayor, Mans Hulden and Gorka Labaka

Conversion of Procedural Morphologies to Finite-State Morphologies: A Case Study of Arabic
Mans Hulden and Younes Samih

A Methodology for Obtaining Concept Graphs from Word Graphs
Marcos Calvo, Jon Ander Gómez, Lluís-F. Hurtado and Emilio Sanchis

16:30–18:00 POSTERS AND COFFEE

20:30 Dinner in the Old Town

Tuesday, July 25th, 2012

9:30–11:00 LONG PAPERS II

11:30–12:30 LONG PAPERS III

12:30–13:30 Business Meeting

Effect of Language and Error Models on Efficiency of Finite-State Spell-Checking and Correction

Tommi A Pirinen
University of Helsinki
Department of Modern Languages
FI-00014 Univ. of Helsinki, PO box 24
tommi.pirinen@helsinki.fi

Sam Hardwick
University of Helsinki
Department of Modern Languages
FI-00014 Univ. of Helsinki, PO box 24
sam.hardwick@helsinki.fi

Abstract

We inspect the viability of finite-state spell-checking and contextless correction of non-word errors in three languages with a large degree of morphological variety. Overviewing previous work, we conduct large-scale tests involving three languages — English, Finnish and Greenlandic — and a variety of error models and algorithms, including proposed improvements of our own. Special reference is made to on-line three-way composition of the input, the error model and the language model. Tests are run on real-world text acquired from freely available sources. We show that the finite-state approaches discussed are sufficiently fast for high-quality correction, even for Greenlandic which, due to its morphological complexity, is a difficult task for non-finite-state approaches.

1 Introduction

In most implementations of spell-checking, efficiency is a limiting factor for selecting or discarding spell-checking solutions. In the case of finite-state spell-checking it is known that finite-state language models can efficiently encode dictionaries of natural languages (Beesley and Karttunen, 2003), even for polysynthetic languages. Most contemporary spell-checking and correction systems are still based on programmatic solutions (e.g. hunspell[1], and its *spell relatives), or at most specialised algorithms for implementing error-tolerant traversal of the finite-state dictionaries (Oflazer, 1996; Huldén, 2009a). There have also been few fully finite-state implementations that both detect and correct errors (Schulz and Mihov, 2002; Pirinen and Lindén, 2010). In this paper we further evaluate the use of finite-state dictionaries with two-tape finite-state automatons as a mechanism for correcting misspellings, and optimisations to the finite-state error models, intending to demonstrate that purely finite-state algorithms can be made sufficiently efficient.

To evaluate the general usability and efficiency of finite-state spell-checking we test a number of possible implementations of such a system with three languages of typologically different morphological features[2] and *reference implementations for contemporary spell-checking applications*: English as a morphologically more isolating language with essentially a word-list approach to spell-checking; Finnish, whose computational complexity has been just beyond the edge of being too hard to implement nicely in eg. hunspell (Pitkänen, 2006); and Greenlandic, a polysynthetic language which is implemented as a finite-state system using Xerox's original finite-state morphology formalism (Beesley and Karttunen, 2003). As a general purpose finite-state library we use HFST[3], which also contains our spell-

[1] http://hunspell.sf.net

[2] We will not go into details regarding the morphological features of these languages. We thank the anonymous reviewer for guiding us to make a rough comparison using a piece of translated text. We observe from the translations of the *Universal Declaration of Human Rights* (with pre-amble included) as follows: the number of word-like tokens for English is 1,746, for Finnish 1,275 and for Greenlandic 1,063. The count of the 15 most frequent tokens are for English 120—28, for Finnish 85—10 and for Greenlandic 38—7.

The average word length is 5.0 characters for English, 7.8 for Finnish and 14.9 for Greenlandic. For the complexity of computational models refer to Table 2 in this article.

[3] http://hfst.sf.net

Proceedings of the 10th International Workshop on Finite State Methods and Natural Language Processing, pages 1–9,
Donostia–San Sebastián, July 23–25, 2012.

checking code.

As neither Finnish nor Greenlandic have been successfully implemented in the hunspell formalism, we mainly use them to evaluate how the complexity of a language model affects the efficiency of finite-state spell-checking. For a full-scale survey on the state-of-the-art non-finite-state spell-checking, refer to Mitton (2009).

The efficiency results are contrasted with the existing research on finite-state spell-checking in Hassan et al. (2008) and the theoretical results on finite-state error-models in Mitankin (2005). Our contribution primarily comprises the addition of morphologically complex languages with actual cyclic dictionary automata (i.e. infinite dictionaries formed by compounding and recurring derivation) and more complex structure in general, compared to those of English and Arabic. Our goal is to demonstrate that finite-state spelling is tractable for these complex languages, to document their implications for performance and to present an algorithm for the task. We also point out that previous approaches have neglected to simultaneously constrain the error model and the dictionary with each other in on-line composition, which affords a significant speed benefit compared to generating the two component compositions.

The rest of the paper is organised as follows. In Section 2 we discuss the spell-checking task, current non-finite-state spell-checkers and previously used finite-state methods for spell-checking and correction and propose some possible speed optimisations for the error models. We also investigate algorithmic limitations of finite-state approaches and ways to remedy them. In Section 3 we present the language models, error models and the testing corpora. In Section 4 we present the comparisons of speed and quality with combinations of different language and error models and corpora for spell-checking. In Section 5 we summarise our findings and results, and outline future goals.

2 Methods

A finite-state spell-checker is typically (Pirinen and Lindén, 2010) composed of at least two finite-state automata; one for the dictionary of the language, or the *language model*, which contains valid strings of the language, and one automaton to map misspelt words into correct strings, or the *error model*. Both the language model and the error model are usually (Pirinen and Lindén, 2010) weighted finite-state automata, where the weights represent the probabilities are of a word being correctly spelled in the language model and of specific misspellings, respectively. We evaluate here the effect of both the language and error model automatons' structure and complexity on the efficiency of the finite-state spelling task.[4]

2.1 Language Models

The most basic language model for a spell-checking dictionary is a list of correctly spelled word forms. One of the easiest ways of creating such a spell-checker is to collect the word forms from a reasonably large corpus of (mostly) correctly spelt texts. Additionally we can count the frequency of words and use that as the likelihood, $P(w) = \frac{c(w)}{\sum_{w \in \mathcal{D}} c(w)}$ where $c(w)$ is the count of the word w and $\mathcal{D}$ is the set of corpus word forms. For morphologically more isolating languages such as English, this is often a sufficient approach (Norvig, 2010), and we use it to create a dictionary for our English spell-checker as well. As a non-finite-state reference point we use hunspell.

For agglutinative languages like Finnish, for which the word-list approach is likely to miss a much greater number of words, one of the most common approaches is to use right-linear grammars, possibly combined with finite-state rule languages to implement morphophonological alterations (Koskenniemi, 1983). This approach also applies to the newest available free / open source and full-fledged finite-state Finnish morphological dictionary we found (Pirinen, 2011). This language model features productive derivations, compounding and rudimentary probabilistic models. We take, as a reference non-finite state language model for Finnish, Voikko's implementation in Malaga, which is currently used as a spell-checking component in open source software. It is implemented in a

[4] The methods introduced in this research as well as all materials are free/libre open source. Please see our svn repository `https://hfst.svn.sf.net/svnroot/trunk/fsmnlp-2012-spellers/` for detailed implementation and scripts to reproduce all the results.

left-associative grammar formalism, which is a potentially less efficient system with more expressive power. It's similar to finite-state formulations in terms of linguistic coverage.

For polysynthetic languages it will be obvious that the coverage of any word-list-based approach will be even lower. Furthermore, most simple extensions to it such as affix stripping (as in hunspell) are not adequate for describing word forms. To our knowledge, the only approaches that have been widely used for spell-checking and morphological analysis of Greenlandic have been based on traditional finite-state solutions, such as the Xerox formalisms. In our case we have obtained a freely available finite-state morphology implementation from the Internet[5]. For further details we refer to the authors' website `http://oqaaserpassualeriffik.org/`.

2.2 Error Models

The ubiquitous formula for modeling typing errors since computer-assisted spelling correction began has been the edit distance metric sometimes attributed to Levenshtein (1966) and/or Damerau (1964). It maps four typical slips of the fingers on a keyboard to events in the fuzzy matching of misspelt word forms to correct ones, that is, the deletion of a character (i.e. failing to press a key), addition of a character (i.e. hitting an extra key accidentally), changing a character (i.e. hitting the wrong key) and transposing adjacent characters (i.e. hitting two keys in the wrong order).

When modeling edit distance as a finite-state automaton, a relatively simple two-tape automaton is sufficient to implement the algorithm (Hassan et al., 2008). The automaton will consist of one arc for each type of error, and additionally one state for each transposition pair. This means that the trivial nondetermistic finite-state automaton implementing the algorithm is of space complexity $S(V, E, \Sigma) = O(|\Sigma|^2|V| + |\Sigma|^2|E|)$, where Σ is the alphabet of language, V is the set vertices in automaton and E is the set of edges in automaton. This edit distance formulation is roughly feature equivalent to hunspell's `TRY` mechanism.

[5] `https://victorio.uit.no/langtech/trunk/st/kal`

To further fine-tune this finite-state formulation of the edit distance algorithm, it is possible to attach a probability to each of the error events as a weight in a weighted finite-state automaton, corresponding to the likelihood of an error, or a confusion factor. This can be used to implement features like keyboard adjacency or an OCR confusion factor to the error correction model. This will not modify the structure of the finite-state error models or the search space—which is why we did not test their effects in this article—, but introduction of non-homogenous weights to the resulting finite-state network may have an effect on search time. This addition is equivalent to hunspell's `KEY` mechanism.

For English language spelling correction there is also an additional type of error model to deal with competence-related misspellings—as opposed to models that mainly deal with mistypings—implemented in the form of phonemic folding and unfolding. This type of error is very specific to certain types of English text and is not in the scope of this experiment. This is the `PHON` part of the hunspell's correction mechanism.

After fine-tuning the error models to reimplement hunspell's feature set, we propose variations of this edit distance scheme to optimise the speed of error correction with little or no negative effect to the quality of the correction suggestions. The time requirement of the algorithm is determined by the size of the search space, i.e. the complexity of the resulting network when the error model is applied to the misspelt string and intersected with the dictionary[6].

To optimise the application of edit distance by limiting the search space, many traditional spell checkers will not attempt to correct the very first letter of the word form. We investigated whether this decision is a particularly effective way to limit the search space, but it does not appear to significantly differ from restricting edits at any other position in the input.

Dividing the states of a dictionary automaton into

[6] For non-finite-state solutions, the search space is simply the number of possible strings given the error corrections made in the algorithm. For finite-state systems the amount of generated strings with cyclic language and error models is infinite, so complexity calculation are theoretically slightly more complex, however for basic edit distance implementations used in this article the search space complexities are always the same and the amount of suggestions generated finite

classes corresponding to the minimum number of input symbols consumed by that state, we found that the average ambiguity in a particular class is somewhat higher for the first input symbols, but then stabilises quickly at a lower level. This was accomplished by performing the following state-categorisation procedure:

1. The start state is assigned to class 0, and all other states are assigned to a candidate pool.
2. All states to which there is an (input) epsilon transition from the start state are assigned to class 0 and removed from the candidate pool.
3. This is repeated for each state in class 0 until no more states are added to class 0. This completes class 0 as the set of states in which the automaton can be before consuming any input.
4. For each state in class 0, states in the candidate pool to which there is a non-epsilon transition are assigned to class 1 and removed from the candidate pool.
5. Class 1 is epsilon-completed as in (2-3).
6. After the completion of class n, class $n + 1$ is constructed. This continues until the candidate pool is empty, which will happen as long as there are no unreachable states.

With this categorisation, we tallied the total number of arcs from states in each class and divided the total by the number of states in the class. This is intended as an approximate measure of the ambiguity present at a particular point in the input. Some results are summarized in Table 1.

Class	Transitions	States	Average
0	156	3	52
1	1,015	109	9.3
2	6,439	1,029	6.3
3	22,436	5,780	3.9
4	38,899	12,785	3.0
5	44,973	15,481	2.9
6	47,808	17,014	2.8
7	47,495	18,866	2.5
8	39,835	17,000	2.3
9	36,786	14,304	2.6
10	45,092	14,633	3.1
11	66,598	22,007	3.0
12	86,206	30,017	2.9

Table 1: State classification by minimum input consumed for the Finnish dictionary

Further, the size of a dictionary automaton that is restricted to have a particular symbol in a particular position does not apparently depend on the choice of position. This result was acquired by intersecting eg. the automaton `e.+` with the dictionary to restrict the first position to have the symbol `e`, the automaton `.e.+` to restrict the second position, and so on. The transducers acquired by this intersection vary in size of the language, number of states and number of transitions, but without any trend depending on the position of the restriction. This is in line with the rather obvious finding that the size of the restricted dictionary in terms of number of strings is similarily position-agnostic.

Presumably, the rationale is a belief that errors predominately occur at other positions in the input. As far as we know, the complete justification for this belief remains to be made with a high-quality, hand-checked error corpus.

On the error model side this optimisation has been justified by findings where between 1.5 % and 15 % of spelling errors happen in the first character of the word, depending on the text type (Bhagat, 2007); the 1.5 % from a small corpus of academic texts (Yannakoudakis and Fawthrop, 1983) and 15 % from dictated corpora (Kukich, 1992). We also performed a rudimentary classification of the errors in the small error corpus of 333 entries from Pirinen et al. (2012), and found errors at the first position in 1.2 % of the entries. Furthermore, we noticed that when evenly splitting the word forms in three parts, 15 % of the errors are in the first third of the word form, while second has 47 % and third 38 %, which would be in favor of discarding initial errors[7].

A second form of optimisation that is used by many traditional spell-checking systems is to apply a lower order edit distance separately before trying higher order ones. This is based on the assumption that the vast majority of spelling errors will be of lower order. In the original account of edit distance for spell-checking, 80 % of the spelling errors were found to be correctable with distance 1 (Pollock and Zamora, 1984).

The third form of optimisation that we test is omitting redundant corrections in error models of higher order than one. Without such an optimisa-

[7]By crude classification we mean that all errors were forced to one of the three classes at weight of one, e.g. a series of three consecutive instances of the same letters was counted as deletion at the first position.

tion, higher order error models will permit adding and deleting the same character in succession at any position, which is obviously futile work for error correction. Performing the optimisation makes the error model larger but reduces the search space, and does not affect the quality of results.

2.3 Algorithms

The obvious baseline algorithm for the task of finding which strings can be altered by the error model in such a way that the alteration is present in the language model is generating all the possible alterations and checking which ones are present in the language model. This was done in Hassan et al. (2008) by first calculating the composition of the input string with the error model and then composing the result with the language model.

If we simplify the error model to one in which only substitutions occur, it can already be seen that this method is quite sensitive to input length and alphabet size. The composition explores each combination of edit sites in the input string. If any number of edits up to d can be made at positions in an input string of length n, there are

$$\sum_{i=1}^{d} \binom{n}{i}$$

ways to choose the edit site, and each site is subject to a choice of $|\Sigma|-1$ edits (the entire alphabet except for the actual input). This expression has no closed form, but as d grows to n, the number of choices has the form 2^n, so the altogether complexity is exponential in input length and linear in alphabet size (quadratic if transpositions are considered).

In practice (when d is small relative to n) it is useful to observe that an increase of 1 in distance results in an additional term to the aforementioned sum, the ratio of which to the previously greatest term is

$$\frac{n!/(d! \cdot (n-d!))}{n!/((d-1)! \cdot (n-d+1)!)} = \frac{n-d+1}{d}$$

indicating that when d is small, increases in it produce an exponential increase in complexity. For an English 26-letter lowercase alphabet, edit distance 2 and the 8-letter word "spelling", 700 strings are stored in a transducer. With transpositions, deletions, insertions and edit weights this grows to $100,215$ different outputs. We have implemented this algorithm for our results by generating the edited strings by lookup, and performing another lookup with the language model on these strings.

Plainly, it would be desirable to improve on this. The intuition behind our improvement is that when editing an input string, say "spellling", it is a wasted effort to explore the remainder after generating a prefix that is not present in the lexicon. For example, after changing the first character to "z" and not editing the second characted, we have the prefix "zp-", which does not occur in our English lexicon. So the remaining possibilities - performing any edits on the remaining 7-character word - can be ignored.

This is accomplished with a three-way composition in which the input, the error model and the language model simultaneously constrain each other to produce the legal correction set. This algorithm is presented in some detail in Lindén et al. (2012). A more advanced and general algorithm is due to Allauzen and Mohri (2009).

3 Material

For language models we have acquired suitable free-to-use dictionaries, readily obtainable on the Internet.

We made our own implementations of the algorithms to create and modify finite-state error models. Our source repository contains a Python script for generating error models and an extensive `Makefile` for exercising it in various permutations.

To test the effect of correctness of the source text to the speed of the spell-checker we have retrieved one of largest freely available open source text materials from the Internet, i.e. Wikipedia. The Wikipedia text is an appropriate real-world material as it is a large body of text authored by many individuals, and may be expected to contain a wide variety of spelling errors. For material with more errors, we have used a simple script to introduce (further, arbitrary) errors at a uniform probability of 1/33 per character; using this method we can also obtain a corpus of errors with correct corrections along them. Finally we have used a text corpus from a language different than the one being spelled to ensure that the majority of words are not in the vocabulary and (almost always) not correctable by standard error models.

The Wikipedia corpora were sourced from `wikimedia.org`. For exact references, see our previously mentioned repository. From the dumps we extracted the contents of the articles and picked the first 100,000 word tokens for evaluation.

In Table 2 we summarize the sizes of automata in terms of structural elements. On the first row, we give the size of the alphabet needed to represent the entire dictionary. Next we give the sizes of automata as nodes and arcs of the finite-state automaton encoding the dictionary. Finally we give the size of the automaton as serialised on the hard disk. While this is not the same amount of memory as its loaded data structures, it gives some indication of memory usage of the program while running the automaton in question. As can be clearly seen from the table, the morphologically less isolating languages do fairly consistently have larger automata in every sense.

Automaton	En	Fi	Kl
Σ set size	43	117	133
Dictionary FSM nodes	49,778	286,719	628,177
Dictionary FSM arcs	86,523	783,461	11,596,911
Dictionary FSM on disk	2.3 MiB	43 MiB	290 MiB

Table 2: The sizes of dictionaries as automata

In Table 3 we give the same figures for the sizes of error models we've generated. The Σ size row here shows the number of symbols left when we have removed the symbols that are usually not considered to be a part of a spell-checking mechanism, such as all punctuation that does not occur word-internally and white-space characters[8]. Note that sizes of error models can be directly computed from their parameters; i.e., the distance, the Σ set size and the optimisation, so this table is provided for reference only.

4 Evaluation

We ran various combinations of language and error models on the corpora described in section 3. We give tabular results of the speed of the system and the effect of the error model on recall. The latter

Automaton	En	Fi	Kl
Σ set size	28	60	64
Edit distance 1 nodes	652	3,308	3,784
Edit distance 1 arcs	2,081	10,209	11,657
Edit distance 2 nodes	1,303	6,615	7,567
Edit distance 2 arcs	4136	20,360	23,252
No firsts ed 1 nodes	652	3,308	3,784
No firsts ed 1 arcs	2,107	10,267	11,719
No firsts ed 2 nodes	1,303	6,615	7,567
No firsts ed 2 arcs	4,162	20,418	23,314
No redundancy and 1st ed 2 nodes	1,303	6,615	7,567
No redundancy and 1st ed 2 arcs	4,162	20,418	23,314
Lower order first ed 1 to 2 arcs	6,217	30,569	34,909
Lower order first ed 1 to 2 nodes	1,955	9,923	11,351

Table 3: The sizes of error models as automata

is to establish that simpler error models lead to degraded recall—and not to more generally evaluate the present system as a spell-checker.

The evaluations in this section are performed on quad-core Intel Xeon E5450 running at 3 GHz with 64 GiB of RAM memory. The times are averaged over five test runs of 10,000 words in a stable server environment with no server processes or running graphical interfaces or other uses. The test results are measured using the `getrusage` C function on a system that supports the maximum resident stack size `ru_maxrss` and user time `ru_utime` fields. The times are also verified with the GNU `time` command. The results for hunspell, Voikkospell and foma processes are only measured with `time` and `top`. The respective versions of the software are Voikkospell 3.3, hunspell 1.2.14, and Foma 0.9.16alpha. The reference systems are tested with default settings, meaning that they will only give some fixed number of suggestions whereas our system will calculate all strings within the given error model.

As a reference implementation for English we use hunspell's en-US dictionary[9] and for a finite-state implementation we use a weighted word-list from Norvig (2010). As a Finnish reference implementation we use Voikko[10], with a LAG-based dictionary using Malaga[11]. The reference correction task for Greenlandic is done with foma's (Huldén, 2009b)

[8]The method described here does not handle run-on words or extraneous spaces, as they introduce lot of programmatic complexity which we believe is irrelevant to the results of this experiment.

[9]`http://wiki.services.openoffice.org/wiki/Dictionaries`

[10]`http://voikko.sf.net`

[11]`http://home.arcor.de/bjoern-beutel/malaga/`

apply med function with default settings[12].

The baseline feature set and the efficiency of spell-checking we are targeting is defined by the currently de facto standard spelling suite in open source systems, hunspell.

In Table 4 we measure the speed of the spell-checking process on native language Wikipedia text with real-world spelling errors and unknown strings. The error model rows are defined as follows: on the *Reference impl.* row, we test the spell-checking speed of the hunspell tool for English, and Voikkospell tool for Finnish. On the *edit distance 2* row we use the basic traditional edit distance 2 without any modifications. On the *No first edits* row we use the error model that does not modify the first character of the word. On the *No redundancy* row we use the edit distance 2 error model with the redundant edit combinations removed. On the *No redundancy and firsts* rows we use the combined error model of *No first edits* and *No redundancy* functionalities. On the row *Lower order first* we apply a lower order edit distance model first, then if no results are found, a higher order model is used. In the tables and formulae we routinely use the language codes to denote the languages: *en* for English, *fi* for Finnish and *kl* for Greenlandic (Kalaallisut).

Error model	En	Fi	Kl
Reference impl.	9.93	7.96	11.42
Generate all edits 2	3818.20	118775.60	36432.80
Edit distance 1	0.26	6.78	4.79
Edit distance 2	7.55	220.42	568.36
No first edits 1	0.44	3.19	3.52
No firsts ed 2	1.38	61.88	386.06
No redundancy ed 2	7.52	4230.94	6420.66
No redundancy and firsts ed 2	1.51	62.05	386.63
Lower order first ed 1 to 2	4.31	157.07	545.91

Table 4: Effect of language and error models to speed (time in seconds per 10,000 word forms)

The results show that not editing the first position does indeed give significant boost to the speed, regardless of language model, which is of course caused by the significant reduction in search space. However, the redundancy avoidance does not seem to make a significant difference. This is most likely because the amount of duplicate paths in the search space is not so proportionally large and their traversal will be relatively fast. The separate application of error models gives the expected timing result between its relevant primary and secondary error models. It should be noteworthy that, when thinking of real world applications, the speed of the most of the models described here is greater than 1 word per second (i.e. 10,000 seconds per 10,000 words).

We measured memory consumption when performing the same tests. Varying the error model had little to no effect. Memory consumption was almost entirely determined by the language model, giving consumptions of 13-7 MiB for English, 0.2 GiB for Finnish and 1.6 GiB for Greenlandic.

To measure the degradation of quality when using different error models we count the proportion of suggestion sets that contain the correct correction among the corrected strings. The suggestion sets are the entire (unrestricted by number) results of correction, with no attempt to evaluate precision[13]. For this test we use automatically generated corpus of spelling errors to get the large-scale results.

Error model	En	Fi	Kl
Edit distance 1	0.89	0.83	0.81
Edit distance 2	0.99	0.95	0.92
Edit distance 3	1.00	0.96	—
No firsts ed 1	0.74	0.73	0.60
No firsts ed 2	0.81	0.82	0.69
No firsts ed 3	0.82	—	—

Table 5: Effect of language and error models to quality (recall, proportion of suggestion sets containing a correctly suggested word)

This test with automatically introduced errors shows us that with uniformly distributed errors the penalty of using an error model that ignores word-initial corrections could be significant. This contrasts to our findings with real world errors, that the distribution of errors tends towards the end of the word, described in 2.2 and (Bhagat, 2007), but it should be noted that degradation can be as bad as given here.

Finally we measure how the text type used will affect the speed of spell-checking. As the best-case scenario we use the unmodified texts of Wikipedia, which contain probably the most realistic native-language-speaker-like typing error dis-

[12]http://code.google.com/p/Foma/

[13]Which, in the absence of suitable error corpora and a more full-fledged language model taking context into account, would be irrelevant for the goal at hand.

tribution available. For text with more errors, where the majority of errors should be recoverable, we introduce automatically generated errors in the Wikipedia texts. Finally to see the performance in the worst case scenario where most of the words have unrecoverable spelling errors we use texts from other languages, in this case English texts for Finnish and Greenlandic spell-checking and Finnish texts for English spell-checking, which should bring us close to the lower bounds on performance. The effects of text type (i.e. frequency of non-words) on speed of spell-checking is given in Table 6. All of the tests in this category were performed with error models under the *avoid redundancy and firsts ed 2* row in previous tables, which gave us the best speed/quality ratio.

Error model	En	Fi	Kl
Native Lang. Corpus	1.38	61.88	386.06
Added automatic errors	6.91	95.01	551.81
Text in another language	22.40	148.86	783.64

Table 6: Effect of text type on error models to speed (in seconds per 10,000 word-forms)

Here we chiefly note that the amount of non-words in text directly reflects the speed of spell-checking. This shows that the dominating factor of the speed of spell-checking is indeed in the correcting of misspelled words.

5 Conclusions and Future Work

In this article, we built a full-fledged finite-state spell-checking system from existing finite-state language models and generated error models. This work uses the system initially described in Pirinen and Lindén (2010) and an algorithm described in Lindén et al. (2012), providing an extensive quantitative evaluation of various combinations of constituents for such a system, and applying it to the most challenging linguistic environments available for testing. We showed that using on-line composition of the word form, error model and dictionary is usable for morphologically complex languages. Furthermore we showed that the error models can be automatically optimised in several ways to gain some speed at cost of recall.

We showed that the memory consumption of the spell-checking process is mainly unaffected by the selection of error model, apart from the need to store a greater set of suggestions for models that generate more suggestions. The error models may therefore be quite freely changed in real world applications as needed.

We verified that correcting only the first input letter affords a significant speed improvement, but that this improvement is not greatly dependent on the position of such a restriction. This practice is somewhat supported by our tentative finding that it may cause the least drop in practical recall figures, at least in Finnish. It is promising especially in conjunction with a fallback model that does correct the first letter.

We described a way to avoid having a finite-state error model perform redundant work, such as deleting and inserting the same letter in succession. The practical improvement from doing this is extremely modest, and it increases the size of the error model.

In this research we focused on differences in automatically generated error models and their optimisations in the case of morphologically complex languages. For future research we intend to study more realistic error models induced from actual error corpora (e.g. Brill and Moore (2000)). Research into different ways to induce weights into the language models, as well as further use of context in finite-state spell-checking (as in Pirinen et al. (2012)), is warranted.

Acknowledgements

We thank the anonymous reviewers for their comments and the HFST research team for fruity discussions on the article's topics. The first author thanks the people of *Oqaaserpassualeriffik* for introducing the problems and possibilities of finite-state applications to the morphologically complex language of Greenlandic.

References

Cyril Allauzen and Mehryar Mohri. 2009. N-way composition of weighted finite-state transducers. *International Journal of Foundations of Computer Science*, 20:613–627.

Kenneth R Beesley and Lauri Karttunen. 2003. *Finite State Morphology*. CSLI publications.

Meenu Bhagat. 2007. Spelling error pattern analysis of punjabi typed text. Master's thesis, Thapar University.

Eric Brill and Robert C. Moore. 2000. An improved error model for noisy channel spelling correction. In *ACL '00: Proceedings of the 38th Annual Meeting on Association for Computational Linguistics*, pages 286–293, Morristown, NJ, USA. Association for Computational Linguistics.

Fred J Damerau. 1964. A technique for computer detection and correction of spelling errors. *Commun. ACM*, (7).

Ahmed Hassan, Sara Noeman, and Hany Hassan. 2008. Language independent text correction using finite state automata. In *Proceedings of the Third International Joint Conference on Natural Language Processing*, volume 2, pages 913–918.

Måns Huldén. 2009a. Fast approximate string matching with finite automata. *Procesamiento del Lenguaje Natural*, 43:57–64.

Måns Huldén. 2009b. Foma: a finite-state compiler and library. In *Proceedings of the 12th Conference of the European Chapter of the Association for Computational Linguistics: Demonstrations Session*, EACL '09, pages 29–32, Stroudsburg, PA, USA. Association for Computational Linguistics.

Kimmo Koskenniemi. 1983. *Two-level Morphology: A General Computational Model for Word-Form Recognition and Production*. Ph.D. thesis, University of Helsinki.

Karen Kukich. 1992. Techniques for automatically correcting words in text. *ACM Comput. Surv.*, 24(4):377–439.

Vladimir I. Levenshtein. 1966. Binary codes capable of correcting deletions, insertions, and reversals. *Soviet Physics—Doklady 10, 707710. Translated from Doklady Akademii Nauk SSSR*, pages 845–848.

Krister Lindén, Erik Axelson, Senka Drobac, Sam Hardwick, Miikka Silfverberg, and Tommi A Pirinen. 2012. Using hfst for creating computational linguistic applications. In *Proceedings of Computational Linguistics - Applications, 2012*, page to appear.

Petar Nikolaev Mitankin. 2005. Universal levenshtein automata. building and properties. Master's thesis, University of Sofia.

Roger Mitton. 2009. Ordering the suggestions of a spellchecker without using context*. *Nat. Lang. Eng.*, 15(2):173–192.

Peter Norvig. 2010. How to write a spelling corrector. referred 2011-01-11, available `http://norvig.com/spell-correct.html`.

Kemal Oflazer. 1996. Error-tolerant finite-state recognition with applications to morphological analysis and spelling correction. *Comput. Linguist.*, 22(1):73–89.

Tommi A Pirinen and Krister Lindén. 2010. Finite-state spell-checking with weighted language and error models. In *Proceedings of the Seventh SaLTMiL workshop on creation and use of basic lexical resources for less-resourced languagages*, pages 13–18, Valletta, Malta.

Tommi Pirinen, Miikka Silfverberg, and Krister Linden. 2012. Improving finite-state spell-checker suggestions with part of speech n-grams. In *Internatational Journal of Computational Linguistics and Applications IJCLA (to appear)*.

Tommi A Pirinen. 2011. Modularisation of finnish finite-state language descriptiontowards wide collaboration in open source development of morphological analyser. In *Proceedings of Nodalida*, volume 18 of *NEALT proceedings*.

Harri Pitkänen. 2006. Hunspell-in kesäkoodi 2006: Final report. Technical report.

Joseph J. Pollock and Antonio Zamora. 1984. Automatic spelling correction in scientific and scholarly text. *Commun. ACM*, 27(4):358–368, April.

Klaus Schulz and Stoyan Mihov. 2002. Fast string correction with levenshtein-automata. *International Journal of Document Analysis and Recognition*, 5:67–85.

Emmanuel J Yannakoudakis and D Fawthrop. 1983. An intelligent spelling error corrector. *Information Processing and Management*, 19(2):101–108.

Practical Finite State Optimality Theory

Dale Gerdemann
University of Tübingen
dg@sfs.nphil.uni-tuebingen.de

Mans Hulden
University of the Basque Country
IXA Group
IKERBASQUE, Basque Foundation for Science
mhulden@email.arizona.edu

Abstract

Previous work for encoding Optimality Theory grammars as finite-state transducers has included two prominent approaches: the so-called 'counting' method where constraint violations are counted and filtered out to some set limit of approximability in a finite-state system, and the 'matching' method, where constraint violations in alternative strings are matched through violation alignment in order to remove suboptimal candidates. In this paper we extend the matching approach to show how not only markedness constraints, but also faithfulness constraints and the interaction of the two types of constraints can be captured by the matching method. This often produces exact and small FST representations for OT grammars which we illustrate with two practical example grammars. We also provide a new proof of nonregularity of simple OT grammars.

1 Introduction

The possibility of representing Optimality Theory (OT) grammars (Prince and Smolensky, 1993) as computational models and finite-state transducers, in particular, has been widely studied since the inception of the theory itself. In particular, constructing an OT grammar step-by-step as the composition of a set of transducers, akin to rewrite rule composition in (Kaplan and Kay, 1994), has offered the attractive possibility of simultaneously modeling OT parsing and generation as a natural consequence of the bidirectionality of finite-state transducers. Two main approaches have received attention as practical options for implementing OT with finite-state transducers: that of Karttunen (1998) and Gerdemann and van Noord (2000).[1] Both approaches model constraint interaction by constructing a GEN-transducer, which is subsequently composed with filtering transducers that mark violations of constraints, and remove suboptimal candidates—candidates that have received more violation marks than the optimal candidate, with the general template:

```
Grammar = Gen .o. MarkC1 .o. FilterC1 ...
                  MarkCN .o. FilterCN
```

In Karttunen's system, auxiliary 'counting' transducers are created that first remove candidates with maximally k violation marks for some fixed k, then $k-1$, and so on, until nothing can be removed without emptying the candidate set, using a finite-state operation called *priority union*. Gerdemann and van Noord (2000) present a similar system that they call a 'matching' approach, but which does not rely on fixing a maximal number of distinguishable violations k. The matching method is a procedure by which we can in many cases (though not always) distinguish between infinitely many violations in a finite-state system—something that is not possible when encoding OT by the alternative approach of counting violations.

In this paper our primary purpose is to both extend and simplify this 'matching' method. We will include interaction of both markedness and faithfulness constraints (MAX, DEP, and IDENT violations)—going beyond both Karttunen (1998) and Gerdemann and van Noord (2000), where only markedness constraints were modeled. We shall also clarify the notation and markup used in the matching approach as well as present a set of generic transducer templates for EVAL by which modeling varying OT grammars becomes a simple matter of modifying the necessary constraint transducers and ordering them correctly in a series of compositions.

[1] Earlier finite-state approaches do exist, see e.g. Ellison (1994) and Hammond (1997).

Proceedings of the 10th International Workshop on Finite State Methods and Natural Language Processing, pages 10–19,
Donostia–San Sebastián, July 23–25, 2012. ©2012 Association for Computational Linguistics

We will first give a detailed explanation of the 'matching' approach in section 2—our encoding, notation, and tools differ somewhat from that of Gerdemann and van Noord (2000), although the core techniques are essentially alike. This is followed by an illustration of our encoding and method through a standard OT grammar example in section 3. In that section we also give examples of debugging OT grammars using standard finite state calculus methods. In section 4 we also present an alternate encoding of an OT account of prosody in Karttunen (2006) illustrating devices where GEN is assumed to add metrical and stress markup in addition to changing, inserting, or deleting segments. We also compare this grammar to both a non-OT grammar and an OT grammar of the same phenomenon described in Karttunen (2006). In section 5, we conclude with a brief discussion about the limitations of FST-based OT grammars in light of the method developed in this paper, as well as show a new proof of nonregularity of some very simple OT constraint systems.

1.1 Notation

All the examples discussed are implemented with the finite-state toolkit *foma* (Hulden, 2009b). The regular expressions are also compilable with the Xerox tools (Beesley and Karttunen, 2003), although some of the tests of properties of finite-state transducers, crucial for debugging, are unavailable. The regular expression formalism used is summarized in table 1.

`AB`	Concatenation
`A|B`	Union
`~A`	Complement
`?`	Any symbol in alphabet
`%`	Escape symbol
`[` and `]`	Grouping brackets
`A:B`	Cross product
`T.l`	Output projection of T
`A -> B`	Rewrite A as B
`A (->) B`	Optionally rewrite A as B
`|| C _ D`	Context specifier
`[..] -> A`	Insert one instance of A
`A -> B ... C`	Insert B and C around A
`.#.`	End or beginning of string

Table 1: Regular expression notation in *foma*.

2 OT evaluation with matching

In order to clarify the main method used in this paper to model OT systems, we will briefly recapitulate the 'matching' approach to filter out suboptimal candidates, or candidates with more violation marks in a string representation, developed in Gerdemann and van Noord (2000).[2]

2.1 Worsening

The fundamental technique behind the finite-state matching approach to OT is a device which we call 'worsening', used to filter out strings from a transducer containing more occurrences of some designated special symbol s (e.g. a violation marker), than some other candidate string in the same pool of strings. This method of transducer manipulation is perhaps best illustrated through a self-contained example.

Consider a simple morphological analyzer encoded as an FST, say of English, that only adds morpheme-boundaries—+-symbols—to input words, perhaps consulting a dictionary of affixes and stems. Some of the mappings of such a transducer could be ambiguous: for example, the words **deconstruction** or **incorporate** could be broken down in two ways by such a morpheme analyzer:

Input	**Output**
deconstruction	de+construct+ion
	deconstruct+ion
incorporate	in+corporate
	incorporate

Suppose our task was now to remove alternate morpheme breakdowns from the transducer so that, if an analysis with a smaller number of morphemes was available for any word, a longer analysis would not be produced. In effect, **deconstruction** should only map to **deconstruct+ion**, since the other alternative has one more morpheme boundary. The worsening trick is based on the idea that we can use the existing set of words from the output side of the morphology, add at least one morpheme boundary to all of them, and use the resulting set of words to filter out longer 'candidates' from the original morphology. For example, one way of adding a +-symbol to **de+construction** produces

[2]Also discussed in Jäger (2002).

de+construct+ion, which coincides with the original output in the morphology, and can now be used to knock out this suboptimal division. This process can be captured through:

```
AddBoundary = [?* 0:%+ ?*]+;
Worsen      =  Morphology .o. AddBoundary;
Shortest    =  Morphology .o. ~Worsen.l;
```

the effect of which is illustrated for the word **deconstruction** in figure 1. Here, `AddBoundary` is a transducer that adds at least one +-symbol to the input. The `Worsen` transducer is simply the original transducer composed with the `AddBoundary` transducer. The `Shortest` morphology is then constructed by extracting the output projection of `Worsen`, and composing its negation with the original morphology.

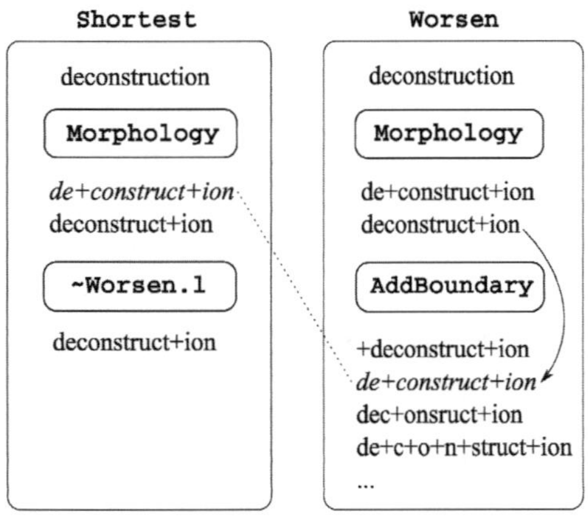

Figure 1: Illustration of a worsening filter for morpheme boundaries.

2.2 Worsening in OT

The above 'worsening' maneuver is what the 'matching' approach to model OT syllabification is based upon. Evaluation of competing candidates with regard to a single OT constraint can be performed in the same manner. This, of course, presupposes that we are using transducers to mark constraint violations in input strings, say by the symbol *. Gerdemann and van Noord (2000) illustrate this by constructing a GEN-transducer that syllabifies words,[3] and another set of transducers that mark violations of some constraint. Then, having a constraint, NOCODA, implemented as a transducer that adds violation marks when syllables end in consonants, we can achieve the following sequence of markup by composition of GEN and NOCODA, for a particular example input **bebop**:

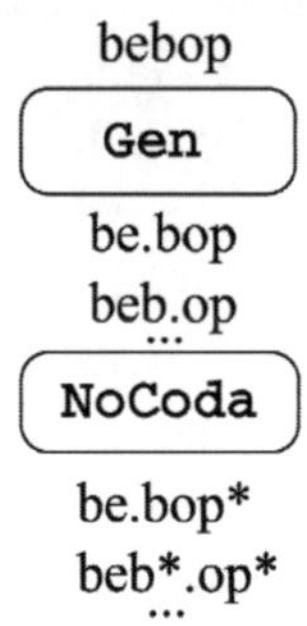

The above transducers could be implemented very simply, by epenthesis replacement rules:

```
# Insert periods arbitrarily inside words
Gen    =  [..] (->) %. || \.#. _ \.#.  ;
# Insert *-marks after C . or C .#.
NoCoda = [..] -> %* || C+ [%. | .#.] _ ;
```

Naturally, at this point in the composition chain we would like to filter out the suboptimal candidates—that is, the ones with fewer violation marks, then remove the marks, and continue with the next constraint, until all constraints have been evaluated. The problem of filtering out the suboptimal candidates is now analogous to the 'worsening' scenario above: we can create a 'worsening'-filter automaton by adding violation marks to the entire set of candidates. In this example, the candidate **be.bop*** would produce a worse candidate **be*.bop***, which (disregarding for the moment syllable boundary marks and the exact position of the violation) can be used to filter out the suboptimal **beb*.op***.

3 An OT grammar with faithfulness and markedness constraints

As previous work has been limited to working with only markedness constraints as well as a somewhat impoverished GEN—one that only syllabifies words—our first task when approaching a more complete finite-state methodology of OT needs to address this point. In keeping with the 'richness of the base'-concept of OT, we require a suitable

[3] Although using a much more complex set of markup symbols than here.

GEN to be able to perform arbitrary deletions (elisions), insertions (epentheses), and changes to the input. A GEN-FST that only performs this task (maps $\Sigma^* \rightarrow \Sigma^*$) on input strings is obviously fairly easy to construct. However, we need to do more than this: we also need to keep track of which parts of the input have been modified by GEN in any way to later be able to pinpoint and mark faithfulness violations—places where GEN has manipulated the input—through an FST.

3.1 Encoding of GEN

Perhaps the simplest possible encoding that meets the above criteria is to have GEN not only change the input, but also mark each segment in its output with a marker whereby we can later distinguish how the input was changed. To do so, we perform the following markup:

- Every surface segment (output) is surrounded by brackets [...].
- Every input segment that was manipulated by GEN is surrounded by parentheses (...).

For example, given the input **a**, GEN would produce an infinite number of outputs, and among them:

`[a]`	GEN did nothing
`(a)[]`	GEN deleted the a
`(a)[e]`	GEN changed the `a` to `e`
`()[d](a)[i]`	GEN inserted a `d` and changed `a` to `i`
...	

This type of generic GEN can be defined through:

```
Gen = S -> %( ... %) %[ (S) %]    ,,
      S -> %[ ... %]              ,,
      [..] (->) [%( %) %[ S %]]*  ;
```

assuming here that `S` represents the set of segments available.

3.2 Evaluation of faithfulness and markedness constraints

As an illustrative grammar, let us consider a standard OT example of word-final obstruent devoicing—as in Dutch or German—achieved through the interaction of faithfulness and markedness constraints. The constraints model the fact that underlyingly voiced obstruents surface as devoiced in word-final position, as in **pad** → **pat**. A set of core constraints to illustrate this include:

- *VF: a markedness constraint that disallows final voiced obstruents.
- IDENTV: a faithfulness constraint that militates against change in voicing.
- VOP: a markedness constraint against voiced obstruents in general.

The interaction of these constraints to achieve devoicing can be illustrated by the following tableau.[4]

bed	*VF	IDENTV	VOP
☞ bet		*	*
pet		**!	
bed	*!		**
ped	*!	*	*

The tableau above represents a kind of shorthand often given in the linguistic literature where, for the sake of conciseness, higher-ranked faithfulness constraints are omitted. For example, there is nothing preventing the candidate **bede** to rank equally with **bet**, were it not for an implicit high-ranked DEP-constraint disallowing epenthesis. As we are building a complete computational model with an unrestricted GEN, and no implicit assumptions, we need to add a few constraints not normally given when arguing about OT models. These include:

- DEP: a faithfulness constraint against epenthesis.
- MAX: a faithfulness constraint against deletion.
- IDENTPL: a faithfulness constraint against changes in place of articulation of segments. This is crucial to avoid e.g. **bat** or **bap** being equally ranked with **bet** in the above example.[5]

[4] The illustration roughly follows (Kager, 1999), p. 42.

[5] Note that a generic higher-ranked IDENT will not do, because then we would never get the desired devoicing in the first place.

Including these constraints explicitly allows us to rule out unwanted candidates that may otherwise rank equal with the candidate where word-final obstruents are devoiced, as illustrated in the following:

bed	DEP	MAX	IDENTPL	*VF	IDENTV	VOP
☞ bet					*	*
pet					**!	
bed				*!		**
ped				*!	*	*
bat			*!		*	*
bep			*!		*	*
be		*!				*
bede	*!					**

Once we have settled for the representation of GEN, the basic faithfulness constraint markup transducers—whose job is to insert asterisks wherever violations occur—can be defined as follows:

```
Dep      = [..] -> {*} || %( %) _ ;
Max      = [..] -> {*} || %[ %] _ ;
Ident    = [..] -> {*} || %( S %) %[ S %] _ ;
```

That is, DEP inserts a *-symbol after ( )-sequences, which is how GEN marks epenthesis. Likewise, MAX-violations are identified by the sequence [ ], and IDENT-violations by a parenthesized segment followed by a bracketed segment. To define the remaining markup transducers, we shall take advantage of some auxiliary template definitions, defined as functions:

```
def Surf(X)        [X .o. [0:%[ ? 0:%]]*].l/
                   [ %( (S) %) | %[ %] ];
def Change(X,Y)  [%( X %) %[ Y %]];
```

Here, `Surf(X)` in effect changes the language `X` so that it can match every possible surface encoding produced by GEN; for example, a surface sequence **ab** may look like **[a][b]**, or **[a](a)[b]**, etc., since it may spring from various different underlying forms. This is a useful auxiliary definition that will serve to identify markedness violations. Likewise `Change(X,Y)` reflects the GEN representation of changing a segment `X` to `Y` needed to concisely identify changed segments. Using the above we may now define the remaining violation markups needed.

```
CVOI      = [b|d|g];
Voiced    = [b|d|g|V];
Unvoiced = [p|t|k];
define VC       Change(Voiced,Unvoiced) |
                Change(Unvoiced,Voiced);
define Place    Change(p,?-b)|Change(t,?-d)|
                Change(k,?-g)|Change(b,?-p)|
                Change(d,?-t)|Change(g,?-k)|
                Change(a,?)|Change(e,?)|
                Change(i,?)|Change(o,?)|
                Change(u,?);

VF       = [..] -> {*} || Surf(CVOI) _ .#.   ;
IdentV   = [..] -> {*} || VC _               ;
VOP      = [..] -> {*} || Surf(CVOI)  _      ;
IdentPl = [..] -> {*} || Place _             ;
```

The final remaining element for a complete implementation concerns the question of 'worsening' and its introduction into a chain of transducer composition. To this end, we include a few more definitions:

```
AddViol =    [?* 0:%* ?*]+;
Worsen  =    [Gen.i .o. Gen]/%* .o. AddViol;
def Eval(X) X .o. ~[X .o. Worsen].l .o. %*->0;
Cleanup =    %[|%] -> 0 .o. %( \%)* %) -> 0;
```

Here, `AddViol` is the basic worsening method discussed above whereby at least one violation mark is added. However, because GEN adds markup to the underlying forms, we need to be a bit more flexible in our worsening procedure when matching up violations. It may be the case that two different competing surface forms have the same underlying form, but the violation marks will not align correctly because of interfering brackets. Given two competing candidates with a different number of violations, for example **(a)[b]*** and **[a]**, we would like the latter to match the former after adding a violation mark since they both originate in the same underlying form **a**. The way to achieve this is to *undo* the effect of GEN, and then redo GEN in every possible configuration before adding the violation marks. The transducer `Worsen`, above, does this by a composition of the inverse GEN, followed by GEN, ignoring already existing violations. For the above example, this leads to representations such as:

$$\texttt{[a]} \stackrel{\texttt{Gen.i}}{\rightarrow} \texttt{a} \stackrel{\texttt{Gen}}{\rightarrow} \texttt{(a)[b]} \stackrel{\texttt{AddViol}}{\rightarrow} \texttt{(a)[b]*}.$$

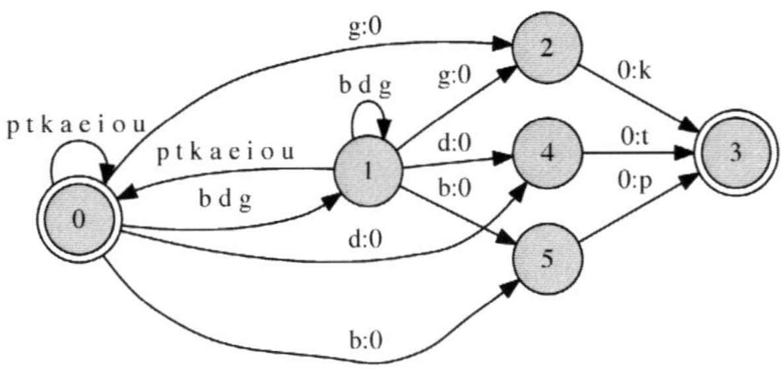

Figure 2: OT grammar for devoicing compiled into an FST.

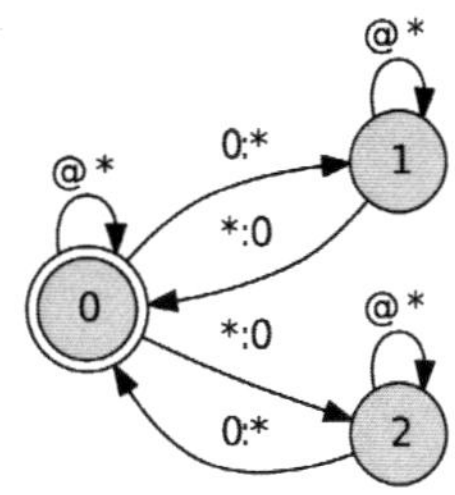


```
Permute = [?* [%*:0 ?* 0:%*|0:%* ?* %*:0]* ?*]*;
```

Figure 3: Violation permutation transducer.

We also define a `Cleanup` transducer that removes brackets and parts of the underlying form.

Now we are ready to compile the entire system into an FST. To apply only GEN and the first constraint, for example, we can calculate:

```
Eval(Gen .o. Dep) .o. Cleanup;
```

and likewise the entire grammar can be calculated by:

```
Eval(Eval(Eval(Eval(Eval(Eval(
Gen .o. Dep) .o. Max) .o. IdentPl) .o.
VF) .o. IdentV) .o. VOP) .o. Cleanup;
```

This yields an FST of 6 states and 31 transitions (see figure 2)—it can be ascertained that the FST indeed does represent a relation where word-final voiced obstruents are always devoiced.

3.3 Permutation of violations

As mentioned in Gerdemann and van Noord (2000), there is an additional complication with the 'worsening'-approach. It is not always the case that in the pool of competing candidates, the violation markers line up, which is a prerequisite for filtering out suboptimal ones by adding violations—although in the above grammar the violations do line up correctly. However, for the vast majority of OT grammars, this can be remedied by inserting a violation-permuting transducer that moves violations markers around before worsening, to attempt to produce a correct alignment. Such a permuting transducer can be defined as in figure 3.

If the need for permutation arises, repeated permutations can be included as many times as warranted in the definition of `Worsen`:

```
Permute = [%*:0 ?* 0:%*|0:%* ?* %*:0]*/?;
Worsen  = [Gen.i .o. Gen]/%* .o.
          Permute .o. ... .o. Permute .o.
          AddViol;
```

Knowing how many permutations are necessary for the transducer to be able to distinguish between any number of violations in a candidate pool is possible as follows: we can can calculate for some constraint `ConsN` in a sequence of constraints,

```
Eval(Eval(Gen .o. Cons1) ... .o. ConsN) .o.
    ConsN .o. \%* -> 0;
```

Now, this yields a transducer that maps every underlying form to n asterisks, n being the number of violations with respect to `ConsN` in the candidates that have successfully survived `ConsN`. If this transducer represents a function (is single-valued), then we know that two candidates with a different number of violations have not survived `ConsN`, and that the worsening yielded the correct answer. Since the question of transducer functionality is known to be decidable (Blattner and Head, 1977), and an efficient algorithm is given in Hulden (2009a), which is included in *foma* (with the command `test functional`) we can address this question by calculating the above for each constraint, if necessary, and then permute the violation markers until the above transducer is functional.

3.4 Equivalence testing

In many cases, the purpose of an OT grammar is to capture accurately some linguistic phenomenon through the interaction of constraints rather than by other formalisms. However, as has been noted by

Karttunen (2006), among others, OT constraint debugging is an arduous task due to the sheer number of unforeseen candidates. One of the advantages in encoding an OT grammar through the worsening approach is that we can produce an exact representation of the grammar, which is not an approximation bounded by the number of constraint violations it can distinguish (as in Karttunen (1998)), or by the length of strings it can handle. This allows us to formally calculate, among other things, the equivalence of an OT grammar represented as an FST and some other transducer. For example, in the above grammar, the intention was to model end-of-word obstruent devoicing through optimality constraints. Another way to model the same thing would be to compile the replacement rule:

```
Rule = b -> p, d -> t, g -> k || _ .#. ;
```

The transducer resulting from this is shown in figure 4.

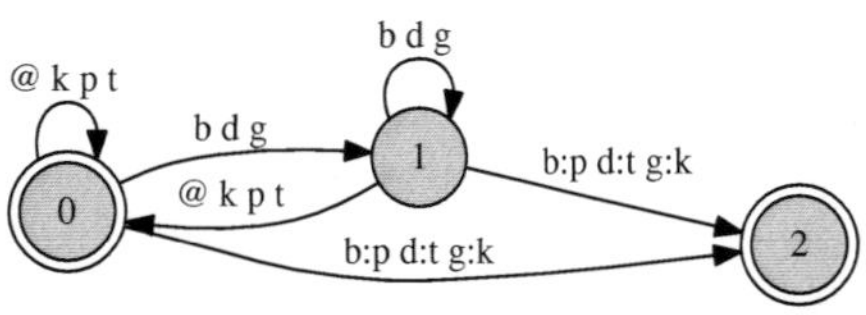

Figure 4: Devoicing transducer compiled through a rule.

As is seen, the OT transducer (figure 2) and the rule transducer (figure 4) are not structurally identical. However, both transducers represent a function—i.e. for any given input, there is always a unique winning candidate. Although transducer equivalence is not testable by algorithm in the general case, it is decidable in the case where one of two transducers is functional. If this is the case it is sufficient to test that domain(τ_1) = domain(τ_2) and that $\tau_2^{-1} \circ \tau_1$ represents identity relations only. As an algorithm to decide if a transducer is an identity transducer is also included in *foma*, it can be used to ascertain that the two above transducers are in fact identical, and that the linguistic generalization captured by the OT constraints is correct:

```
regex Rule.i .o. Grammar;
test identity
```

which indeed returns TRUE. For a small grammar, such as the devoicing grammar, determining the correctness of the result by other means is certainly feasible. However, for more complex systems the ability to test for equivalence becomes a valuable tool in analyzing constraint systems.

4 Variations on GEN: an OT grammar of stress assignment

Most OT grammars that deal with phonological phenomena with faithfulness and markedness grammars are implementable through the approach given above, with minor variations according to what specific constraints are used. In other domains, however, in may be the case that GEN, as described above, needs modification. A case in point are grammars that mark prosody or perform syllabification that often take advantage of only markedness constraints. In such cases, there is often no need for GEN to insert, change, and delete material if all faithfulness constraints are assumed to outrank all markedness constraints. Or alternatively, if the OT grammar is assumed to operate on a different stratum where no faithfulness constraints are present. However, GEN still needs to insert material into strings, such as stress marks or syllable boundaries.

To test the approach with a larger 'real-world' grammar we have reimplemented a Finnish stress assignment grammar, originally implemented through the counting approach of Karttunen (1998) in Karttunen (2006), following a description in Kiparsky (2003). The grammar itself contains nine constraints, and is intended to give a complete account of stress placement in Finnish words. Without going into a line-by-line analysis of the grammar, the crucial main differences in this implementation to that of the previous sections are:

- GEN only inserts symbols `(` `)` `ˋ and ˊ` to mark feet and stress
- Violations need to be permuted in `Worsen` to yield an exact representation
- GEN syllabifies words correctly through a replacement rule (no constraints are given in the grammar to model syllabification; this is assumed to be already performed)

```
kainostelijat      ->   (ka´i.nos).(te`.li).jat
kalastelemme       ->   (ka´.las).te.(le`m.me)
kalasteleminen     ->  *(ka´.las).te.(le`.mi).nen
kalastelet         ->   (ka´.las).(te`.let)
kuningas           ->   (ku´.nin).gas
strukturalismi     ->   (stru´k.tu).ra.(li`s.mi)
ergonomia          ->   (e´r.go).(no`.mi).a
matematiikka       ->   (ma´.te).ma.(ti`ik.ka)
```

Figure 5: Example outputs of matching implementation of Finnish OT.

Compiling the entire grammar through the same procedure as above outputs a transducer with 134 states, and produces the same predictions as Karttunen's counting OT grammar.[6] As opposed to the previous devoicing grammar, compiling the Finnish prosody grammar requires permutation of the violation markers, although only one constraint requires it (STRESS-TO-WEIGHT, and in that case, composing `Worsen` with one round of permutation is sufficient for convergence).

Unlike the counting approach, the current approach confers two significant advantages. The first is that we can compile the entire grammar into an FST that does not restrict the inputs in any way. That is, the final product is a stand-alone transducer that accepts as input *any* sequence of any length of symbols in the Finnish alphabet, and produces an output where the sequence is syllabified, marked with feet, and primary and secondary stress placement (see figure 5). The counting method, in order to compile at all, requires that the set of inputs be fixed to some very limited set of words, and that the maximum number of distinguishable violations (and indirectly word length) be fixed to some k.[7] The second advantage is that, as mentioned before, we are able to formally compare the OT grammar (because it is not an approximation), to a rule-based grammar (FST) that purports to capture the same phenomena. For example, Karttunen (2006), apart from the counting OT implementation, also provides a rule-based account of Finnish stress, which he discovers to be distinct from an OT account by finding two words where their respective predictions differ. However, by virtue of having an exact transducer, we can formally analyze the OT account together with the rule-based account to see if they differ in their predictions for *any* input, without having to first intuit a differing example:

```
regex RuleGrammar.i .o. OTGrammar;
test identity
```

Further, we can subject the two grammars to the usual finite-state calculus operations to gain possible insight into what kinds of words yield different predictions with the two—something useful for linguistic debugging. Likewise, we can use similar techniques to analyze for redundancy in grammars. For example, we have assumed that the VOP-constraint plays no role in the above devoicing tableaux. Using finite-state calculus, we can prove it to be so for any input if the grammar is constructed with the method presented here.

5 Limits on FST implementation

We shall conclude the presentation here with a brief discussion of the limits of FST representability, even of simple OT grammars. Previous analyses have shown that OT systems are beyond the generative capacity of finite-state systems, under some assumptions of what GEN looks like. For example, Frank and Satta (1998) present such a constraint system where GEN is taken to be defined through a transduction equivalent to:[8]

```
Gen = [a:b|b:a]* | [a|b]*;
```

That is, a relation which *either* maps all a's to b's and vice versa, or leaves the input unchanged. Now, let us assume the presence of a single markedness constraint *a, militating against the letter a. In that case, given an input of the format a^*b^* the effective mapping of the entire system is one that is an identity relation if there are fewer a's than b's; otherwise the a's and b's are swapped. As is easily seen, this is not a regular relation.

One possible objection to this analysis of non-regularity is that linguistically GEN is usually assumed to perform any transformation to the input

[6] Including replicating errors in Kiparsky's OT analysis discovered by Karttunen, as seen in figure 5.

[7] Also, compiling the grammar is reasonably quick: 7.04s on a 2.8MHz Intel Core 2, vs. 2.1s for a rewrite-rule-based account of the same phenomena.

[8] The idea is attributed to Markus Hiller in the article.

whatsoever—not just limiting itself to a proper subset of $\Sigma^* \to \Sigma^*$. However, it is indeed the case that even with a canonical GEN-function, some very simple OT systems fall outside the purview of finite-state expressibility, as we shall illustrate by a different example here.

5.1 A simple proof of OT nonregularity

Assume a grammar that has four very basic constraints: IDENT, forbidding changes, DEP, forbidding epenthesis, $^*ab$, a markedness constraint against the sequence ab, and MAX, forbidding deletion, ranked IDENT,DEP $\gg$ $^*ab$ $\gg$ MAX. We assume GEN to be as general as possible—performing arbitrary deletions, insertions, and changes.

It is clear, as is illustrated in table 2, that for all inputs of the format $a^n b^m$ the grammar in question describes a relation that deletes all the a's or all the b's depending on which there are fewer instances of, i.e. $a^n b^m \to a^n$ if $m < n$, and $a^n b^m \to b^m$ if $n < m$. This can be shown by a simple pumping argument to not be realizable through an FST.

aaabb	IDENT	DEP	*ab	MAX
aaaaa	*!*			
aaacbb		*!		
aaabb			*!	
aaab			*!	*
bb				***!
☞ aaa				**

Table 2: *Illustrative tableau for a simple constraint system not capturable as a regular relation.*

Implementing this constraint system with the methods presented here is an interesting exercise and serves to examine the behavior of the method.

We define GEN, DEP, MAX, and IDENT as before, define a universal alphabet (excluding markup symbols), and the constraint *ab naturally as:

```
S        = ? - %( - %) - %[ - %] - %* ;
NotAB    = [..] -> {*} || Surf(a b) _ ;
```

Now, with one round of permutation of the violation markers in `Worsen` as follows:

```
Worsen =   [Gen.i .o. Gen]/{*} .o.
           AddViol .o. Permute;
```

we calculate

```
define Grammar Eval(Eval(Eval(Eval(
       Gen .o. Ident) .o. Dep) .o. NotAB) .o.
       Max) .o. Cleanup;
```

which produces an FST that cannot distinguish between more than two a's or b's in a string. While it correctly maps **aab** to **aa** and **abb** to **bb**, the tableau example of **aaabb** is mapped to both **aaa** and **bb**. However, with one more round of permutation in `Worsen`, we produce an FST that can indeed cover the example, mapping **aaabb** uniquely to **bb**, while failing with **aaaabbb** (see figure 6). This illustrates the approximation characteristic of the matching method: for some grammars (probably most natural language grammars) the worsening approach will at some point of permutation of the violation markers terminate and produce an exact FST representation of the grammar, while for some grammars such convergence will never happen. However, if the permutation of markers terminates and produces a functional transducer when testing each violation as described above, the FST is guaranteed to be an exact representation.

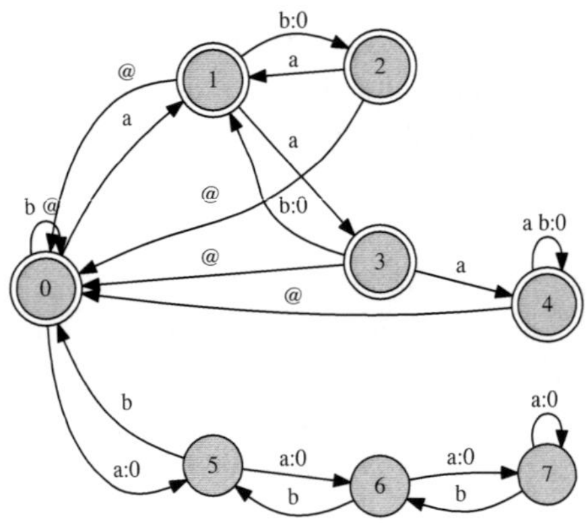

Figure 6: An non-regular OT approximation.

It is an open question if it is decidable by examining a grammar whether it will yield an exact FST representation. We do not expect this question to be easy, since it cannot be determined by the nature of the constraints alone. For example, the above four-constraint system does have an exact FST representation in some orderings of the constraints, but not in the particular one given above.

6 Conclusion

We have presented a practical method of implementing OT grammars as finite-state transducers. The examples, definitions, and templates given should be sufficient and flexible enough to encode a wide variety of OT grammars as FSTs. Although no method can encode all OT grammars as FSTs, the fundamental advantage with the system outlined is that for a large majority of practical cases, an FST can be produced which is not an approximation that can only tell apart a limited number of violations. As has been noted elsewhere (e.g. Eisner (2000b,a)), some OT constraints, such as Generalized Alignment constraints, are on the face of it not suitable for FST implementation. We may add to this that some very simple constraint systems, assuming a canonical GEN, and only using the most basic faithfulness and markedness constraints, are likewise not encodable as regular relations, and seem to have the generative power to encode phenomena not found in natural language. However, for most practical purposes—and this includes modeling actual phenomena in phonology and morphology—the present approach offers a fruitful way to implement, analyze, and debug OT grammars.

References

Beesley, K. R. and Karttunen, L. (2003). *Finite State Morphology*. CSLI Publications, Stanford, CA.

Blattner, M. and Head, T. (1977). Single-valued a-transducers. *Journal of Computer and System Sciences*, 15(3):328–353.

Eisner, J. (2000a). Directional constraint evaluation in optimality theory. In *Proceedings of the 18th conference on Computational linguistics*, pages 257–263. Association for Computational Linguistics.

Eisner, J. (2000b). Easy and hard constraint ranking in optimality theory. In *Finite-state phonology: Proceedings of the 5th SIGPHON*, pages 22–33.

Ellison, T. M. (1994). Phonological derivation in optimality theory. In *Proceedings of COLING'94—Volume 2*, pages 1007–1013.

Frank, R. and Satta, G. (1998). Optimality theory and the generative complexity of constraint violability. *Computational Linguistics*, 24(2):307–315.

Gerdemann, D. and van Noord, G. (2000). Approximation and exactness in finite state optimality theory. In *Proceedings of the Fifth Workshop of the ACL Special Interest Group in Computational Phonology*.

Hammond, M. (1997). Parsing syllables: Modeling OT computationally. *Rutgers Optimality Archive (ROA)*, 222-1097.

Hulden, M. (2009a). *Finite-state Machine Construction Methods and Algorithms for Phonology and Morphology*. PhD thesis, The University of Arizona.

Hulden, M. (2009b). Foma: a finite-state compiler and library. In *EACL 2009 Proceedings*, pages 29–32.

Jäger, G. (2002). Gradient constraints in finite state OT: the unidirectional and the bidirectional case. *More than Words. A Festschrift for Dieter Wunderlich*, pages 299–325.

Kager, R. (1999). *Optimality Theory*. Cambridge University Press.

Kaplan, R. M. and Kay, M. (1994). Regular models of phonological rule systems. *Computational Linguistics*, 20(3):331–378.

Karttunen, L. (1998). The proper treatment of optimality theory in computational phonology. In *Finite-state Methods in Natural Language Processing*.

Karttunen, L. (2006). The insufficiency of paper-and-pencil linguistics: the case of Finnish prosody. *Rutgers Optimality Archive*.

Kiparsky, P. (2003). Finnish noun inflection. *Generative approaches to Finnic linguistics. Stanford: CSLI*.

Prince, A. and Smolensky, P. (1993). Optimality theory: Constraint interaction in generative grammar. *ms. Rutgers University Cognitive Science Center*.

Riggle, J. (2004). *Generation, recognition, and learning in finite state Optimality Theory*. PhD thesis, University of California, Los Angeles.

Handling Unknown Words in Arabic FST Morphology

Khaled Shaalan and Mohammed Attia
Faculty of Engineering & IT,
The British University in Dubai
khaled.shaalan@buid.ac.ae
mohammed.attia@buid.ac.ae

Abstract

A morphological analyser only recognizes words that it already knows in the lexical database. It needs, however, a way of sensing significant changes in the language in the form of newly borrowed or coined words with high frequency. We develop a finite-state morphological guesser in a pipelined methodology for extracting unknown words, lemmatizing them, and giving them a priority weight for inclusion in a lexicon. The processing is performed on a large contemporary corpus of 1,089,111,204 words and passed through a machine-learning-based annotation tool. Our method is tested on a manually-annotated gold standard of 1,310 forms and yields good results despite the complexity of the task. Our work shows the usability of a highly non-deterministic finite state guesser in a practical and complex application.

1 Introduction

Due to the complex and semi-algorithmic nature of the Arabic morphology, it has always been a challenge for computational processing and analysis (Kiraz, 2001; Beesley 2003; Shaalan et al., 2012). A lexicon is an indispensable part of a morphological analyser (Dichy and Farghaly, 2003; Attia, 2006; Buckwalter, 2004; Beesley, 2001), and the coverage of the lexical database is a key factor in the coverage of the morphological analyser. This is why an automatic method for updating a lexical database is crucially important.

We present the first attempt, to the best of our knowledge, to address lemmatization of Arabic unknown words. The specific problem with lemmatizing unknown words is that they cannot be matched against a morphological lexicon. We develop a rule-based finite-state morphological guesser and use a machine learning disambiguator, MADA (Roth et al., 2008), in a pipelined approach to lemmatization.

This paper is structured as follows. The remainder of the introduction reviews previous work on Arabic unknown word extraction and lemmatization, and explains the data used in our experiments. Section 2 presents the methodology followed in extracting and analysing unknown words. Section 3 provides details on the morphological guesser we have developed to help deal with the problem. Section 4 shows and discusses the testing and evaluation results, and finally Section 5 gives the conclusion.

1.1 Previous Work

Lemmatization of Arabic words has been addressed in (Roth et al., 2008; Dichy, 2001). Lemmatization of unknown words has been addressed for Slovene in (Erjavec and Džerosk, 2004), for Hebrew in (Adler at al., 2008) and for English, Finnish, Swedish and Swahili in (Lindén, 2008). Lemmatization means the normalization of text data by reducing surface forms to their canonical underlying representations, which, in Arabic, means verbs in their perfective, indicative, 3rd person, masculine, singular forms, such as شَكَرَ

Proceedings of the 10th International Workshop on Finite State Methods and Natural Language Processing, pages 20–24,
Donostia–San Sebastián, July 23–25, 2012.

$akara "to thank"; and nominals in their nominative, singular, masculine forms, such as طالِب TAlib "student"; and nominative plural for *pluralia tantum* nouns (or nouns that appear only in the plural form and are not derived from a singular word), such as ناس nAs "people". To the best of our knowledge, the study presented here is the first to address lemmatization of Arabic unknown words. The specific problem with lemmatizing unknown words is that they cannot be matched against a lexicon. In our method, we use a machine learning disambiguator, develop a rule-based finite-state morphological guesser, and combine them in a pipelined process of lemmatization. We test our method against a manually created gold standard of 1,310 types (unique forms) and show a significant improvement over the baseline. Furthermore, we develop an algorithm for weighting and prioritizing new words for inclusion in a lexicon depending on three factors: number of form variations of the lemmas, cumulative frequency of the forms, and POS tags.

1.2 Data Used

In our work we rely on a large-scale corpus of 1,089,111,204 words, consisting of 925,461,707 words from the Arabic Gigaword Fourth Edition (Parker et al., 2009), and 163,649,497 words from news articles collected from the Al-Jazeera web site.[1] In this corpus, unknown words appear at a rate of between 2% of word tokens (when we ignore possible spelling variants) and 9% of word tokens (when possible spelling variants are included).

2 Methodology

To deal with unknown words, or out-of-vocabulary words (OOVs), we use a pipelined approach, which predicts part-of-speech tags and morpho-syntactic features before lemmatization. First, a machine learning, context-sensitive tool is used. This tool, MADA (Roth et al., 2008), performs POS tagging and morpho-syntactic analysis and disambiguation of words in context. MADA internally uses the Standard Arabic Morphological Analyser (SAMA) (Maamouri et al., 2010), an updated version of Buckalter Arabic Morphological Analyser (BAMA) (Buckwalter, 2004). Second, we develop a finite-state morphological guesser that gives all possible interpretations of a given word. The morphological guesser first takes an Arabic form as a whole and then strips off all possible affixes and clitics one by one until all potential analyses are exhausted. As the morphological guesser is highly non-deterministic, all the interpretations are matched against the morphological analysis of MADA that receives the highest probabilistic scores. The guesser's analysis that bears the closest resemblance (in terms of morphological features) with the MADA analysis is selected.

These are the steps followed in extracting and lemmatizing Arabic unknown words:

- A corpus of 1,089,111,204 is analysed with MADA. The number of types for which MADA could not find an analysis in SAMA is 2,116,180.
- These unknown types are spell checked by the Microsoft Arabic spell checker using MS Office 2010. Among the unknown types, the number of types accepted as correctly spelt is 208,188.
- We then select types with frequency of 10 or more. This leave us with 40,277 types.
- We randomly select 1,310 types and manually annotate them with the gold lemma, the gold POS and lexicographic preference for inclusion in a dictionary.
- We use the full POS tags and morpho-syntactic features produced by MADA.
- We use the finite-state morphological guesser to produce all possible morphological interpretations and corresponding lemmatizations.
- We compare the POS tags and morpho-syntactic features in MADA output with the output of the morphological guesser and choose the one with the highest matching score.

3 Morphological Guesser

We develop a morphological guesser for Arabic that analyses unknown words with all possible clitics, morpho-syntactic affixes and all relevant alteration operations that include insertion, assimilation, and deletion. Beesley and Karttunen

[1] http://aljazeera.net/portal. Collected in January 2010.

(2003) show how to create a basic guesser. The core idea of a guesser is to assume that a stem is composed of any arbitrary sequence of Arabic non-numeric characters, and this stem can be prefixed and/or suffixed with a predefined set of prefixes, suffixes or clitics. The guesser marks clitic boundaries and tries to return the stem to its underlying representation, the lemma. Due to the nondeterministic nature of the guesser, there will be a large number of possible lemmas for each form.

The XFST finite-state compiler (Beesley and Karttunen, 2003) uses the "substitute defined" command for creating the guesser. The XFST commands in our guesser are stated as follows.

```
define PossNounStem
[[Alphabet]^{2,24}] "+Guess":0;
define PossVerbStem
[[Alphabet]^{2,6}] "+Guess":0;
```

This rule states that a possible noun stem is defined as any sequence of Arabic non-numeric characters of length between 2 and 24 characters. A possible verb stem is between 2 and 6 characters. The length is the only constraint applied to an Arabic word stem. This word stem is surrounded by prefixes, suffixes, proclitics and enclitics. Clitics are considered as independent tokens and are separated by the '@' sign, while prefixes and suffixes are considered as morpho-syntactic features and are interpreted with tags preceded by the '+' sign. Below we present the analysis of the unknown noun وَالمُسَوِّقونَ wa-Al-musaw~iquwna "and-the-marketers".

MADA output:
form:wAlmswqwn num:p gen:m per:na
case:n asp:na mod:na vox:na pos:noun
prc0:Al_det prc1:0 prc2:wa_conj
prc3:0 enc0:0 stt:d

Finite-state guesser output:
والمسوقون +adjوالمسوق+Guess+masc+pl+nom@
والمسوقون +adjوالمسوقون+Guess+sg@
والمسوقون +nounوالمسوق+Guess+masc+pl+nom@
والمسوقون +nounوالمسوقون+Guess+sg@
والمسوقون و+conj@ال+defArt@+adjمسوق
+Guess+masc+pl+nom@
والمسوقون و+conj@ال+defArt@+adjمسوقون
+Guess+sg@
والمسوقون و+conj@ال+defArt@+nounمسوق
+Guess+masc+pl+nom@
والمسوقون و+conj@ال+defArt@+nounمسوقون
+Guess+sg@
والمسوقون و+conj@+adjالمسوق+Guess+masc
+pl+nom@
والمسوقون و+conj@+adjالمسوقون+Guess+sg@
والمسوقون و+conj@+nounالمسوق+Guess+masc
+pl+nom@
والمسوقون و+conj@+nounالمسوقون+Guess+sg@

For a list of 40,277 word types, the morphological guesser gives an average of 12.6 possible interpretations per word. This is highly non-deterministic when compared to AraComLex morphological analyser (Attia et al. 2011) which has an average of 2.1 solutions per word. We also note that 97% of the gold lemmas are found among the finite-state guesser's choices.

4 Testing and Evaluation

To evaluate our methodology we create a manually annotated gold standard test suite of randomly selected surface form types. For these surface forms, the gold lemma and part of speech are manually given. Besides, the human annotator gives a preference on whether or not to include the entry in a dictionary. This feature helps to evaluate our lemma weighting equation. The annotator tends to include nouns, verbs and adjectives, and only proper nouns that have a high frequency. The size of the test suite is 1,310.

4.1 Evaluating Lemmatization

In the evaluation experiment we measure accuracy calculated as the number of correct tags divided by the count of all tags. The baseline is given by the assumption that new words appear in their base form, i.e., we do not need to lemmatize them. The baseline accuracy is 45% as shown in Table 1. The POS tagging baseline proposes the most frequent tag (proper name) for all unknown words. In our test data this stands at 45%. We notice that MADA POS tagging accuracy is unexpectedly low (60%). We use Voted POS Tagging, that is when a lemma gets a different POS tag with a higher frequency, the new tag replaces the old low frequency tag.

This method has improved the tagging results significantly (69%).

		Accuracy
	POS tagging	
1	POS Tagging baseline	45%
2	MADA POS tagging	60%
3	Voted POS Tagging	69%

Table 1. Evaluation of POS tagging

As for the lemmatization process itself, we notice that our experiment in the pipelined lemmatization approach gains a higher (54%) score than the baseline (45%) as shown in Table 2. This score significantly rises to 63% when the difference in the definite article 'Al' is ignored. The testing results indicate significant improvements over the baseline.

	Lemmatization	
1	Lemmas found among corpus forms	64%
2	Lemmas found among FST guesser forms	97%
3	Lemma first-order baseline	45%
4	Pipelined lemmatization (first-order decision) with strict definite article matching	54%
5	Pipelined lemmatization (first-order decision) ignoring definite article matching	63%

Table 2. Evaluation of lemmatization

4.2 Evaluating Lemma Weighting

In our data we have 40,277 unknown token types. After lemmatization they are reduced to 18,399 types (that is 54% reduction of the surface forms) which are presumably ready for manual validation before being included in a lexicon. This number is still too big for manual inspection. In order to facilitate human revision, we devise a weighting algorithm for ranking so that the top *n* number of words will include the most lexicographically relevant words. We call surface forms that share the same lemma 'sister forms', and we call the lemma that they share the 'mother lemma'. This weighting algorithm is based on three criteria: frequency of the sister forms, number of sister forms, and a POS factor which penalizes proper nouns (due to their disproportionate high frequency). The parameters of the weighting algorithm has been tuned through several rounds of experimentation.

```
Word Weight = ((number of sister
forms having the same mother
lemma * 800) + cumulative sum of
frequencies of sister forms
having the same mother lemma) /
2 + POS factor
```

Good words	In top 100	In bottom 100
relying on Frequency alone (baseline)	63	50
relying on number of sister forms * 800	87	28
relying on POS factor	58	30
using the combined criteria	78	15

Table 3. Evaluation of lemma weighting and ranking

Table 3 shows the evaluation of the weighting criteria. We notice that the combined criteria gives the best balance between increasing the number of good words in the top 100 words and reducing the number of good words in the bottom 100 words.

5 Conclusion

We develop a methodology for automatically extracting unknown words in Arabic and lemmatizing them in order to relate multiple surface forms to their base underlying representation using a finite-state guesser and a machine learning tool for disambiguation. We develop a weighting mechanism for simulating a human decision on whether or not to include the new words in a general-domain lexical database. We show the feasibility of a highly non-deterministic finite state guesser in an essential and practical application.

Out of a word list of 40,255 unknown words, we create a lexicon of 18,399 lemmatized, POS-tagged and weighted entries. We make our unknown word lexicon available as a free open-source resource[2].

Acknowledgments

This research is funded by the UAE National Research Foundation (NRF) (Grant No. 0514/2011).

[2] http://arabic-unknowns.sourceforge.net/

References

Adler, M., Goldberg, Y., Gabay, D. and Elhadad, M. 2008. Unsupervised Lexicon-Based Resolution of Unknown Words for Full Morpholological Analysis. In: Proceedings of Association for Computational Linguistics (ACL), Columbus, Ohio.

Attia, M. 2006. An Ambiguity-Controlled Morphological Analyzer for Modern Standard Arabic Modelling Finite State Networks. In: Challenges of Arabic for NLP/MT Conference, The British Computer Society, London, UK.

Attia, Mohammed, Pavel Pecina, Lamia Tounsi, Antonio Toral, Josef van Genabith. 2011. An Open-Source Finite State Morphological Transducer for Modern Standard Arabic. International Workshop on Finite State Methods and Natural Language Processing (FSMNLP). Blois, France.

Beesley, K. R. 2001. Finite-State Morphological Analysis and Generation of Arabic at Xerox Research: Status and Plans in 2001. In: The ACL 2001 Workshop on Arabic Language Processing: Status and Prospects, Toulouse, France.

Beesley, K. R., and Karttunen, L.. 2003. Finite State Morphology: CSLI studies in computational linguistics. Stanford, Calif.: Csli.

Buckwalter, T. 2004. Buckwalter Arabic Morphological Analyzer (BAMA) Version 2.0. Linguistic Data Consortium (LDC) catalogue number LDC2004L02, ISBN1-58563-324-0

Dichy, J. 2001. On lemmatization in Arabic, A formal definition of the Arabic entries of multilingual lexical databases. ACL/EACL 2001 Workshop on Arabic Language Processing: Status and Prospects. Toulouse, France.

Dichy, J., and Farghaly, A. 2003. Roots & Patterns vs. Stems plus Grammar-Lexis Specifications: on what basis should a multilingual lexical database centred on Arabic be built? In: The MT-Summit IX workshop on Machine Translation for Semitic Languages, New Orleans.

Erjavec, T., and Džerosk, S. 2004. Machine Learning of Morphosyntactic Structure: Lemmatizing Unknown Slovene Words. *Applied Artificial Intelligence*, 18:17–41.

Kiraz, G. A. 2001. *Computational Nonlinear Morphology: With Emphasis on Semitic Languages*. Cambridge University Press.

Lindén, K. 2008. A Probabilistic Model for Guessing Base Forms of New Words by Analogy. In CICling-2008, 9th International Conference on Intelligent Text Processing and Computational Linguistics, Haifa, Israel, pp. 106-116.

Maamouri, M., Graff, D., Bouziri, B., Krouna, S., and Kulick, S. 2010. LDC Standard Arabic Morphological Analyzer (SAMA) v. 3.1. LDC Catalog No. LDC2010L01. ISBN: 1-58563-555-3.

Parker, R., Graff, D., Chen, K., Kong, J., and Maeda, K. 2009. Arabic Gigaword Fourth Edition. LDC Catalog No. LDC2009T30. ISBN: 1-58563-532-4.

Roth, R., Rambow, O., Habash, N., Diab, M., and Rudin, C. 2008. Arabic Morphological Tagging, Diacritization, and Lemmatization Using Lexeme Models and Feature Ranking. In: Proceedings of Association for Computational Linguistics (ACL), Columbus, Ohio.

Shaalan, K., Magdy, M., Fahmy, A., Morphological Analysis of Il-formed Arabic Verbs for Second Language Learners, In Eds. McCarthy P., Boonthum, C., *Applied Natural Language Processing: Identification, Investigation and Resolution*, PP. 383-397, IGI Global, PA, USA, 2012.

Urdu – Roman Transliteration via Finite State Transducers

Tina Bögel
University of Konstanz
Konstanz, Germany
Tina.Boegel@uni-konstanz.de

Abstract

This paper introduces a two-way Urdu–Roman transliterator based solely on a non-probabilistic finite state transducer that solves the encountered scriptural issues via a particular architectural design in combination with a set of restrictions. In order to deal with the enormous amount of overgenerations caused by inherent properties of the Urdu script, the transliterator depends on a set of phonological and orthographic restrictions and a word list; additionally, a default component is implemented to allow for unknown entities to be transliterated, thus ensuring a large degree of flexibility in addition to robustness.

1 Introduction

This paper introduces a way of **t**ransliterating **U**rdu and **R**oman via a non-probabilistic **f**inite state transducer (**TURF**), thus allowing for easier machine processing.[1] The TURF transliterator was originally designed for a grammar of Hindi/Urdu (Bögel et al., 2009), based on the grammar development platform XLE (Crouch et al., 2011). This grammar is written in Roman script to serve as a bridge/pivot language between the different scripts used by Urdu and Hindi. It is in principle able to parse input from both Hindi and Urdu and can generate output for both of these language varieties. In order to achieve this goal, transliterators converting the scripts of Urdu and Hindi, respectively, into the common Roman representation are of great importance.

[1] I would like to thank Tafseer Ahmed and Miriam Butt for their help with the content of this paper. This research was part of the Urdu ParGram project funded by the Deutsche Forschungsgemeinschaft.

The TURF system presented in this paper is concerned with the Urdu–Roman transliteration. It deals with the Urdu-specific orthographic issues by integrating certain restrictional components into the finite state transducer to cut down on overgeneration, while at the same time employing an architectural design that allows for a large degree of flexibility. The transliterator is based solely on a non-probabilistic finite state transducer implemented with the Xerox finite state technology (XFST) (Beesley and Karttunen, 2003), a robust and easy-to-use finite state tool.

This paper is organized as follows: In section 2, one of the (many) orthographic issues of Urdu is introduced. Section 3 contains a short review of earlier approaches. Section 4 gives a brief introduction into the transducer and the set of restrictions used to cut down on overgeneration. Following this is an account of the architectural design of the transliteration process (section 5). The last two sections provide a first evaluation of the TURF system and a final conclusion.

2 Urdu script issues

Urdu is an Indo-Aryan language spoken mainly in Pakistan and India. It is written in a version of the Persian alphabet and includes a substantial amount of Persian and Arabic vocabulary. The direction of the script is from right to left and the shapes of most characters are context sensitive; i.e., depending on the position within the word, a character assumes a certain form.

Urdu has a set of diacritical marks which appear above or below a character defining a particular vowel, its absence or compound forms. In total, there are 15 of these diacritics (Malik, 2006, 13);

Proceedings of the 10th International Workshop on Finite State Methods and Natural Language Processing, pages 25–29,
Donostia–San Sebastián, July 23–25, 2012.

the four most frequent ones are shown in Table 1 in combination with the letter ب 'b'.

ب + diacritic	Name	Roman transliteration
بَ	Zabar	ba
بِ	Zer	bi
بُ	Pesh	bu
بّ	Tashdid	bb

Table 1: The four most frequently used diacritics

When transliterating from the Urdu script to another script, these diacritics present a huge problem because in standard Urdu texts, the diacritics are rarely used. Thus, for example, we generally are only confronted with the letter ب 'b' and have to guess at the pronunciation that was intended. Take, e.g., the following example, where the word کتا kuttA 'dog' is to be transliterated. Without diacritics, the word consists of three letters: *k*, *t* and *A*. If in the case of transliteration, the system takes a guess at possible short vowels and geminated consonants, the output contains multiple possibilities ((1)).

(1)
```
fst[1]: up کتا
kuttA
kutA
kittA
kitA
kattA
katA
```

In addition to the correct transliteration *kuttA*, the transliterator proposes five other possibilities for the missing diacritics. These examples show that this property of the Urdu script makes it extremely difficult for any transliterator to correctly transliterate undiacriticized input without the help of word lists.

3 Earlier approaches

Earlier approaches to Urdu transliteration almost always have been concerned with the process of transliterating Urdu to Hindi *or* Hindi to Urdu (see, e.g., Lehal and Saini (2010) (Hindi → Urdu), Malik et al. (2009) (Urdu → Hindi), Malik et al. (2010) (Urdu → Roman) or Ahmed (2009) (Roman → Urdu). An exception is Malik (2006), who explored the general idea of using finite state transducers and an intermediate/pivot language to deal with the issues of the scripts of Urdu and Hindi.

All of these approaches are highly dependent on word lists due to the properties of the Urdu script and the problems arising with the use of diacritics. Most systems dealing with undiacriticized input are faced with low accuracy rates: The original system of Malik (2006), e.g., drops from approximately 80% to 50% accuracy (cf. Malik et al. (2009, 178)) – others have higher accuracy rates at the cost of being unidirectional.

While Malik et al. (2009) have claimed that the non-probabilistic finite state model is not able to handle the orthographic issues of Urdu in a satisfying way, this paper shows that there are possibilities for allowing a high accuracy of interpretation, even if the input text does not include diacritics.

4 The TURF Transliterator

The TURF transliterator has been implemented as a non-probabilistic finite state transducer compiled with the **lexc** language (Lexicon Compiler), which is explicitly designed to build finite state networks and analyzers (Beesley and Karttunen, 2003, 203). The resulting network is completely compatible with one that was written with, e.g., regular expressions, but has the advantage in that it is easily readable. The transliteration scheme used here was developed by Malik et al. (2010), following Glassman (1986).

As has been shown in section 1, Urdu transliteration with simple character-to-character mapping is not sufficient. A default integration of short vowels and geminated consonants will, on the other hand, cause significant overgeneration. In order to reduce this overgeneration and to keep the transliterator as efficient as possible, the current approach integrates several layers of restrictions.

4.1 The word list

When dealing with Urdu transliteration it is not possible to *not* work with a word list in order to exclude a large proportion of the overgenerated output. In contrast to other approaches, which depend on Hindi or Urdu wordlists, TURF works with a Roman wordlist. This wordlist is derived from an XFST finite state morphology (Bögel et al., 2007) independently created as part of the Urdu ParGram development effort for the Roman intermediate language (Bögel et al., 2009).

4.2 Regular expression filters

The regular expression filters are based on knowledge about the phonotactics of the language and are a powerful tool for reducing the number of possibilities proposed by the transliterator. As a concrete example, consider the filter in (2).

(2) [~[y A [a |i |u]]]

In Urdu a combination of *[y A short vowel]* is not allowed (~). A filter like in (2) can thus be used to disallow any generations that match this sequence.

4.3 Flag diacritics

The XFST software also provides the user with a method to store 'memory' within a finite state network (cf. Beesley and Karttunen (2003, 339)). These so-called *flag diacritics* enable the user to enforce desired constraints within a network, keeping the transducers relatively small and simple by removing illegal paths and thus reducing the number of possible analyses.

5 The overall TURF architecture

However, the finite state transducer should also be able to deal with unknown items; thus, the constraints on transliteration should not be too restrictive, but should allow for a default transliteration as well. Word lists in general have the drawback that a matching of a finite state transducer output against a word list will delete any entities not on the word list. This means that a methodology needs to be found to deal with unknown but legitimate words without involving any further (non-finite state) software. Figure 1 shows the general architecture to achieve this goal. For illustrative purposes two words are transliterated: كتاب kitAb 'book' and كت, which transliterates to an unknown word *kt*, potentially having the surface forms *kut, kat* or *kit*.

5.1 Step 1: Transliteration Part 1

The finite state transducer itself consists of a network containing the Roman–Urdu character mapping with the possible paths regulated via flag diacritics. Apart from these regular mappings, the network also contains a default Urdu and a default Roman component where the respective characters are simply matched against themselves (e.g. k:k, r:r). On top of this network, the regular expression filters provide further restrictions for the output form.

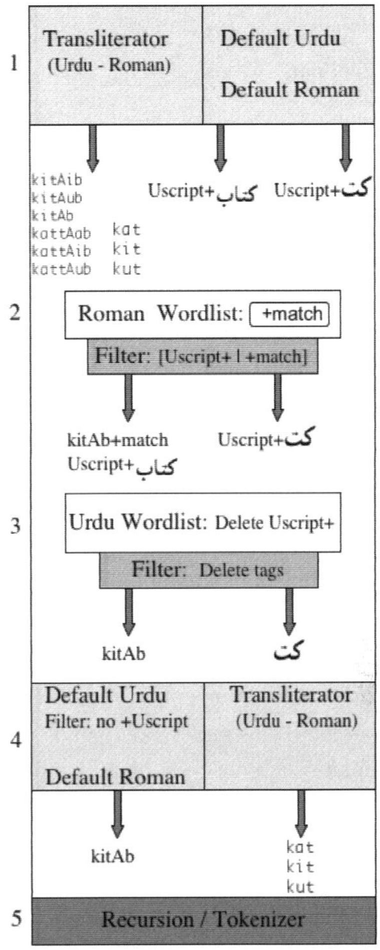

Figure 1: Transliteration of كت and كتاب

The Urdu script default 1-1 mappings are marked with a special identification tag (`[+Uscript]`) for later processing purposes. Thus, an Urdu script word will not only be transliterated into the corresponding Roman script, but will also be 'transliterated' into itself plus an identificational tag.

The output of the basic transliterator shows part of the vast overgeneration caused by the underspecified nature of the script, even though the restricting filters and flags are compiled into this component.

5.2 Step 2: Word list matching and tag deletion

In step 2, the output is matched against a Roman word list. In case there is a match, the respective word is tagged `[+match]`. After this process, a filter is applied, erasing all output forms that contain neither a `[+match]` nor a `[Uscript+]` tag. This way we are left with two choices for the word کتاب – one transliterated 'matched' form and one default Urdu form – while the word کتب is left with only the default Urdu form.

5.3 Step 3: Distinguishing unknown and overgenerated entities

The Urdu word list applied in step 3 is a transliteration of the original Roman word list (4.1), which was transliterated via the TURF system. Thus, the Urdu word list is a mirror image of the Roman word list. During this step, the Urdu script words are matched against the Urdu word list, this time *deleting* all the words that *find* a match. As was to be expected from matching against a mirror word list of the original Roman word list, all of the words that found a match in the Roman word list will also find a match in the Urdu word list, while all unknown entities fail to match. As a result, any Urdu script version of an already correctly transliterated word is deleted, while the Urdu script unknown entity is kept for further processing – the system has now effectively separated known from unknown entities.

In a further step, the tags of the remaining entities are deleted, which leaves us with the correct transliteration of the known word *kitAb* and the unknown Urdu script word کتب.

5.4 Step 4: Transliteration Part 2

The remaining words are once again sent into the finite state transducer of step 1. The Roman transliteration *kitAb* passes unhindered through the Default Roman part. The Urdu word on the other hand is transliterated to all possible forms (in this case three) within the range of the restrictions applied by flags and filters.

5.5 Step 5: Final adjustments

Up to now, the transliterator is only applicable to single words. With a simple (recursive) regular expression it can be designed to apply to larger strings containing more than one word.

The ouput can then be easily composed with a standard tokenizer (e.g. Kaplan (2005)) to enable smooth machine processing.

6 Evaluation

A first evaluation of the TURF transliterator with unseen texts resulted in an accuracy of 86%, if the input was *not* diacriticized. The accuracy rate for undiacriticized text always depends on the size of the word list. The word list used in this application is currently being extended from formerly 20.000 to 40.000 words; thus, a significant improvement of the accuracy rate can be expected within the next few months.

If the optional inclusion of short vowels is removed from the network, the accuracy rate for diacriticized input is close to 97%.

When transliterating from Roman to Urdu, the accuracy rate is close to a 100%, iff the Roman script is written according to the transliteration scheme proposed by Malik et al. (2010).

Transliteration	$U \rightarrow R$	$U \rightarrow R$	$R \rightarrow U$
Input	diacritics	no diacritics	
Diacritics	opt. / compuls.	optional	
Accuracy	86% / 97%	86%	$\sim$ 100%

Table 2: Accuracy rates of the TURF transliterator

7 Conclusion

This paper has introduced a finite state transducer for Urdu $\leftrightarrow$ Roman transliteration. Furthermore, this paper has shown that it is possible for applications based *only* on non-probabilistic finite state technology to return output with a high state-of-the-art accuracy rate; as a consequence, the application profits from the inherently fast and small nature of finite state transducers.

While the transliteration from Roman to Urdu is basically a simple character to character mapping, the transliteration from Urdu to Roman causes a substantial amount of overgeneration due to the underspecified nature of the Urdu script. This was solved by applying different layers of restrictions.

The specific architectural design enables TURF to distinguish between unknown-to-the-word-list and overgenerated items; thus, when matched against a word list, unknown items are not deleted along with the overgenerated items, but are transliterated along with the known items. As a consequence, a transliteration is always given, resulting in an efficient, highly accurate and robust system.

References

Tafseer Ahmed. 2009. Roman to Urdu transliteration using wordlist. In *Proceedings of the Conference on Language and Technology 2009 (CLT09)*, CRULP, Lahore.

Kenneth R. Beesley and Lauri Karttunen. 2003. *Finite State Morphology*. CSLI Publications, Stanford, CA.

Tina Bögel, Miriam Butt, Annette Hautli, and Sebastian Sulger. 2007. Developing a finite-state morphological analyzer for Urdu and Hindi. In T. Hanneforth und K. M. Würzner, editor, *Proceedings of the Sixth International Workshop on Finite-State Methods and Natural Language Processing*, pages 86–96, Potsdam. Potsdam University Press.

Tina Bögel, Miriam Butt, Annette Hautli, and Sebastian Sulger. 2009. Urdu and the modular architecture of ParGram. In *Proceedings of the Conference on Language and Technology 2009 (CLT09)*, CRULP, Lahore.

Dick Crouch, Mary Dalrymple, Ron Kaplan, Tracy King, John Maxwell, and Paula Newman. 2011. *XLE Documentation*. Palo Alto Research Center, Palo Alto, CA. URL: http://www2.parc.com/isl/groups/nltt/xle/doc/xle_toc.html.

Eugene H. Glassman. 1986. *Spoken Urdu*. Nirali Kitaben Publishing House, Lahore, 6 edition.

Ronald M. Kaplan. 2005. A method for tokenizing text. In *Festschrift in Honor of Kimmo Koskenniemi's 60th anniversary*. CSLI Publications, Stanford, CA.

Gurpreet S. Lehal and Tejinder S. Saini. 2010. A Hindi to Urdu transliteration system. In *Proceedings of ICON-2010: 8th International Conference on Natural Language Processing*, Kharagpur.

Abbas Malik, Laurent Besacier, Christian Boitet, and Pushpak Bhattacharyya. 2009. A hybrid model for Urdu Hindi transliteration. In *Proceedings of the 2009 Named Entities Workshop, ACL-IJCNLP*, pages 177–185, Suntec, Singapore.

Muhammad Kamran Malik, Tafseer Ahmed, Sebastian Sulger, Tina Bögel, Atif Gulzar, Ghulam Raza, Sarmad Hussain, and Miriam Butt. 2010. Transliterating Urdu for a Broad-Coverage Urdu/Hindi LFG Grammar. In *Proceedings of the Seventh Conference on International Language Resources and Evaluation (LREC 2010)*. European Language Resources Association (ELRA).

Abbas Malik. 2006. Hindi Urdu machine transliteration system. Master's thesis, University of Paris.

Integrating Aspectually Relevant Properties of Verbs into a Morphological Analyzer for English

Katina Bontcheva
Heinrich-Heine-University
Düsseldorf
bontcheva@phil.uni-duesseldorf.de

Abstract

The integration of semantic properties into morphological analyzers can significantly enhance the performance of any tool that uses their output as input, e.g., for derivation or for syntactic parsing. In this paper will be presented my approach to the integration of aspectually relevant properties of verbs into a morphological analyzer for English.

1 Introduction

Heid, Radtke and Klosa (2012) have recently surveyed morphological analyzers and interactive online dictionaries for German and French. They have established that most of them do not utilize semantic properties. The integration of semantic properties into morphological analyzers can significantly enhance the performance of any tool that uses their output as input, e.g., for derivation or for syntactic parsing. In this paper will be presented my approach to the integration of aspectually relevant properties of verbs into a morphological analyzer for English.

In section 2 I will describe a prototypical finite-state morphological analyzer for English that doesn't utilize semantic properties. Some classifications of English verbs with respect to the aspectually relevant properties that they lexicalize will be outlined in section 3. In section 4 will be presented my approach to the integration the semantic classes in the lexicon. I will describe the modified morphological analyzer for English in section 5 and point out in section 6 the challenges that inflectionally-rich languages present to the techniques outlined in section 4.

Finally, in section 7 I will draw some conclusions and outline future work on other languages.

2 A Prototypical Finite-State Morphological Analyzer for English

English is an inflectionally-poor language which for this reason has been chosen to illustrate my approach to the integration of grammatically relevant lexicalized meaning into morphological analyzers. It has a finite number of irregular (strong) verbs. The rest of the verbs are regular and constitute a single inflectional class.

This prototypical morphological analyzer for English has parallel implementations in *xfst* (cf. Beesley and Karttunen (2003)) and *foma* (cf. Hulden (2009a) and (2009b)). It consists of a lexicon that describes the morphotactics of the language, and of phonological and orthographical alternations and realizational rules that are handled by finite-state replace rules elsewhere. The bases of the regular verbs are stored in a single text file. Here is an excerpt from the *lexc* lexicon without semantic features:

```
LEXICON Root
                      Verb ;
...
LEXICON Verb
^VREG      VerbReg ;
...
LEXICON VerbReg
+V:0        VerbRegFlex ;
...
! This lexicon contains the morpho-
tactic rules.

LEXICON VerbRegFlex
< ["+Pres"] ["+3P"] ["+Sg"]   > # ;
< ["+Pres"] ["+Non3PSg"]   > # ;
< ["+Past"] >    # ;
< ["+PrPart"|"+PaPart"] >   # ;
< ["+Inf"] >  # ;
```


Proceedings of the 10th International Workshop on Finite State Methods and Natural Language Processing, pages 30–34, Donostia–San Sebastián, July 23–25, 2012. ©2012 Association for Computational Linguistics

3 Aspectually Relevant Properties of Verbs

The information that is provided by the prototypical analyzer described above contains lemma, W(ord)-features (morphosyntactic features that exhibit different specifications in different cells of the same inflectional paradigm) and L(exeme)-features that "specify a lexeme's invariant **morphosyntactic** properties" (e.g., gender of nouns, cf. Stump (2001), p. 137, emphasis mine).

L-features should not be confused with lexicalized meaning. I adopt the definition in Rappaport Hovav and Levin (2010), p. 23: "In order to distinguish **lexicalized meaning** from inferences derived from particular uses of verbs in sentences, we take lexicalized meaning to be those **components of meaning** that are entailed in all uses of (a single sense of) a verb, regardless of context" (emphasis mine). Obviously, this definition is applicable not only to verbs but to all word classes.

However, in this paper I will limit myself to the description of lexicalized aspectually relevant properties of verbs.

3.1 Vendler's Classification

In his famous paper "Verbs and Times" Vendler (1957) introduced his "time schemata presupposed by various verbs" (ibid.). He proposes four time schemata: **states, activities**, **accomplishments** and **achievements**.

It is important to point out from the beginning that although he didn't declare explicitly that he was classifying VPs, he did imply this: "Obviously these differences **cannot be explained in terms of time alone: other factors, like the presence or absence of an object, conditions, intended state of affairs, also enter the picture.**" (ibid., p. 143, emphasis mine).

The properties that are often used to define Vendler's classes are **dynamicity, duration** and **telicity**. States are non-dynamic, achievements are non-durative. States and activities are inherently unbounded (non-telic); accomplishments and achievements are inherently bounded. Since three features are needed to differentiate between only four classes that cannot be represented as, e.g., a right-branching tree one wonders if these are the right features to be used for the classification.

Vendler's classification was widely accepted and is used in most current studies on aspect. However, Vendlerian classes cannot be implemented in a *lexc* lexicon for the following reasons:

- Vendler does not classify verbs but VPs
- Part of the features used to differentiate between the classes are not lexicalized by the verb but can be determined at the VP level
- This classification allows multiple class membership even for the same word sense. Thus *run* can be activity and accomplishment, cf. above *running/running a mile*.

3.2 Levin and Rappaport Hovav's Approach to English Verb classes

Sets of semantically related verbs that share a range of linguistic properties form verb classes. There are different criteria for grouping and granularity, e.g., Levin (1993) classifies the verbs in two ways: a) according to semantic content with 48 broad classes and 192 smaller classes; b) according to their participation in argument alternations with 79 alternations. The account of Beth Levin and Malka Rappaport Hovav for verb classes developed over the years in a steady and consistent way that can be trailed in the following publications: (Levin 1993; Levin and Rappaport Hovav 1991, 1995, 2005; Rappaport Hovav 2008; Rappaport Hovav and Levin 1998, 2001, 2005, 2010), among others.

Here I will just summarize the most important ideas and implications for the non-stative verbs:

- Dynamic verbs either lexicalize scales (scalar verbs) or do not (non-scalar verbs)
- Non-scalar verbs lexicalize manner
- Scalar verbs lexicalize result
- Scalar verbs lexicalize two major types of scales – multi-point scales and two-point scales
- The chosen aspectually relevant properties are complementary
- All lexical distinctions described here have grammatical consequences which are relevant to aspectual composition.

This interpretation of non-stative verbs has some very attractive properties:

- The verbs fall into disjunctive classes. There is no multiple class membership (for the same word sense).
- The aspectual properties are lexicalized exclusively by the verb and are not computed at the VP level.

- The lexicalized aspectual properties constrain the syntactical behavior of the verb.
- Manner verbs in English show a uniform argument-realization pattern: they can appear with unspecified and non-subcategorized objects.
- Result verbs are more constrained and less uniform in their argument realization patterns. Transitivity (in contrast to the manner verbs) is an issue.

4 Intersection of Semantic Classes and Inflectional Classes

The main difficulties here arise from the fact that the set of bases that belong to one inflectional class of verbs usually is not identical with the set of bases that lexicalize a particular aspectually relevant property. As a rule, it has intersections with more than one semantic class. The situation is relatively manageable in inflectionally-poor languages like English but becomes very complicated in inflectionally-rich languages.

The distribution of verbs in inflectional classes is in general complementary. There are some exceptions that will not be discussed here.

Vendler's approach to the verb classification described in 3.1 has the undesirable property that most of the verbs have multiple class membership, while the approach of Levin and Rappaport Hovav described in 3.2 has advantages which make the task easier.

Thus, for English we have the set of bases of regular verbs that is monolithic, and the same set of bases but this time divided into complementary subsets of aspectual semantic classes in the sense of Levin and Rappaport Hovav. The cross product of the number of subsets in the first set and the number of subsets in the second set equals the number of aspectual semantic classes since there is only one inflectional class of regular verbs.

5 The modified Prototypical Lexicon for English

The following modifications need to be introduced to the lexicon in order to incorporate the aspectual properties of English verbs.

The single placeholder pointing to the single file containing the bases of regular verbs must be replaced with several placeholders that point to the files containing the complementary subsets of bases of verbs belonging to the different aspectual classes.

New continuation lexicons introducing each aspectual class must be added immediately after LEXICON Verb. Since the union of the sets of aspectual-class bases of regular verbs is identical with the set of the bases of the regular verbs, all aspectual-class lexicons have the same continuation lexicon: LEXICON VerbRegFlex. Irregular verbs get the semantic tags added to the lexical entry and suppletive verbs get them in the master lexicon.

```
Multichar_Symbols
+V +VIrrTT %<manner%>
...

LEXICON Root
          Verb ;
          VerbSuppl ;
...

LEXICON VerbSuppl
go%<resmulpo%>+V+Inf:go  # ;
go%<resmulpo%>+V+Pres+3P+Sg:goes # ;
go%<resmulpo%>+V+Pres+Non3PSg:go # ;
go%<resmulpo%>+V+Past:went  # ;
go%<resmulpo%>+V+PaPart:gone  # ;
go%<resmulpo%>+V+PrPart:going # ;
...

LEXICON Verb
^VREGM      VerbRegManner ;
...
LEXICON VerbRegManner
+V%<manner%>:0       VerbRegFlex ;

LEXICON VerbRegFlex
...
```

Below is an excerpt from the file holding the bases of irregular verbs that build identical past-tense and perfect-participle forms by adding *'-t'*:

```
...
{creep<manner>}:{creep} |
{feel} |
{keep} |
{sleep} |
{sweep<manner>}:{sweep} |
...
```

In order to be able to rewrite the semantic-class tags, which appear only on the lexical (upper) side of the transducer containing the lexicon, I invert the network, apply the semantic-tag rewriting rules and invert the resulting net again. The network is then composed with the realization rules and the phonological and orthographical alternations that operate on the surface (lower) side of the transducer:

```
! Semantic-features tag-rewriting
define LEX2 [LEX1.i] ;
define LEX2 [LEX1.i] ;
define Mnr [ %< m a n n e r %> ->
       %<%+SV%>%<%+SVO%>%<%+SVOOC%> ] ;

! alternative RRG tags
!define Mnr  [%< m a n n e r %> ->
!%<do´ %(x%, %[predicate´ %(x%) or
!              %(x%, y%)%]%)%>] ;

define LEX3 [LEX2 .o. Mnr] ;
define LEX  [LEX3.i] ;

! Inflectional morphology: realization
...
```

Here is the output of the analysis of *'swept'* with dependency-grammar valency-pattern tags (S=subject, V=verb, O=object, OC=object complement):

```
swept
sweep<+SV><+SVO><+SVOOC>+V+Past
sweep<+SV><+SVO><+SVOOC>+V+PaPart
```

and the alternative output with Role and Reference Grammar logical structures:

```
swept
sweep<do´(x,[predicate´(x)or(x,y)])>+V+Past
sweep<do´(x,[predicate´(x)or(x,y)])>+V+PaPart
```

Valency information is necessary for syntactic parsing and has been used in Constraint Grammar shallow parsers and in dependency parsers. The advantage of this approach to already existing morphological analyzers for English is that the valency-pattern tags are added to classes of verbs rather than to individual lexical entries. The ability to provide alternative outputs for the integrated aspectually relevant semantic information is a novelty of this morphological analyzer.

6 Beyond English: the Challenges of Inflectionally-Rich Languages

We have seen a simplified example that shows the modeling and the implementation of a morphological analyzer that utilizes semantic-class tags for aspectually relevant lexical properties of English verbs.

Things become much more challenging if we want to model inflectionally-rich languages such as Bulgarian, Russian or Finnish. Bulgarian verbs, for example, can be divided (depending on the modeling) into some 15 complementary inflectional classes. This number multiplied by 4 Levin-Rappaport-Hovav classes would result in some 60 sets of verb bases that share the same inflectional class and Levin-Rappaport-Hovav class. If a finer-grained semantic classification is adopted, the number of classes will considerably increase and this will lead to a lexicon that exclusively requires manual lexicographical work.

7 Conclusion

This paper illustrates the integration of aspectually relevant properties of verbs into a morphological analyzer for English. I showed that these features can be integrated while the computational efficiency of the analyzer can still be maintained if the linguistic modelling is adequate. However, this only scratches the surface of the challenge of integrating semantic features into morphological analyzers. In the future, it is planned (together with other researchers) to extend the integration of semantic features to nouns, adjectives and adverbs. We also plan to model and implement morphological analyzers for other languages such as German, Russian, Polish and Bulgarian.

References

Kenneth R. Beesley and Lauri Karttunen. 2003. Finite State Morphology. Palo Alto, CA: CSLI Publications

David Dowty. 1979. Word Meaning and Montague Grammar. Dordrecht: Reidel.

William Foley and Robert Van Valin, Jr. 1984. Functional Syntax and Universal Grammar. Cambridge: Cambridge University Press.

Ulrich Heid, Janina Radtke and Anette Klosa. 2012. Morphology and Semantics: A Survey of Morphological Analyzers and Interactive Online Dictionaries – and Proposals for their Improvement. 15th International Morphology Meeting. Morphology and Meaning. Vienna, February 9-12, 2012

Mans Hulden. 2009a. Finite-State Machine Construction Methods and Algorithms for Phonology and Morphology. PhD Thesis, University of Arizona.

Mans Hulden. 2009b. Foma: a Finite-State Compiler and Library. In: Proceedings of the EACL 2009 Demonstrations Session, pp. 29-32.

Beth Levin. 1993. English Verb Classes and Alternations: A Preliminary Investigation. Chicago, IL: University of Chicago Press..

Beth Levin and Malka Rappaport Hovav. 1991. Wiping the Slate Clean: A Lexical Semantic Exploration. In: B. Levin and S. Pinker, (eds.). Special Issue on Lexical and Conceptual Semantics. Cognition 41, pp. 123-151.

Beth Levin and Malka Rappaport Hovav. 1995. Unaccusativity: At the Syntax-Lexical Semantics Interface. Cambridge, MA : MIT Press.

Beth Levin and Malka Rappaport Hovav. 2005. Argument Realization. Cambridge, UK: Cambridge University Press.

Malka Rappaport Hovav. 2008. Lexicalized Meaning and the Internal Temporal Structure of Events. In: S. Rothstein, (ed.), Theoretical and Crosslinguistic Approaches to the Semantics of Aspect. Amsterdam: John Benjamins, pp. 13-42.

Malka Rappaport Hovav and Beth Levin. 1998. Building Verb Meanings. In: M. Butt and W. Geuder, (eds.). The Projection of Arguments: Lexical and Compositional Factors. Stanford, CA: CSLI Publications, pp. 97-134.

Malka Rappaport Hovav and Beth Levin. 2001. An Event Structure Account of English Resultatives. Language 77, pp. 766-797.

Malka Rappaport Hovav and Beth Levin. 2005. Change of State Verbs: Implications for Theories of Argument Projection. In: N. Erteschik-Shir and T. Rapoport (eds.) The Syntax of Aspect. Oxford: Oxford University Press, pp. 274-286.

Malka Rappaport Hovav and Beth Levin. 2010. Reflections on Manner/Result Complementarity. In: M. Rappaport Hovav, E. Doron, and I. Sichel (eds.). Syntax, Lexical Semantics, and Event Structure. Oxford: Oxford University Press, pp. 21–38.

Gregory Stump. 2001. Inflectional Morphology: A Theory of Paradigm Structure. Cambridge: Cambridge University Press.

Zeno Vendler. 1957. Verbs and Times. The Philosophical Review, Vol. 66, No. 2., pp. 143-60

Finite-state technology in a verse-making tool

Manex Agirrezabal, Iñaki Alegria, Bertol Arrieta
University of the Basque Country (UPV/EHU)
maguirrezaba008@ikasle.ehu.es, i.alegria@ehu.es, bertol@ehu.es
Mans Hulden
Ikerbasque (Basque Science Foundation)
mhulden@email.arizona.edu

Abstract

This paper presents a set of tools designed to assist traditional Basque verse writers during the composition process. In this article we are going to focus on the parts that have been created using finite-state technology: this includes tools such as syllable counters, rhyme checkers and a rhyme search utility.

1 The BAD tool and the Basque singing tradition

The BAD tool is an assistant tool for verse-makers in the Basque *bertsolari* tradition. This is a form of improvised verse composition and singing where participants are asked to produce impromptu compositions around themes which are given to them following one of many alternative verse formats. The variety of verse schemata that exist all impose fairly strict structural requirements on the composer. Verses in the *bertsolari* tradition must consist of a specified number of lines, each with a fixed number of syllables. Also, strict rhyme patterns must be followed. The structural requirements are considered the most difficult element in the *bertsolaritza*—however, well-trained *bertsolaris* can usually produce verses that fulfill the structural prerequisites in a very limited time.

The BAD tool presented here is mainly directed at those with less experience in the tradition such as students. One particular target group are the *bertso-eskola*-s (verse-making schools) that have been growing in popularity—these are schools found throughout the Basque Country that train young people in the art of *bertsolaritza*.

The primary functionality of the tool is illustrated in figure 1 which shows the main view of the utility. The user is offered a form in which a verse can be written, after which the system checks the technical correctness of the poem. To perform this task, several finite state transducer-based modules, are used, some of them involving the metrics (syllable counter) of the verse, and others the rhyme (rhyme searcher and checker). The tool has support for 150 well known verse meters.

In the following sections, we will outline the technology used in each of the parts in the system.

2 Related work

Much of the existing technology for Basque morphology and phonology uses finite-state technology, including earlier work on rhyme patterns (Arrieta et al., 2001). In our work, we have used the Basque morphological description (Alegria et al., 1996) in the rhyme search module. Arrieta et al. (2001) develop a system where, among other things, users can search for words that rhyme with an introduced pattern. It is implemented in the formalism of two-level morphology (Koskenniemi, 1983) and compiled into finite-state transducers.

We have used the open-source *foma* finite-state compiler to develop all the finite-state based parts of our tool.[1]. After compiling the transducers, we use them in our own application through the C/C++ API provided with *foma*.

3 Syllable counter

As mentioned, each line in a verse must contain a specified number of syllables. The syllable counter module that checks whether this is the case consists of a submodule that performs the syllabification itself as well as a module that yields variants produced by optional apocope and syncope effects. For the syllabification itself, we use the approach described in Hulden (2006), with some modifications to capture Basque phonology.

[1] In our examples, FST expressions are written using *foma* syntax. For details, visit http://foma.googlecode.com

Proceedings of the 10th International Workshop on Finite State Methods and Natural Language Processing, pages 35–39,
Donostia–San Sebastián, July 23–25, 2012. ©2012 Association for Computational Linguistics

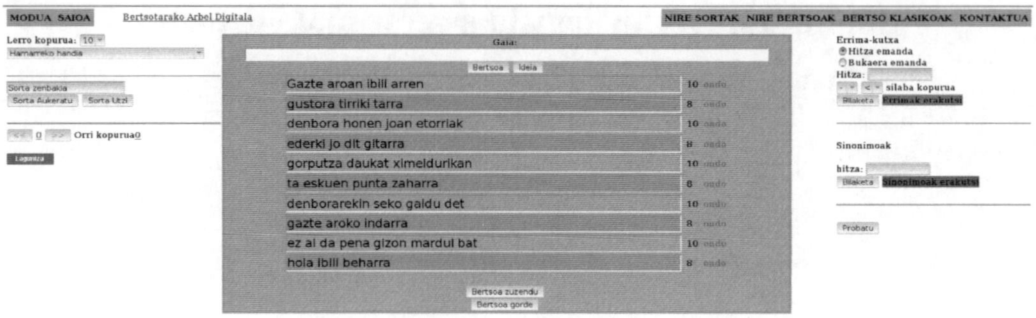

Figure 1: A verse written in the BAD web application.

3.1 Syllabification

Basque syllables can be modeled by assuming a maximum onset principle together with a sonority hierarchy where obstruents are the least sonorous element, followed in sonority by the liquids, the nasals and the glides. The syllable nuclei are always a single vowel (a,e,i,o,u) or a combination of a low vowel (a,e) and a high vowel (i,o,u) or a high vowel and another high vowel.

The syllabifier relies on a chain of composed replacement rules (Beesley and Karttunen, 2003) compiled into finite-state transducers. These definitions are shown in figure 2. The overall strategy is to first mark off the nuclei in a word by the rule `MarkNuclei` which takes advantage of a left-to-right longest replacement rule. This is to ensure that diphthongs do not get split into separate syllables by the subsequent syllabification process. Following this, syllables are marked off by the `markSyll`-rule, which inserts periods after legitimate syllables. This rule takes advantage of the shortest-leftmost replacement strategy—in effect minimizing the coda and maximizing the size of the onset of a syllable to the extent permitted by the allowed onsets and codas, defined in `Onset` and `Coda`, respectively.

To illustrate this process, supposing that we are syllabifying the Basque word **intransitiboa**. The first step in the syllabification process is to mark the nuclei in the word, resulting in **{i}ntr{a}ns{i}t{i}b{o}{a}**. In the more complex syllabification step, the `markSyll` rule assures that the juncture **ntr** gets divided as **n.tr** because **nt.r** would produce a non-maximal onset, and **i.ntr** would in turn produce an illegal onset in the second syllable. The final syllabification, after markup removal by the `Cleanup` rule, is then **in.tran.si.ti.bo.a**. This process is illustrated in figure 3

```
define Obs         [f|h|j|k|p|s|t|t s|t z|t x|x|
                    z|b|d|g|v|d d|t t];
define LiqNasGli   [l|r|r r|y|n|m];
define LowV        [a|e|o];
define HighV       [i|u];
define V           LowV | HighV;
define Nucleus     [V | LowV HighV |
                   [HighV HighV - [i i] - [u u]]];
define Onset       (Obs) (LiqNasGli);
define Coda        C^<4;

define MarkNuclei Nucleus @-> %{ ... %};
define Syll        Onset %{ Nucleus %} Coda;
define markSyll    Syll @> ... "." || _ Syll ;
define cleanUp     %{|%} -> 0;

regex MarkNuclei .o. markSyll .o. cleanUp;
```

Figure 2: Syllable definition

In *bertsolaritza*, Basque verse-makers follow this type of syllable counting in the majority if cases; however, there is some flexibility as regards the syllabification process. For example, suppose that the phrase **ta lehenengo urtian** needs to fit a line which must contain six syllables. If we count the syllables using the algorithm shown above, we receive a count of eight (**ta le.hen.en.go ur.ti.an**). However, in the word **lehenengo** we can identify the syncope pattern **vowel-h-vowel**, with the two vowels being identical. In such cases, we may simply replace the entire sequence by a single vowel (ehe $\rightarrow$ e). This is phonetically equivalent to shortening the *ehe*-sequence (for those dialects where the orthographical **h** is silent). With this modification, we can fit the line in a 7 syllable structure. We can, however, further reduce the line to 6 syllables by a second type of process that merges the last syllable of one word with the first of the next one and then resyllabifying. Hence, **ta lehenengo urtian**, using the modifications explained above, could be reduced to **ta.le.nen.gour.ti.an**, which would fit the 6 syllable structure. This production of syllabification variants is shown in figure 4.

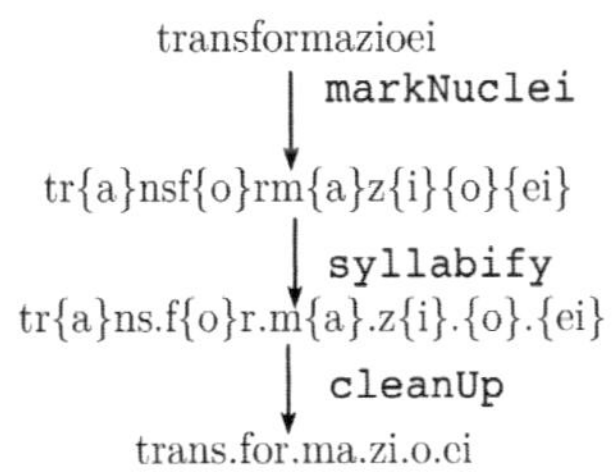

Figure 3: Normal syllabification.

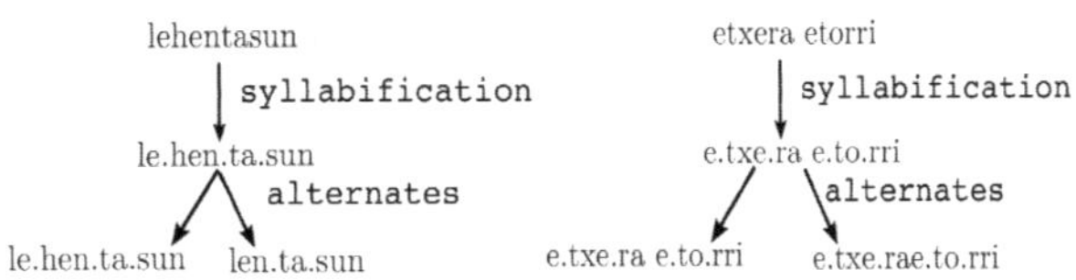

Figure 4: Flexible syllabification.

4 Finite-state technology for rhymes

4.1 Basque rhyme patterns and rules

Similar to the flexibility in syllabification, Basque rhyme schemes also allows for a certain amount of leeway that *bertsolaris* can take advantage of. The widely consulted rhyming dictionary *Hiztegi Errimatua* (Amuriza, 1981) contains documented a number of phonological alternations that are acceptable as off-rhymes: for example the stops **p**, **t**, and **k** are often interchangeable, as are some other phonological groups. Figure 5 illustrates the definitions for interchangeable phonemes when rhyming. The interchangeability is done as a prelude to rhyme checking, whereby phonemes in certain groups, such as **p**, are replaced by an abstract symbol denoting the group (e.g. **PTK**).

4.2 Rhyme checker

The rhyme checker itself in BAD was originally developed as a *php*-script, and then reimplemented as

```
define plosvl       [p | t | k];
define rplosv       [b | d | g | r];
define sib          [s | z | x];
define nas          [n | m];

define plosvlconv   ptk -> PTK;
define rplosvconv   bdgr -> BDGR;
define sibconv      sib -> SZX;
define nasconv      nas -> NM;

define phoRules     plosvlconv .o. rplosvconv .o.
                    sibconv    .o. nasconv ;
```

Figure 5: Conflation of consonant groups before rhyme checking.

a purely finite-state system. In this section we will focus on the finite-state based one.

As the *php* version takes advantage of syllabification, the one developed with transducers does not. Instead, it relies on a series of replacement rules and the special `_eq()` operator available in *foma*. An implementation of this is given in figure 6. As input to the system, the two words to be checked are assumed to be provided one after the other, joined by a hyphen. Then, the system (by rule `rhympat1`) identifies the segments that do not participate in the rhyme and marks them off with "{" and "}" symbols (e.g. **landa-ganga** $\rightarrow$ <{**l**}**anda**>-<{**g**}**anga**>).

The third rule (`rhympat3`) removes everything that is between "{" and "}", leaving us only with the segments relevant for the rhyming pattern (e.g. <**anda**>-<**anga**>). Subsequent to this rule, we apply the phonological grouping reductions mentioned above in section 4.1, producing, for example (<**aNMBDGRa**>-<**aNMBDGRa**>).

After this reduction, we use the `_eq(X,L,R)`-operator in *foma*, which from a transducer `X`, filters out those words in the output where material between the specified delimiter symbols `L` and `R` are unequal. In our case, we use the < and > symbols as delimiters, yielding a final transducer that does not accept non-rhyming words.

4.3 Rhyme search

The BAD tool also includes a component for searching words that rhyme with a given word. It is developed in *php* and uses a finite-state component likewise developed with *foma*.

Similarly to the techniques previously described, it relies on extracting the segments relevant to the

```
define rhympat1    [0:"{" ?* 0:"}"
  [[[V+ C+]  (V) V] | [(C) V V]] C* ];
# constraining V V C pattern
define rhympat2  ~[?* V "}" V C];
# cleaning non-rhyme part
define rhympat3  "{" ?* "}" -> 0;
define rhympat rhympat1 .o. rhympat2 .o.
  rhympat3;

# rhyming pattern on each word
# and phonological changes
define MarkPattern rhympat .o.
       phoRules  .o. patroiak;
# verifying if elements between < and >
# are equal
define    MarkTwoPatterns
    0:%< MarkPattern 0:%> %-
    0:%< MarkPattern 0:%> ;
define Verify  _eq(MarkTwoPatterns, %<, %>)
regex Verify .o. Clean;
```

Figure 6: Rhyme checking using *foma*.

rhyme, after which phonological rules are applied (as in 4.1) to yield phonetically related forms. For example, introducing the pattern **era**, the system returns four phonetically similar forms **era**, **eda**, **ega**, and **eba**. Then, these responses are fed to a transducer that returns a list of words with the same endings. To this end, we take advantage of a finite-state morphological description of Basque (Alegria et al., 1996).

As this transducer returns a set of words which may be very comprehensive—including words not commonly used, or very long compounds—we then apply a frequency-based filter to reduce the set of possible rhymes. To construct the filter, we used a newspaper corpus, (Egunkaria[2]) and extracted the frequencies of each word form. Using the frequency counts, we defined a transducer that returns a word's frequency, using which we can extract only the n-most frequent candidates for rhymes. The system also offers the possibility to limit the number of syllables that desired rhyming words may contain. The syllable filtering system and the frequency limiting parts have been developed in *php*. Figure 7 shows the principle of the rhyme search's finite-state component.

5 Evaluation

As we had available to us a rhyme checker written in *php* before implementing the finite-state version,

[2]http://berria.info

```
regex phoRules .o. phoRules.i .o.
      0:?* ?* .o. dictionary ;
```

Figure 7: Rhyme search using *foma*

it allowed for a comparison of the application speed of each. We ran an experiment introducing 250,000 pairs of words to the two rhyme checkers and measured the time each system needed to reply. The FST-based checker was roughly 25 times faster than the one developed in *php*.

It is also important to mention that these tools are going to be evaluated in an academic environment. As that evaluation has not been done yet, we made another evaluation in our NLP group in order to detect errors in terms of syllabification and rhyme quality. The general feeling of the experiment was that the BAD tool works well, but we had some efficiency problems when many people worked together. To face this problem some tools are being implemented as a server.

6 Discussion & Future work

Once the main tools of the BAD have been developed, we intend to focus on two different lines of development. The first one is to extend to flexibility of rhyme checking. There are as of yet patterns which are acceptable as rhymes to *bertsolaris* that the system does not yet recognize. For example, the words **filma** and **errima** will not be accepted by the current system, as the two rhymes **ilma** and **ima** are deemed to be incompatible. In reality, these two words are acceptable as rhymes by *bertsolaris*, as the **l** is not very phonetically prominent. However, adding flexibility also involves controlling for overgeneration in rhymes. Other reduction patterns not currently covered by the system include phenomena such as synaloepha—omission of vowels at word boundaries when one word ends and the next one begins with a vowel.

Also, we intend to include a catalogue of melodies in the system. These are traditional melodies that usually go along with a specific meter. Some 3,000 melodies are catalogued (Dorronsoro, 1995). We are also using the components described in this article in another project whose aim is to construct a robot capable to find, generate and sing verses automatically.

Acknowledgments

This research has been partially funded by the Spanish Ministry of Education and Science (OpenMT-2, TIN2009-14675-C03) and partially funded by the Basque Government (Research Groups, IT344-10).

We would like to acknowledge Aitzol Astigarraga for his help in the development of this project. He has been instrumental in our work, and we intend to continue working with him. Also we must mention the Association of Friends of Bertsolaritza, whose verse corpora has been used to test and develop these tools and to develop new ones.

References

Alegria, I., Artola, X., Sarasola, K., and Urkia, M. (1996). Automatic morphological analysis of Basque. *Literary and Linguistic Computing*, 11(4):193–203.

Amuriza, X. (1981). *Hiztegi errimatua [Rhyme Dictionary]*. Alfabetatze Euskalduntze Koordinakundea.

Arrieta, B., Alegria, I., and Arregi, X. (2001). An assistant tool for verse-making in Basque based on two-level morphology. *Literary and linguistic computing*, 16(1):29–43.

Beesley, K. R. and Karttunen, L. (2003). *Finite state morphology*. CSLI.

Dorronsoro, J. (1995). *Bertso doinutegia [Verse melodies repository]*. Euskal Herriko Bertsolari Elkartea.

Hulden, M. (2006). Finite-state syllabification. *Finite-State Methods and Natural Language Processing*, pages 86–96.

Koskenniemi, K. (1983). Two-level morphology: A general computational model for word-form production and generation. *Publications of the Department of General Linguistics, University of Helsinki. Helsinki: University of Helsinki.*

DAGGER: A Toolkit for Automata on Directed Acyclic Graphs

Daniel Quernheim
Institute for Natural Language Processing
Universität Stuttgart, Germany
Pfaffenwaldring 5b, 70569 Stuttgart
daniel@ims.uni-stuttgart.de

Kevin Knight
University of Southern California
Information Sciences Institute
Marina del Rey, California 90292
knight@isi.edu

Abstract

This paper presents DAGGER, a toolkit for finite-state automata that operate on *directed acyclic graphs* (dags). The work is based on a model introduced by (Kamimura and Slutzki, 1981; Kamimura and Slutzki, 1982), with a few changes to make the automata more applicable to natural language processing. Available algorithms include membership checking in bottom-up dag acceptors, transduction of dags to trees (bottom-up dag-to-tree transducers), k-best generation and basic operations such as union and intersection.

1 Introduction

Finite string automata and finite tree automata have proved to be useful tools in various areas of natural language processing (Knight and May, 2009). However, some applications, especially in semantics, require graph structures, in particular *directed acyclic graphs* (dags), to model reentrancies. For instance, the dags in Fig. 1 represents the semantics of the sentences "The boy wants to believe the girl" and "The boy wants the girl to believe him." The double role of "the boy" is made clear by the two parent edges of the BOY node, making this structure non-tree-like.

Powerful graph rewriting systems have been used for NLP (Bohnet and Wanner, 2010), yet we consider a rather simple model: finite dag automata that have been introduced by (Kamimura and Slutzki, 1981; Kamimura and Slutzki, 1982) as a straightforward extension of tree automata. We present the toolkit DAGGER (written in PYTHON) that can be used to visualize dags and to build dag acceptors

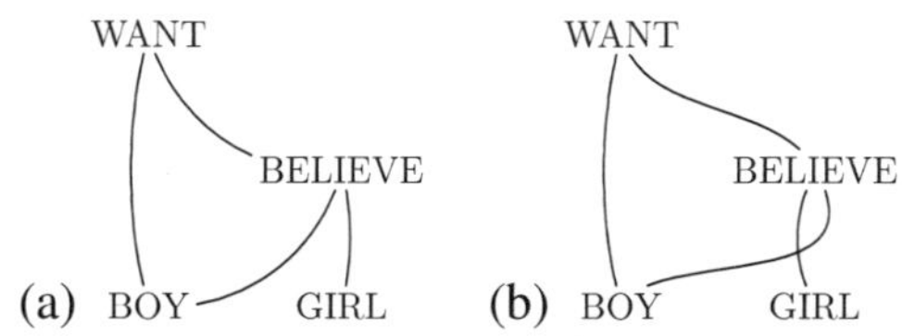

Figure 1: (a) "The boy wants to believe the girl." and (b) "The boy wants the girl to believe him." First edge represents `:agent` role, second edge represents `:patient` role.

and dag-to-tree transducers similar to their model. Compared to those devices, in order to use them for actual NLP tasks, our machines differ in certain aspects:

- We do not require our dags to be planar, and we do not only consider derivation dags.
- We add weights from any commutative semiring, e.g. real numbers.

The toolkit is available under an open source licence.[1]

2 Dags and dag acceptors

DAGGER comes with a variety of example dags and automata. Let us briefly illustrate some of them. The dag of Fig. 1(a) can be defined in a human-readable format called PENMAN (Bateman, 1990):

```
(1 / WANT
    :agent (2 / BOY)
    :patient (3 / BELIEVE
                :agent 2
                :patient (4 / GIRL)))
```

[1] http://www.ims.uni-stuttgart.de/~daniel/dagger/

Proceedings of the 10th International Workshop on Finite State Methods and Natural Language Processing, pages 40–44,
Donostia–San Sebastián, July 23–25, 2012.

```
s
s -> (WANT :agent i :patient s)
s -> (BELIEVE :agent i :patient s)
i -> (0)
s -> (0)
i -> (GIRL)
i -> (BOY)
s -> (GIRL)
s -> (BOY)
i i -> (GIRL)
i i -> (BOY)
i s -> (GIRL)
i s -> (BOY)
s s -> (GIRL)
s s -> (BOY)
```

Figure 2: Example dag acceptor `example.bda`.

```
s
s -> (WANT :agent i :patient s) @ 0.6
s -> (BELIEVE :agent i :patient s) @ 0.4
i -> (0) @ 0.2
s -> (0) @ 0.4
i -> (GIRL) @ 0.3
s -> (GIRL) @ 0.3
i -> (BOY) @ 0.2
s -> (BOY) @ 0.2
i i -> (2=1 :arg e) @ 0.3
i s -> (2=1 :arg e) @ 0.3
s s -> (2=1 :arg e) @ 0.3
e -> (GIRL) @ 0.4
e -> (BOY) @ 0.6
```

Figure 3: Simplified dag acceptor `simple.bda`.

In this format, every node has a unique identifier, and edge labels start with a colon. The tail node of an edge is specified as a whole subdag, or, in the case of a reentrancy, is referred to with its identifier.

Fig. 2 shows a dag acceptor. The first line contains the final state, and the remaining lines contain rules. Mind that the rules are written in a top-down fashion, but are evaluated bottom-up for now. Let us consider a single rule:

```
s -> (WANT :agent i :patient s)
```

The right-hand side is a symbol (`WANT :agent :patient`) whose tail edges are labeled with states (`i` and `s`), and after applying the rule, its head edges are labeled with new states (`s`). All rules are height one, but in the future we will allow for larger subgraphs.

In order to deal with symbols of arbitrary head rank (i.e. symbols that can play multiple roles), we can use rules using special symbols such as `2=1` and `3=1` that split one edge into more than one:

```
i s -> (2=1 :arg e)
```

Using these state-changing rules, the ruleset can be simplified (see Fig. 3), however the dags look a bit different now:

```
(1 / WANT
    :agent (2 / 2=1
              :arg (3 / BOY))
    :patient (4 / BELIEVE
                 :agent 2
                 :patient (5 / GIRL)))
```

Note that we also added weights to the ruleset now. Weights are separated from the rest of a rule by the `@` sign. The weight semantics is the usual one, where weights are multiplied along derivation steps, while the weights of alternative derivations are added.

2.1 Membership checking and derivation forests

DAGGER is able to perform various operations on dags. The instructions can be given in a simple expression language. The general format of an expression is:

```
(command f1 .. fm p1 .. pn)
```

Every command has a number of (optional) features f_i and a fixed number of arguments p_i. Most commands have a short and a long name; we will use the short names here to save space. In order to evaluate a expression, you can either

- supply it on the command-line:

  ```
  ./dagger.py -e EXPRESSION
  ```

- or read from a file:

  ```
  ./dagger.py -f FILE
  ```

We will now show a couple of example expressions that are composed of smaller expressions. Assume that the dag acceptor of Fig. 2 is saved in the file `example.bda`, and the file `boywants.dag` contains the example dag in PENMAN format. We can load the dag with the expression `(g (f boywants.dag))`, and the acceptor with the expression `(a w (f example.bda))` where `w` means that the acceptor is weighted. We could also specify the dag directly in PENMAN format using `p` instead of `f`. We can use the command `r`:

```
(r (a w (f example.bda)) (g (f
boywants.dag)))
```

to check whether `example.bda` recognizes `boywants.dag`. This will output one list item

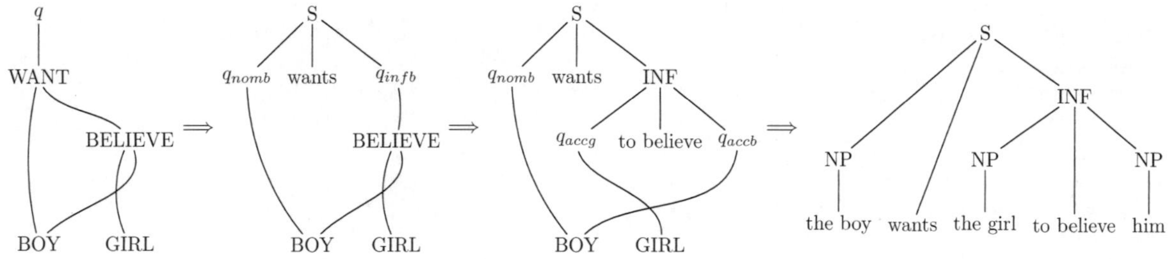

Figure 4: Derivation from graph to tree "the boy wants the girl to believe him".

```
q
q.S(x1 wants x2)) -> (WANT :agent nomb.x1 :patient inf.x2)
inf.INF(x1 to believe x2) -> (BELIEVE :agent accg.x1 :patient accb.x2)
accg.NP(the girl) -> (GIRL)
nomb.NP(the boy) accb.(him) -> (BOY)
```

Figure 5: Example dag-to-tree-transducer `example.bdt`.

for each successful derivation (and, if the acceptor is weighted, their weights), in this case: `('s', '0.1', 0, '0')`, which means that the acceptor can reach state `s` with a derivation weighted 0.1. The rest of the output concerns dag-to-tree transducers and will be explained later.

Note that in general, there might be multiple derivations due to ambiguity (non-determinism). Fortunately, the whole set of derivations can be efficiently represented as another dag acceptor with the `d` command. This *derivation forest acceptor* has the set of rules as its symbol and the set of configurations (state-labelings of the input dag) as its state set.

```
(d (a w (f example.bda)) (g f
boywants.dag)))
```

will write the derivation forest acceptor to the standard output.

2.2 k-best generation

To obtain the highest-weighted 7 dags generated by the example dag acceptor, run:

```
(k 7 (a w (f example.bda)))
```

```
(1 / BOY)
(1 / GIRL)
(1 / BELIEVE :agent (2 / GIRL) :patient 2)
(1 / WANT :agent (2 / GIRL) :patient 2)
(1 / 0)
(1 / BELIEVE :agent (2 / BOY) :patient 2)
(1 / WANT :agent (2 / BOY) :patient 2)
```

If the acceptor is unweighted, the smallest dags (in terms of derivation steps) are returned.

```
(1 / 0)
(1 / BOY)
(1 / GIRL)
(1 / BELIEVE :agent (2 / GIRL) :patient 2)
(1 / BELIEVE :agent (2 / BOY) :patient 2)
(1 / BELIEVE :agent (2 / GIRL) :patient
    (3 / 0))
(1 / BELIEVE :agent (2 / GIRL) :patient
    (3 / GIRL))
```

2.3 Visualization of dags

Both dags and dag acceptors can be visualized using GRAPHVIZ[2]. For this purpose, we use the `q` (query) command and the `v` feature:

```
(v (g (f boywants.dag)) boywants.pdf)
(v (a (f example.bda)) example.pdf)
```

Dag acceptors are represented as hypergraphs, where the nodes are the states and each hyperedge represents a rule labeled with a symbol.

2.4 Union and intersection

In order to construct complex acceptors from simpler building blocks, it is helpful to make use of union (`u`) and intersection (`i`). The following code will intersect two acceptors and return the 5 best dags of the intersection acceptor.

```
(k 5 (i (a (f example.bda)) (a (f
someother.bda))))
```

Weighted union, as usual, corresponds to sum, weighted intersection to product.

[2]available under the Eclipse Public Licence from `http://www.graphviz.org/`

	string automata	tree automata	dag automata
compute	...strings (sentences)	...(syntax) trees	...semantic representations
k-best	...paths through a WFSA (Viterbi, 1967; Eppstein, 1998)	...derivations in a weighted forest (Jiménez and Marzal, 2000; Huang and Chiang, 2005)	✓
EM training	Forward-backward EM (Baum et al., 1970; Eisner, 2003)	Tree transducer EM training (Graehl et al., 2008)	?
Determinization	...of weighted string acceptors (Mohri, 1997)	...of weighted tree acceptors (Borchardt and Vogler, 2003; May and Knight, 2006a)	?
Transducer composition	WFST composition (Pereira and Riley, 1997)	Many transducers not closed under composition (Maletti et al., 2009)	?
General tools	AT&T FSM (Mohri et al., 2000), Carmel (Graehl, 1997), OpenFST (Riley et al., 2009)	Tiburon (May and Knight, 2006b), ForestFIRE (Cleophas, 2008; Strolenberg, 2007)	DAGGER

Table 1: General-purpose algorithms for strings, trees and feature structures.

3 Dag-to-tree transducers

Dag-to-tree transducers are dag acceptors with tree output. In every rule, the states on the right-hand sides have tree variables attached that are used to build one tree for each state on the left-hand side. A fragment of an example dag-to-tree transducer can be seen in Fig. 5.

Let us see what happens if we apply this transducer to our example dag:

```
(r (a t (f example.bdt)) (g (f
boywants.dag)))
```

All derivations including output trees will be listed:

```
('q', '1.0',
S(NP(the boy) wants INF(NP(the girl)
to believe NP(him))),
'the boy wants the girl to believe
him')
```

A graphical representation of this derivation (top-down instead of bottom-up for illustrative purposes) can be seen in Fig. 4.

3.1 Backward application and force decoding

Sometimes, we might want to see which dags map to a certain input tree in a dag-to-tree transducer. This is called *backward application* since we use the transducer in the reverse direction: We are currently implementing this by "generation and checking", i.e. a process that generates dags and trees at the same time. Whenever a partial tree does not match the input tree, it is discarded, until we find a derivation and a dag for the input tree. If we also restrict the dag part, we have *force decoding*.

4 Future work

This work describes the basics of a dag automata toolkit. To the authors' knowledge, no such implementation already exists. Of course, many algorithms are missing, and there is a lot of room for improvement, both from the theoretical and the practical viewpoint. This is a brief list of items for future research (Quernheim and Knight, 2012):

- Complexity analysis of the algorithms.
- Closure properties of dag acceptors and dag-to-tree transducers as well as composition with tree transducers.
- Extended left-hand sides to condition on a larger semantic context, just like extended top-down tree transducers (Maletti et al., 2009).
- Handling flat, unordered, sparse sets of relations that are typical of feature structures. Currently, rules are specific to the rank of the nodes. A first step in this direction could be gone by getting rid of the explicit `n=m` symbols.
- Hand-annotated resources such as (dag, tree) pairs, similar to treebanks for syntactic representations as well as a reasonable probabilistic model and training procedures.
- Useful algorithms for NLP applications that exist for string and tree automata (cf. Table 1). The long-term goal could be to build a semantics-based machine translation pipeline.

Acknowledgements

This research was supported in part by ARO grant W911NF-10-1-0533. The first author was supported by the German Research Foundation (DFG) grant MA 4959/1–1.

References

John A. Bateman. 1990. Upper modeling: organizing knowledge for natural language processing. In *Proc. Natural Language Generation Workshop*, pages 54–60.

L. E. Baum, T. Petrie, G. Soules, and N. Weiss. 1970. A maximization technique occurring in the statistical analysis of probabilistic functions of Markov chains. *Ann. Math. Statist.*, 41(1):164171.

Bernd Bohnet and Leo Wanner. 2010. Open source graph transducer interpreter and grammar development environment. In *Proc. LREC*.

Björn Borchardt and Heiko Vogler. 2003. Determinization of finite state weighted tree automata. *J. Autom. Lang. Comb.*, 8(3):417–463.

Loek G. W. A. Cleophas. 2008. *Tree Algorithms: Two Taxonomies and a Toolkit*. Ph.D. thesis, Department of Mathematics and Computer Science, Eindhoven University of Technology.

Jason Eisner. 2003. Learning non-isomorphic tree mappings for machine translation. In *Proc. ACL*, pages 205–208.

David Eppstein. 1998. Finding the k shortest paths. *SIAM J. Comput.*, 28(2):652–673.

Jonathan Graehl, Kevin Knight, and Jonathan May. 2008. Training tree transducers. *Comput. Linguist.*, 34(3):391–427.

Jonathan Graehl. 1997. Carmel finite-state toolkit. `http://www.isi.edu/licensed-sw/carmel`.

Liang Huang and David Chiang. 2005. Better k-best parsing. In *Proc. IWPT*.

Víctor M. Jiménez and Andrés Marzal. 2000. Computation of the n best parse trees for weighted and stochastic context-free grammars. In *Proc. SSPR/SPR*, pages 183–192.

Tsutomu Kamimura and Giora Slutzki. 1981. Parallel and two-way automata on directed ordered acyclic graphs. *Inf. Control*, 49(1):10–51.

Tsutomu Kamimura and Giora Slutzki. 1982. Transductions of dags and trees. *Math. Syst. Theory*, 15(3):225–249.

Kevin Knight and Jonathan May. 2009. Applications of weighted automata in natural language processing. In Manfred Droste, Werner Kuich, and Heiko Vogler, editors, *Handbook of Weighted Automata*. Springer.

Andreas Maletti, Jonathan Graehl, Mark Hopkins, and Kevin Knight. 2009. The power of extended top-down tree transducers. *SIAM J. Comput.*, 39(2):410–430.

Jonathan May and Kevin Knight. 2006a. A better n-best list: Practical determinization of weighted finite tree automata. In *Proc. HLT-NAACL*.

Jonathan May and Kevin Knight. 2006b. Tiburon: A weighted tree automata toolkit. In Oscar H. Ibarra and Hsu-Chun Yen, editors, *Proc. CIAA*, volume 4094 of *LNCS*, pages 102–113. Springer.

Mehryar Mohri, Fernando C. N. Pereira, and Michael Riley. 2000. The design principles of a weighted finite-state transducer library. *Theor. Comput. Sci.*, 231(1):17–32.

Mehryar Mohri. 1997. Finite-state transducers in language and speech processing. *Computational Linguistics*, 23(2):269–311.

Fernando Pereira and Michael Riley. 1997. Speech recognition by composition of weighted finite automata. In *Finite-State Language Processing*, pages 431–453. MIT Press.

Daniel Quernheim and Kevin Knight. 2012. Towards probabilistic acceptors and transducers for feature structures. In *Proc. SSST*. (to appear).

Michael Riley, Cyril Allauzen, and Martin Jansche. 2009. OpenFST: An open-source, weighted finite-state transducer library and its applications to speech and language. In *Proc. HLT-NAACL (Tutorial Abstracts)*, pages 9–10.

Roger Strolenberg. 2007. ForestFIRE and FIREWood. a toolkit & GUI for tree algorithms. Master's thesis, Department of Mathematics and Computer Science, Eindhoven University of Technology.

Andrew Viterbi. 1967. Error bounds for convolutional codes and an asymptotically optimum decoding algorithm. *IEEE Transactions on Information Theory*, 13(2):260–269.

WFST-based Grapheme-to-Phoneme Conversion: Open Source Tools for Alignment, Model-Building and Decoding

Josef R. Novak, Nobuaki Minematsu, Keikichi Hirose
Graduate School of Information Science and Technology
The University of Tokyo, Japan
{novakj,mine,hirose}@gavo.t.u-tokyo.ac.jp

Abstract

This paper introduces a new open source, WFST-based toolkit for Grapheme-to-Phoneme conversion. The toolkit is efficient, accurate and currently supports a range of features including EM sequence alignment and several decoding techniques novel in the context of G2P. Experimental results show that a combination RNNLM system outperforms all previous reported results on several standard G2P test sets. Preliminary experiments applying Lattice Minimum Bayes-Risk decoding to G2P conversion are also provided. The toolkit is implemented using OpenFst.

1 Introduction

Grapheme-to-Phoneme (G2P) conversion is an important problem related to Natural Language Processing, Speech Recognition and Spoken Dialog Systems development. The primary goal of G2P conversion is to accurately predict the pronunciation of a novel input word given only the spelling. For example, we would like to be able to predict,

PHOENIX → /f i n I k s/

given only the input spelling and a G2P model or set of rules. This problem is straightforward for some languages like Spanish or Italian, where pronunciation rules are consistent. For languages like English and French however, inconsistent conventions make the problem much more challenging.

In this paper we present a fully data-driven, state-of-the-art, open-source toolkit for G2P conversion, *Phonetisaurus* [1]. It includes a novel modified Expectation-Maximization (EM)-driven G2P sequence alignment algorithm, support for joint-sequence language models, and several decoding solutions. The paper also provides preliminary investigations of the applicability of Lattice Minimum Bayes-Risk (LMBR) decoding [2; 3] and N-best rescoring with a Recurrent Neural Network Language Model (RNNLM) [4; 5] to G2P conversion. The Weighted Finite-State Transducer (WFST) framework is used throughout, and the open source implementation relies on OpenFst [6]. Experimental results are provided illustrating the speed and accuracy of the proposed system.

The remainder of the paper is structured as follows. Section 2 provides background, Section 3 outlines the alignment approach, Section 4 describes the joint-sequence LM. Section 5 describes decoding approaches. Section 6 discusses preliminary experiments, Section 7 provides simple usage commands and Section 8 concludes the paper.

2 G2P problem outline

Grapheme-to-Phoneme conversion has been a popular research topic for many years. Many different approaches have been proposed, but perhaps the most popular is the joint-sequence model [6]. Most joint-sequence modeling techniques focus on producing an initial alignment between corresponding grapheme and phoneme sequences, and then modeling the aligned dictionary as a series of joint tokens. The gold standard in this area is the EM-driven joint-sequence modeling approach described in [6] that simultaneously infers both alignments and subsequence chunks. Due to space constraints the reader is referred to [6] for a detailed background of previous research.

The G2P conversion problem is typically broken down into several sub-problems: (1) Sequence alignment, (2) Model training and, (3) Decoding. The goal of (1) is to align the grapheme and phoneme sequence pairs in a training dictionary. The goal of (2) is to produce a model able to generate new pronunciations for novel words, and the

Proceedings of the 10th International Workshop on Finite State Methods and Natural Language Processing, pages 45–49,
Donostia–San Sebastián, July 23–25, 2012.

goal of (3) is to find the most likely pronunciation given the model.

3 Alignment

The proposed toolkit implements a modified WFST-based version of the EM-driven multiple-to-multiple alignment algorithm proposed in [7] and elaborated in [8]. This algorithm is capable of learning natural G-P relationships like `igh`→/`AY`/ which were not possible with previous 1-to-1 algorithms like [9].

The proposed alignment algorithm includes three modifications to [7]: (1) A constraint is imposed such that only `m-to-one` and `one-to-m` arcs are considered during training. (2) During initialization a joint alignment lattice is constructed for each input entry, and any unconnected arcs are deleted. (3) All arcs, including deletions and insertions are initialized to and constrained to maintain a non-zero weight.

These minor modifications appear to result in a small but consistent improvement in terms of Word Accuracy (WA) on G2P tasks. The Expectation and Maximization steps for the EM training procedure are outlined in Algorithms 2, 3. The EM algorithm

Algorithm 1: EM-driven M2One/One2M

Input: x^T, y^V, mX, mY, dX, dY
Output: γ, AlignedLattices
1 **foreach** *sequence pair* (x^T, y^V) **do**
2 | InitFSA(x^T, y^V, mX, mY, dX, dY)
3 **foreach** *sequence pair* (x^T, y^V) **do**
4 | Expectation(x^T, y^V, mX, mY, γ)
5 Maximization(γ)

is initialized by generating an alignment FSA for each dictionary entry, which encodes all valid G-P alignments, given max subsequence parameters supplied by the user. Any unconnected arcs are deleted and all remaining arcs are initialized with a non-zero weight. In Algorithm 2 lines 2-3 compute the forward and backward probabilities. Lines 4-8 compute the arc posteriors and update the current model. In Algorithm 3 lines 1-2 normalize the probability distribution. Lines 3-6 update the alignment lattice arc weights with the new model.

Algorithm 2: Expectation step

Input: *AlignedLattices*
Output: γ, *total*
1 **foreach** *FSA alignment lattice F* **do**
2 | $\alpha \leftarrow$ ShortestDistance(F)
3 | $\beta \leftarrow$ ShortestDistance(F^R)
4 | **foreach** *state* $q \in Q[F]$ **do**
5 | | **foreach** *arc* $e \in E[q]$ **do**
6 | | | $v \leftarrow ((\alpha[q] \otimes w[e]) \otimes \beta[n[e]]) \oslash \beta[0]$;
7 | | | $\gamma[i[e]] \leftarrow \gamma[i[e]] \oplus v$;
8 | | | $total \leftarrow total \oplus v$;

Algorithm 3: Maximization step

Input: γ, *total*
Output: AlignedLattices
1 **foreach** *arc* e *in* $E[\gamma]$ **do**
2 | $\gamma_{new}[i[e]] \leftarrow w[e]/total$; $\gamma[i[e]] \leftarrow 0$;
3 **foreach** *FSA alignment lattice F* **do**
4 | **foreach** *state* $q \in Q[F]$ **do**
5 | | **foreach** *arc* $e \in E[q]$ **do**
6 | | | $w[e] \leftarrow \gamma_{new}[i[e]]$;

4 Joint Sequence N-gram model

The pronunciation model implemented by the toolkit is a straightforward joint N-gram model. The training corpus is constructed by extracting the best alignment for each entry, e.g.:

```
a}x b}b a}@ c|k}k
a}x b}b a}@ f}f t}t
```

The training procedure is then, (1) Convert aligned sequence pairs to sequences of aligned joint label pairs, $(g_1{:}p_1, g_2{:}p_2, ..., g_n{:}p_n)$; (2) Train an N-gram model from (1); (3) Convert the N-gram model to a WFST. Step (3) may be performed with any language modeling toolkit. In this paper *mitlm* [11] is utilized.

5 Decoding

The proposed toolkit provides varying support for three different decoding schemes. The default decoder provided by the distribution simply extracts the shortest path through the phoneme lattice created via composition with the input word,

$$H_{best} = ShortestPath(Project_o(w \circ M)) \quad (1)$$

where H_{best} refers to the lowest cost path, $Project_o$ refers to projecting the output labels, w refers to the input word, M refers to the G2P model, and $\circ$ indicates composition.

5.1 RNNLM N-best rescoring

Recurrent Neural Network Language Models have recently enjoyed a resurgence in popularity in the context of ASR applications [4]. In another recent publication we investigated the applicability of this approach to G2P conversion with joint sequence models by providing support for the `rnnlm toolkit` [5]. The training corpus for the G2P LM is a corpus of joint sequences, thus it can be used without modification to train a parallel RNNLM. N-best reranking is then accomplished with the proposed toolkit by causing the decoder to output the N-best joint G-P sequences, and employing `rnnlm` to rerank the the N-best joint sequences,

$$\begin{aligned} H_{Nbest} =& NShortestPaths(w \circ M) \\ H_{best} =& Project_o(Rescore_{rnn}(H_{Nbest})). \end{aligned} \tag{2}$$

In practice the `rnnlm` models require considerable tuning, and somewhat more time to train, but provide a consistent WA boost. For further details on algorithm as well as tuning for G2P see [4; 10].

5.2 Lattice Minimum Bayes-Risk decoding for G2P

In [2] the authors note that the aim of MBR decoding is to find the hypothesis that has the "least expected loss under the model". MBR decoding was successfully applied to Statistical Machine Translation (SMT) lattices in [2], and significantly improved in [3]. Noting the similarities between G2P conversion and SMT, we have begun work implementing an integrated LMBR decoder for the proposed toolkit.

Our approach closely follows that described in [3], and the algorithm implementation is summarized in Algorithm 4. The inputs are the full phoneme lattice that results from composing the input word with the G2P model and projecting output labels, an exponential scale factor α, and N-gram precision factors θ_{0-N}. The θ_n are computed using a linear corpus BLEU [2] N-gram precision p, and a match ratio r using the following equations, $\theta_0 = -1/T;\ \theta_n = 1/(NTpr^{n-1})$. T is a constant

Algorithm 4: G2P Lattice MBR-Decode

Input: $\mathcal{E} \leftarrow Project_o(w \circ M)$, α, θ_{0-n}

1 $\mathcal{E} \leftarrow$ScaleLattice$(\alpha \times \mathcal{E})$
2 $\mathcal{N}_N \leftarrow$ExtractN-grams$(\mathcal{E})$
3 **for** $n \leftarrow 1$ **to** N **do**
4     $\Phi_n \leftarrow$ MakeMapper$(\mathcal{N}_n)$
5     $\Psi_n^R \leftarrow$ MakePathCounter$(\mathcal{N}_n)$
6     $\mathcal{U}_n \leftarrow Opt((\mathcal{E} \circ \Phi_n) \circ \Psi_n^R)$
7     $\Omega_n = \Phi_n$
8   **for** *state* $q \in Q[\Omega_n]$ **do**
9   **for** *arc* $e \in E[q]$ **do**
10             $w[e] \leftarrow \theta_n \times \mathcal{U}(o[e])$
11 $\mathcal{P} \leftarrow Project_{input}(\mathcal{E}_{\theta_0} \circ \Omega_1)$
12 **for** $n \leftarrow 2$ **to** N **do**
13     $\mathcal{P} \leftarrow Project_{input}(\mathcal{P} \circ \Omega_n)$
14 $\mathcal{H}_{best} = ShortestPath(\mathcal{P})$

which does not affect the MBR decision [2]. Line 1 applies α to the raw lattice. In effect this controls how much we trust the raw lattice weights. After applying α, $\mathcal{E}$ is normalized by pushing weights to the final state and removing any final weights. In line 2 all unique N-grams up to order N are extracted from the lattice. Lines 4-10 create, for each order, a context-dependency FST (Φ_n) and a special path-posterior counting WFST (Ψ_n^R), which are then used to compute N-gram posteriors ($\mathcal{U}_n$), and finally to create a decoder WFST (Ω_n). The full MBR decoder is then computed by first making an unweighted copy of $\mathcal{E}$, applying θ_0 uniformly to all arcs, and iteratively composing and input-projecting with each Ω_n. The MBR hypothesis is then the best path through the result $\mathcal{P}$. See [2; 3] for further details.

6 Experimental results

Experimental evaluations were conducted utilizing three standard G2P test sets. These included replications of the NetTalk, CMUdict, and OALD English language dictionary evaluations described in detail in [6]. Results comparing various configuration of the proposed toolkit to the joint sequence model *Sequitur* [6] and an alternative discriminative training toolkit *direcTL+* [8] are described in Table 1. Here *m2m-P* indicates the proposed toolkit using the alignment algorithm from [7], *m2m-fst-P*

System	NT15k	CMUdict	OALD
Sequitur [6]	66.20	75.47	82.51
direcTL+ [8]	~	75.52	83.32
m2m-P	66.39	75.08	81.20
m2m-fst-P	66.41	75.25	81.86
rnnlm-P	**67.77**	**75.56**	**83.52**

Table 1: Comparison of G2P WA(%) for previous systems and variations of the proposed toolkit.

indicates the alternative FST-based alignment algorithm, and *rnnlm-P* indicates the use of RNNLM N-best reranking.

The results show that the improved alignment algorithm contributes a small but consistent improvement to WA, while RNNLM reranking contributes a further small but significant boost to WA which produces state-of-the-art results on all three test sets.

The WA gains are interesting, however a major plus point for the toolkit is speed. Table 2 compares training times for the proposed toolkit with previously reported results. The *m2m-fst-P* for system for

System	NETtalk-15k	CMUdict
Sequitur [6]	Hours	Days
direcTL+ [8]	Hours	Days
m2m-P	2m56s	21m58s
m2m-fst-P	1m43s	13m06s
rnnlm-P	20m	2h

Table 2: Training times for the smallest (15k entries) and largest (112k entries) training sets.

CMUdict performs %0.27 worse than the state-of-the-art, but requires just a tiny fraction of the training time. This turn-around time may be very important for rapid system development. Finally, Figure. 1 plots WA versus decoding time for *m2m-fst-P* on the largest test set, further illustrating the speed of the decoder, and the impact of using larger models.

Preliminary experiments with the LMBR decoder were also carried out using the smaller NT15k dataset. The θ_n values were computed using p, r, and T from [2] while α was tuned to 0.6. Results are described in Table 3. The system matched the basic WA for N=6, and achieved a small improvement in PA over *m2m-fst-P* (%91.80 versus %91.82). Tuning the loss function for the G2P task should improve performance.

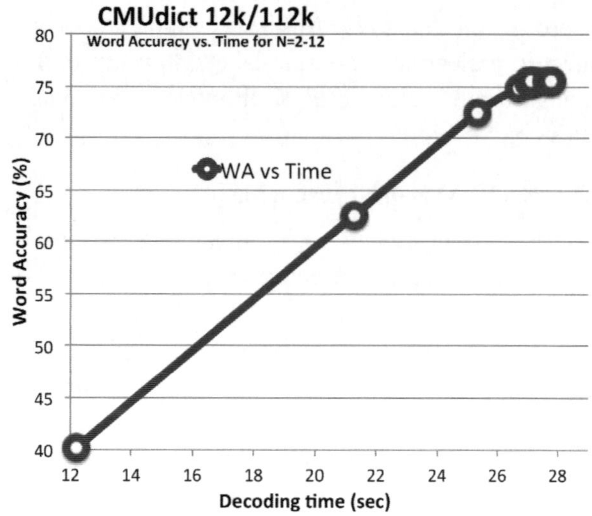

Figure 1: Decoding speed vs. WA plot for various N-gram orders for the CMUdict 12k/112k test/train set. Times averaged over 5 run using `ctime`.

NT15k	N=1	N=2	N=3	N=4	N=5	N=6
WA	28.88	65.48	66.03	66.41	66.37	**66.50**
PA	83.17	91.74	91.79	91.87	91.82	**91.82**

Table 3: LMBR decoding Word Accuracy (WA) and Phoneme Accuracy (PA) for order N=1-6.

7 Toolkit distribution and usage

The preceding sections introduced various theoretical aspects of the toolkit as well as preliminary experimental results. The current section provides several introductory usage commands.

The toolkit is open source and released under the liberal BSD license. It is available for download from [1], which also includes detailed compilation instructions, tutorial information and additional examples. The examples that follow utilize the NETTalk dictionary.

Align a dictionary:

```
$ phonetisaurus-align --input=test.dic \
   --ofile=test.corpus
```

Train a 7-gram model with mitlm:

```
$ estimate-ngram -o 7 -t test.corpus \
   -wl test.arpa
```

Convert the model to a WFSA

```
$ phonetisaurus-arpa2fst --input=test.arpa \
   --prefix=test
```

Apply the default decoder

```
$ phonetisaurus-g2p --model=test.fst \
   --input=abbreviate --nbest=3 --words
abbreviate 25.66 @ b r i v i e t
```

```
abbreviate 28.20 @ b i v i e t
abbreviate 29.03 x b b r i v i e t
```

Apply the LMBR decoder

```
$ phonetisaurus-g2p --model=test.fst \
   --input=abbreviate --nbest=3 --words \
   --mbr --order=7
abbreviate 1.50 @ b r i v i e t
abbreviate 2.62 x b r i v i e t
abbreviate 2.81 a b r i v i e t
```

8 Conclusion and Future work

This work introduced a new Open Source WFST-driven G2P conversion toolkit which is both highly accurate as well as efficient to train and test. It incorporates a novel modified alignment algorithm. To our knowledge the RNNLM N-best reranking and LMBR decoding are also novel applications in the context of G2P.

Both the RNNLM N-best reranking and LMBR decoding are promising but further work is required to improve usability and performance. In particular RNNLM training requires considerable tuning, and we would like to automate this process. The provisional LMBR decoder achieved a small improvement but further work will be needed to tune the loss function. Several known optimizations are also planned to speed up the LMBR decoder.

Nevertheless the current release of the toolkit provides several novel G2P solutions, achieves state-of-the-art WA on several test sets and is efficient for both training and decoding.

References

J. Novak, et al. [1]. `http://code.google.com/p/phonetisaurus`

R. Tromble and S. Kumar and F. Och and W. Macherey. [2]. *Lattice Minimum Bayes-Risk Decoding for Statistical Machine Translation*, Proc. EMNLP 2007, pp. 620-629.

G. Blackwood and A. Gispert and W. Byrne. [3]. *Efficient path counting transducers for minimum bayes-risk decoding of statistical machine translation lattices*, Proc. ACL 2010, pp. 27-32.

T. Mikolov and M. Karafiat and L. Burget and J. Černocký and S. Khundanpur. [4]. *Recurrent Neural Network based Language Model*, Proc. InterSpeech, 2010.

T. Mikolov and S. Kombrink and D. Anoop and L. Burget and J. Černocký. [5]. *RNNLM - Recurrent Neural Network Language Modeling Toolkit*, ASRU 2011, demo session.

C. Allauzen and M. Riley and J. Schalkwyk and W. Skut and M. Mohri. [6]. *OpenFST: A General and Efficient Weighted Finite-State Transducer Library*, Proc. CIAA 2007, pp. 11-23.

M. Bisani and H. Ney. [6]. *Joint-sequence models for grapheme-to-phoneme conversion*, Speech Communication 50, 2008, pp. 434-451.

S. Jiampojamarn and G. Kondrak and T. Sherif. [7]. *Applying Many-to-Many Alignments and Hidden Markov Models to Letter-to-Phoneme Conversion*, NAACL HLT 2007, pp. 372-379.

S. Jiampojamarn and G. Kondrak. [8]. *Letter-to-Phoneme Alignment: an Exploration*, Proc. ACL 2010, pp. 780-788.

E. Ristad and P. Yianilos. [9]. *Learning String Edit Distance*, IEEE Trans. PRMI 1998, pp. 522-532.

J. Novak and P. Dixon and N. Minematsu and K. Hirose and C. Hori and H. Kashioka. [10]. *Improving WFST-based G2P Conversion with Alignment Constraints and RNNLM N-best Rescoring*, Interspeech 2012 (Accepted).

B. Hsu and J. Glass. [11]. *Iterative Language Model Estimation: Efficient Data Structure & Algorithms*, Proc. Interspeech 2008.

Kleene, a Free and Open-Source Language for Finite-State Programming

Kenneth R. Beesley
SAP Labs, LLC
P.O. Box 540475
North Salt Lake, UT 84054
USA
ken.beesley@sap.com

Abstract

Kleene is a high-level programming language, based on the OpenFst library, for constructing and manipulating finite-state acceptors and transducers. Users can program using regular expressions, alternation-rule syntax and right-linear phrase-structure grammars; and Kleene provides variables, lists, functions and familiar program-control syntax. Kleene has been approved by SAP AG for release as free, open-source code under the Apache License, Version 2.0, and will be available by August 2012 for downloading from http://www.kleene-lang.org. The design, implementation, development status and future plans for the language are discussed.

1 Introduction

Kleene[1] is a finite-state programming language in the tradition of the AT&T Lextools (Roark and Sproat, 2007),[2] the SFST-PL language (Schmid, 2005),[3] the Xerox/PARC finite-state toolkit (Beesley and Karttunen, 2003)[4] and FOMA (Huldén, 2009b),[5] all of which provide higher-level programming formalisms built on top of low-level finite-state libraries. Kleene itself is built on the OpenFst library (Allauzen et al., 2007),[6] developed by Google Labs and NYU's Courant Institute.

The design and implementation of the language were motivated by three main principles, summarized as Syntax Matters, Licensing Matters and Open Source Matters. As for the syntax, Kleene allows programmers to specify weighted or unweighted finite-state machines (FSMs)—including acceptors that encode regular languages and two-projection transducers that encode regular relations—using regular expressions, alternation-rule syntax and right-linear phrase-structure grammars. The regular-expression operators are borrowed, as far as possible, from familiar Perl-like and academic regular expressions, and the alternation rules are based on the "rewrite rules" made popular by Chomsky and Halle (Chomsky and Halle, 1968). Borrowing from general-purpose programming languages, Kleene also provides variables, lists and functions, plus nested code blocks and familiar control structures such as `if-else` statements and `while` loops.

As for the licensing, Kleene, like the OpenFst library, is released under the Apache License, Version 2.0, and its other dependencies are also released under this and similar permissive licenses that allow commercial usage. In contrast, many notable finite-state implementations, released under the GPL and similar licenses, are restricted to academic and other non-commercial use. The Kleene code is also open-source, allowing users to examine, correct, augment and even adopt the code if the project should ever be abandoned by its original maintainer(s).

[1] Kleene is named after American mathematician Stephen Cole Kleene (1909–1994), who investigated the properties of regular sets and invented the metalanguage of regular expressions.

[2] http://www.research.att.com/~alb/lextools/

[3] http://www.ims.uni-stuttgart.de/projekte/gramotron/SOFTWARE/SFST.html

[4] http://www.fsmbook.com

[5] http://code.google.com/p/foma/

[6] http://www.openfst.org

Proceedings of the 10th International Workshop on Finite State Methods and Natural Language Processing, pages 50–54,
Donostia–San Sebastián, July 23–25, 2012.

It is hoped that Kleene will provide an attractive development environment for experts and students. Pre-edited Kleene scripts can be run from the command line, but a graphical user interface is also provided for interactive learning, programming, testing and drawing of FSMs.

Like comparable implementations of finite-state machines, Kleene can be used to implement a variety of useful applications, including spell-checking and -correction, phonetic modeling, morphological analysis and generation, and various kinds of pattern matching. The paper continues with a brief description the Kleene language, the current state of development, and plans for the future.

2 Implementation

The Java-language Kleene parser, implemented with JavaCC and JJTree (Copeland, 2007),[7] is Unicode-capable and portable. Successfully parsed statements are reduced to abstract syntax trees (ASTs), which are interpreted by calling C++ functions in the OpenFst library via the Java Native Interface (JNI).

3 Kleene Syntax

3.1 Regular Expressions

Basic assignment statements have a regular expression on the right-hand side, as shown in Table 1. As in Perl regular expressions, simple alphabetic characters are literal, and concatenation is indicated by juxtaposition, with no overt operator. Parentheses can be used to group expressions. The postfixed `*` (the "Kleene star"), + (the "Kleene plus"), and `?` denote zero-or-more, one-or-more, and optionality, respectively. Square-bracketed expressions have their own internal syntax to denote character sets, including character ranges such as `[A-Z]`. The union operator is `|`. Basic regular operations missing from Perl regular expressions include composition (`o` or `_o_`), crossproduct (`:`), language intersection (`&`), language negation (~) and language subtraction (`-`). Weights are indicated inside angle brackets, e.g. <0.1>.

Special characters can be literalized with a preceding backslash or inside double quotes, e.g. `\*` or `"*"` denotes a literal asterisk rather than the Kleene plus. To improve the readability of expressions, spaces are not significant, unless they appear inside square brackets or are explicitly literalized inside double quotes or with a preceding backslash.

In a language like Kleene where alphabetic symbols are literal, and the expression `dog` denotes three literal symbols, *d*, *o* and *g*, concatenated together, there must be a way to distinguish variable names from simple concatenations. The Kleene solution is to prefix variable names that are bound to FSM values with a dollar-sign sigil, e.g. `$myvar`. Once defined, a variable name can be used inside subsequent regular expressions, as in the following example, which models a fragment of Esperanto verb morphology.

```
$vroot = don | dir | pens | ir ;
// "give", "say", "think", "go"
$aspect = ad ;
// optional repeated aspect
$vend = as | is | os | us | u | i ;
// pres, past, fut, cond, subj, inf
$verbs = $vroot $aspect? $vend ;
// use of pre-defined variables
```

Similarly, names of functions that return FSMs are distinguished with the `$^` sigil. To denote less common operations, rather than inventing and proliferating new and arguably cryptic regular-expression operators, Kleene provides a set of predefined functions including

`$^reverse`(*regexp*)
`$^invert`(*regexp*)
`$^inputProj`(*regexp*)
`$^outputProj`(*regexp*)
`$^contains`(*regexp*)
`$^ignore`(*regexp*, *regexp*)
`$^copy`(*regexp*)

Users can also define their own functions, and function calls are regular expressions that can appear as operands inside larger regular expressions.

3.2 Alternation-Rule Syntax

Kleene provides a variety of alternation-rule types, comparable to Xerox/PARC Replace Rules (Beesley and Karttunen, 2003, pp. 130–82), but implemented using algorithms by Måns Huldén (Huldén, 2009a).

[7] https://javacc.dev.java.net

```
$var = dog ;
$var = d o g ;          // equivalent to dog
$var = ~( a+ b* c? ) ;
$var = \~ \+ \* \? ;    // literalized special characters
$var = "~+*?";          // literalized characters inside double quotes
$var = "dog" ;          // unnecessary literalization, equivalent to dog
$myvar = (dog | cat | horse) s? ;
$yourvar = [A-Za-z] [A-Za-z0-9]* ;
$hisvar = ([A-Za-z]-[aeiouAEIOU])+ ;
$hervar = (bird|cow|elephant|pig) & (pig|ant|bird) ;
$ourvar = (dog):(chien) o (chien):(Hund) ;
$theirvar = [a-z]+ ( a <0.91629> | b <0.1> ) ;   // weights in brackets
```

Table 1: Kleene Regular-Expression Assignment Examples.

input-expression -> output-expression / left-context _ right-context

Table 2: The Simplest Kleene Alternation-Rule Template.

The simplest rules have the template shown in Table 2, and are interpreted into transducers that map the input to the output in the specified context. Such rules, which cannot be reviewed in detail here, are commonly used to model phonetic and orthographical alternations.

3.3 Right-Linear Phrase Structure Grammars

While regular expressions are formally capable of describing any regular language or regular relation, some linguistic phenomena—especially productive morphological compounding and derivation—can be awkward to describe this way. Kleene therefore provides right-linear phrase-structure grammars that are similar in semantics, if not in syntax, to the Xerox/PARC `lexc` language (Beesley and Karttunen, 2003, pp. 203–78).

A Kleene phrase-structure grammar is defined as a set of productions, each assigned to a variable with a `$>` sigil. Productions may include right-linear references to themselves or to other productions, which might not yet be defined. The productions are parsed immediately but are not evaluated until the entire grammar is built into an FSM via a call to the built-in function `$^start()`, which takes one production variable as its argument and treats it as the starting production of the whole grammar. The following example models a fragment of Esperanto noun morphotactics, including noun-root compounding.

```
$>Root = (kat | hund | elefant | dom)
            ( $>Root | $>AugDim ) ;
$>AugDim = ( eg | et )? $>Noun ;
$>Noun = o $>Plur ;
$>Plur = j? $>Case ;
$>Case = n? ;

$net = $^start($>Root) ;
```

The syntax on the right-hand side of productions is identical to the regular-expression syntax, but allowing right-linear references to productions of the form `$>`*Name*.

4 Kleene FSMs

Each Kleene finite-state machine consists of a standard OpenFst FSM, under the default Tropical Semiring, wrapped with a Java object[8] that stores the private alphabet[9] of each machine.

In Kleene, it is not necessary or possible to declare the characters being used; characters appearing in regular expressions, alternation rules and right-linear phrase-structure grammars are stored automatically as FSM arc labels using their Unicode

[8]Each Java object of the class Fst contains a long integer field that stores a pointer to the OpenFst machine, which actually resides in OpenFst's C++ memory space.

[9]The alphabet, sometimes known as the *sigma*, contains just the symbols that appear explicitly in the labels of the FSM.

code point value, and this includes Unicode supplementary characters. Programmer-defined multi-character symbols, represented in the syntax with surrounding single quotes, e.g. `'+Noun'` and `'+Verb'`, or, using another common convention, `'[Noun]'` and `'[Verb]'`, also need no declaration and are automatically stored using code point values taken from a Unicode Private Use Area.

The dot (`.`) denotes *any* character, and it translates non-trivially into reserved arc labels that represent OTHER (i.e. unknown) characters.[10]

5 Status

5.1 Currently Working

As of the date of writing, Kleene is an advanced beta project offering the following:

- Compilation of regular expressions, right-linear phrase-structure grammars, and several alternation-rule variations into FSMs.
- Robust handling of Unicode, including supplementary characters, plus support for user-defined multi-character symbols.
- Variables and maintenance of symbol tables in a frame-based environment.
- Pre-defined and user-defined functions.
- Handling of lists of FSMs, iteration over lists, and functions that handle and return lists.
- A graphical user interface, including tools to draw FSMs and test them manually.
- File I/O of FSMs in an XML format.
- Interpretation of arithmetic expressions, arithmetic variables and functions, including boolean functions; and `if-then` statements and `while` loops that use boolean operators and functions.

[10]The treatment of FSM-specific alphabets and the handling of OTHER characters is modeled on the Xerox/PARC implementation (Beesley and Karttunen, 2003, pp. 56–60).

5.2 Future Work

The work remaining to be done includes:

- Completion of the implementation of alternation-rule variations.
- Writing of runtime code and APIs to apply FSMs to input and return output.
- Conversion of FSMs into stand-alone executable code, initially in Java and C++.
- Expansion to handle semirings other than the default Tropical Semiring of OpenFst.
- Testing in non-trivial applications to determine memory usage and performance.

6 History and Licensing

Kleene was begun informally in late 2006, became part of a company project in 2008, and was under development until early 2011, when the project was canceled. On 4 May 2012, SAP AG released Kleene as free, open-source code under the Apache License, Version 2.0.[11]

The Kleene source code will be repackaged according to Apache standards and made available for download by August of 2012 at `http://www.kleene-lang.org`. A user manual, currently over 100 pages, and an engineering manual will also be released. Precompiled versions will be provided for Linux, OS X and, if possible, Windows.

Acknowledgments

Sincere thanks are due to the OpenFst team and all who made that library available. A special personal thanks goes to Måns Huldén, who graciously released his algorithms for interpreting alternation rules and language-restriction expressions, and who went to great lengths to help me understand and reimplement them. I also acknowledge my SAP Labs colleagues Paola Nieddu and Phil Sours, who contributed to the design and implementation of Kleene, and my supervisor Michael Wiesner, who supported the open-source release. Finally, I thank Lauri Karttunen, who introduced me to finite-state linguistics and has always been a good friend and mentor.

[11]`http://www.apache.org/licenses/LICENSE-2.0.html`

References

Cyril Allauzen, Michael Riley, Johan Schalkwyk, Wojciech Skut, and Mehryar Mohri. 2007. OpenFst: A general and efficient weighted finite-state transducer library. In *Proceedings of the Ninth International Conference on Implementation and Application of Automata (CIAA 2007)*, volume 4783 of *Lecture Notes in Computer Science*, pages 11–23. Springer.

Kenneth R. Beesley and Lauri Karttunen. 2003. *Finite State Morphology*. CSLI Publications, Palo Alto, CA.

Noam Chomsky and Morris Halle. 1968. *The Sound Pattern of English*. Harper and Row, New York.

Tom Copeland. 2007. *Generating Parsers with JavaCC*. Centennial Books, Alexandria, VA.

Måns Huldén. 2009a. *Finite-State Machine Construction Methods and Algorithms for Phonology and Morphology*. Ph.D. thesis, The University of Arizona, Tucson, AZ.

Måns Huldén. 2009b. Foma: a finite-state compiler and library. In *Proceedings of the EACL 2009 Demonstrations Session*, pages 29–32, Athens, Greece.

Brian Roark and Richard Sproat. 2007. *Computational Approaches to Morphology and Syntax*. Oxford Surveys in Syntax & Morphology. Oxford University Press, Oxford.

Helmut Schmid. 2005. A programming language for finite state transducers. In *FSMNLP'05*, Helskinki.

Implementation of replace rules using preference operator

Senka Drobac, Miikka Silfverberg, and Anssi Yli-Jyrä
University of Helsinki
Department of Modern Languages
Unioninkatu 40 A
FI-00014 Helsingin yliopisto, Finland
{senka.drobac, miikka.silfverberg, anssi.yli-jyra}@helsinki.fi

Abstract

We explain the implementation of replace rules with the .r-glc. operator and preference relations. Our modular approach combines various preference constraints to form different replace rules. In addition to describing the method, we present illustrative examples.

1 Introduction

The idea of HFST - Helsinki Finite-State Technology (Lindén et al. 2009, 2011) is to provide open-source replicas of well-known tools for building morphologies, including XFST (Beesley and Karttunen 2003). HFST's lack of replace rules such as those supported by XFST, prompted us to implement them using the present method, which replicates XFST's behavior (with minor differences which will be detailed in later work), but will also allow easy expansion with new functionalities.

The semantics of replacement rules mixes contextual conditions with replacement strategies that are specified by replace rule operators. This paper describes the implementation of replace rules using a preference operator, *.r-glc.*, that disambiguates alternative replacement strategies according to a preference relation. The use of preference relations (Yli-Jyrä 2008b) is similar to the *worsener* relations used by Gerdemann (2009). The current approach was first described in Yli-Jyrä (2008b), and is closely related to the matching-based finite-state approaches to optimality in OT phonology (Noord and Gerdemann 1999; Eisner 2000). The preference operator, *.r-glc.*, is the reversal of generalized lenient composition (glc), a preference operator construct proposed by Jäger (2001). The implementation is developed using the HFST library, and is now a part of the same.

The purpose of this paper is to explain a general method of compiling replace rules with *.r-glc.* operator and to show how preference constraints described in Yli-Jyrä (2008b) can be combined to form different replace rules.

2 Notation

The notation used in this paper is the standard regular expression notation extended with replace rule operators introduced and described in Beesley and Karttunen (2003).

In a simple rule

$$a\ op\ b\ dir\ L_1\ \_\ R_1, \dots, L_n\ \_\ R_n$$

op is a replace rule operator such as: →, (→), @→, @>, ←, (←), …; $a \subseteq \Sigma^*$ is the set of patterns in the input text that are overwritten in the output text by the alternative patterns, which are given as set $b \subseteq \Sigma^*$, where Σ^* is a universal language and Σ set of alphabetical symbols; L_n and R_n are left and right contexts and *dir* is context direction (||, //, \\ and \/).

Rules can also be parallel. Then they are divided with double comma (,,), or alternately with single comma if context is not specified.

Operation	Name
X Y	The concatenation of Y after X
X | Y	The disjunction of X and Y
X:Y	The cross product of X and Y, where X and Y denote languages
X .o. Y	The composition of X and Y, where X and Y denote relations
X^+	The Kleene plus
X^*	The Kleene star
$proj_1(X)$	The projection of the input language of the relation X
$proj_2(X)$	The projection of the output language of the relation X

Table 1 – List of operations

Proceedings of the 10th International Workshop on Finite State Methods and Natural Language Processing, pages 55–59, Donostia–San Sebastián, July 23–25, 2012.

Operators used in the paper are listed in Table 1, where X and Y stand for regular expressions.

Additionally, parenthesis ( ) are used to mark optionality, squared brackets [ ] for precedence and question mark ? is used to denote set Σ in regular expressions.

3 Method

The general idea for compiling replace rules with the *.r-glc.* operator and preference constraints is shown in Figure 1.

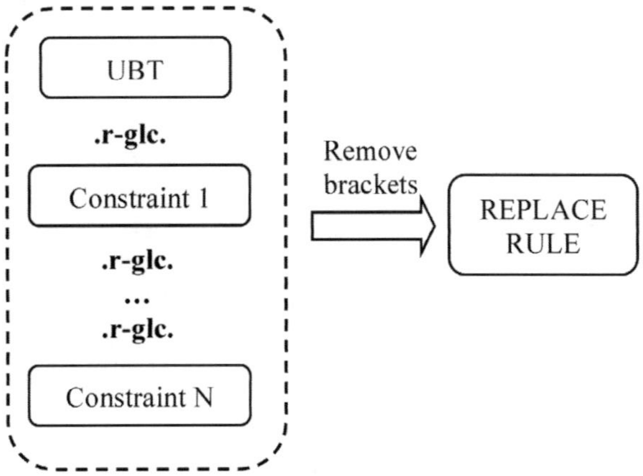

Figure 1: General method of building a replace rule

The method consists of the following steps:

1. Building an Unconstrained Bracketed Transducer (UBT) – a transducer which applies or skips contextually valid replacements freely in all possible portions of the inputs. Every application of the replacement rule is marked with special brackets. Similar replace rules that differ only with respect to their replacement strategies will use the same UBT. Thus, the compilation of UBT is independent of the replacement strategy, which increases the modularity of the compilation algorithm.
2. Implement the functionality of the replace rule operator by constraining the UBT with the respective preference relation.
3. Remove brackets from the transducer.

The major advantage of this method is its modularity. The algorithm is divided into small components which are combined in the desired way. This approach allows every part of the algorithm to be separately and clearly defined, tested and changed. Furthermore, modularity makes it possible to easily integrate new functionalities such as weighted replace rules or two level contexts.

3.1 Unconstrained Bracketed Transducer

As mentioned earlier, it is first necessary to build the UBT. This step can be seen as a variant of Yli-Jyrä and Koskenniemi's (2007) method for compiling contextually restricted changes in two-level grammars. The main difference now is that the rule applications cannot overlap because they will be marked with brackets.

Step 1: Bracketed center

The first step is to create a bracketed center, $center_B$ – the replace relation surrounded by brackets $\{\langle, \rangle\}$. For optional replacement, it is necessary that $center_B$ also contains the upper side of the relation bracketed with another pair of brackets $B_2 = \{\llbracket, \rrbracket\}$. This is necessary for filtering out all the results without any brackets (see later filter T_{MOST+}) and getting non optional replacement.

$$center_B = \bigcup_{i \leq n} \langle a_i : b_i \rangle \cup \llbracket a_i \rrbracket$$

In case of parallel replace rules, bracketed center is the union of all individual bracketed centers. Like XFST, this implementation requires parallel replace rules to have the same replace operator (and optionality) in all replacements.

Step 2: The change centers in free context

The second step is to expand bracketed center to be valid in any context.

If $B = \{\langle, \rangle, \llbracket, \rrbracket\}$, we can define:

$$\mathcal{U} = [\Sigma - B \cup center_B]^*$$

Then, center in free context is:

$$center_{FREE} = \mathcal{U} \diamond center_B \, \mathcal{U}$$

where ⋄ is diamond, which is used to align centers and contexts during compilation.

Step 3: Expanded center in context

The next step is to compile contexts. The method used for constructing $center_{CONTXT}$ depends on whether the context must match on the upper or the lower side. Since it is possible to have multiple contexts, each replacement should be surrounded with all applicable contexts:

$$center_{CONTXT} = c_1 | \, c_2 \, | \dots | \, c_n$$

Center surrounded with one context is:

$$c_1 = [L \mid L'] \diamond center_B \, [R \mid R'],$$

where L and R are left and right contexts from the replace rule, and L' and R' are expanded contexts, depending on which side the context matches. In the case when context must match on the upper side, L' and R' are:

$$L' = \big[[\mathcal{U}\, L] \ll \mathrm{B}\big]\,.\mathrm{o.}\ \mathcal{U}$$
$$R' = \big[[R\ \mathcal{U}] \ll \mathrm{B}\big]\,.\mathrm{o.}\ \mathcal{U}$$

If they must match on the lower side:

$$L' = \mathcal{U}.\mathrm{o.}\big[[\mathcal{U}\, L] \ll \mathrm{B}\big]$$
$$R' = \mathcal{U}.\mathrm{o.}\big[[R\ \mathcal{U}] \ll \mathrm{B}\big]$$

where brackets are freely inserted ($\ll$) in the contexts and then composed with $\mathcal{U}$.

In this example:

$$a \rightarrow b \parallel c\,\_\,d$$

both contexts should match on the upper side of the replacement, so $center_{CONTXT}$ is:

$$L' = \big[[\mathcal{U}\ \mathrm{c}] \ll \mathrm{B}\big]\,.\mathrm{o.}\ \mathcal{U}$$
$$R' = \big[[\mathrm{d}\ \mathcal{U}] \ll \mathrm{B}\big]\,.\mathrm{o.}\ \mathcal{U}$$
$$c_1 = (\,c \mid L'\,)\ \diamond\ \langle a : b\rangle \cup [\![a]\!]\ (\,d \mid R'\,)$$
$$center_{CONTXT} = c_1$$

This way of compiling contexts allows every rule in a parallel replace rule to have its own context direction (||, //, \\, \/). Therefore, rules like the following one are valid in this implementation:

$$a \rightarrow b \backslash\backslash c\,\_\,d\,,, b \rightarrow c\,//\,c\,\_\,d$$

Steps 4: Final operations

Finally, to get the unconstrained replace transducer it is necessary to subtract $center_{CONTXT}$ from $center_{FREE}$, remove diamond and do a negation of that relation.

Let $V = \big[[\Sigma - B - \diamond] \cup center_B\big]^*$, then:

$$V\ - d_{\diamond}[\,center_{FREE}\ \text{-}\ center_{CONTXT}\,]$$

where $d_{\diamond}$ denotes removal of diamond.

3.2 Constraints

All the preference constraints were defined in Yli-Jyrä (2008), but since they were mostly difficult to interpret and implement, here is the list of the constraints written with regular expressions over the set of finite binary relations.

First, let us define RP – a regular expression often used in the restraints:

$$RP = \ [B{:}0 \mid 0{:}B \mid ?{-}B\,]^*$$

The left most preference is achieved by:

$$T_{LM} = \ ?^* <:0\ [B{:}\,0]^*[?\ -B]\ RP$$

Right most preference:

$$T_{RM} = \ RP\ [?{-}B]^+\ \ \rangle : 0\ ?^*$$

Longest match left to right:

$$L_L = \ [?{-}B] \mid [0{:}\langle\ | 0{:}\langle \mid \langle :0 \mid B\,][?{-}B]^+$$
$$T_{LRLONG} = ?^*\ \langle\ \ [?\ - B\,]^+\ 0:\rangle\ L_L\ RP$$

Longest match right to left:

$$L_R = \ [?{-}B]\ |[?{-}B]^+\ [0{:}\langle\ |0 : \rangle|\ \rangle : 0|\ B\,]$$
$$T_{RLLONG} = \ RP\ L_R\ 0 : \langle\ \ [?\ - B\,]^+ \rangle\ ?^*$$

Shortest match left to right:

$$S_L = \ [?{-}B] \mid [\,0 : \langle \mid \rangle : 0 \mid \langle{:}0 \mid B\,][?{-}B]^+$$
$$T_{LRSHORT} = ?^*\ \langle\ \ [?\ - B\,]^+\ \ \rangle : 0\ S_L\ RP$$

Shortest match right to left:

$$S_L = \ [?{-}B] \mid [?{-}B]^+\ [\,0 : \langle \mid \rangle : 0 \mid \langle{:}0 \mid B\,]$$
$$T_{RLSHORT} = \ RP\ S_R\ \langle : 0\ [?\ - B\,]^+\langle\ \ ?^*$$

For compiling epenthesis rules, to avoid more than one epsilon in the row:

$$B_L = \{\langle\,, [\![\ \}$$
$$B_R = \{\ \rangle,\ ]\!]\}$$
$$T_{NO\ REP}{}' = ?^*\ B_L B_R B_L B_R\ ?^*$$

For non-optional replacements:

$$T_{MOST+} = ?^*\ [B_L{:}0\ \ [?{-}B]^+\ B_R{:}0\ ?^*\,]^+$$

To remove paths containing B_2, where $B_2 = \{\ [\![,]\!]\}$:

$$T_{LEST}{}' = ?^*\ B_2\ ?^*$$

Since $T_{NO\ REP}{}'$ and $T_{LEST}{}'$ are reflexive, they are not preference relation. Instead, they are filters applied after preference relations.

3.3 Applying constraints with *.r-glc.* operator

To apply a preference constraint in order to restrict transducer *t*, we use *.r-glc.* operator. The *.r-glc.* operation between transducer *t* and a *constraint* is shown in Figure 2. Input language of a transducer is noted as $proj_1$ and output language as $proj_2$.

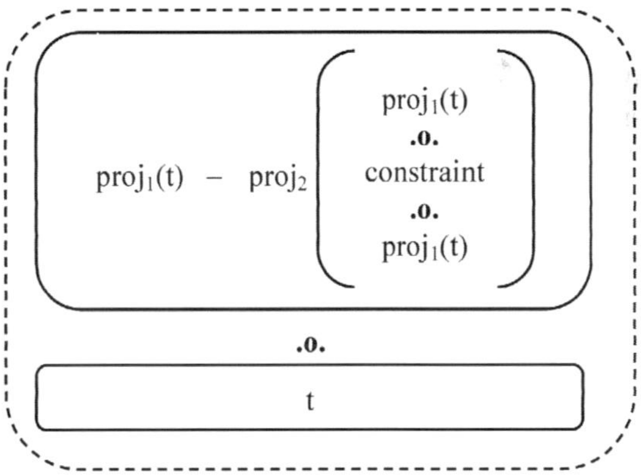

Figure 2: Breakdown of the operation: *t .r-glc. constraint*

Contraints combinations

As shown in Figure 1, in order to achieve desired replace rules, it is often necessary to use several constraints. For example, to achieve left to right longest match, it is necessary to combine T_{LM} and

T_{LRLONG}. If the same longest match contains epenthesis, $T_{NO\ REP}$ constraint should also be used.

3.4 Removing brackets

Removing brackets is simply achieved by applying $T_{LEST} = ?^* \ B \ ?^*$ constraint, where B is set of brackets we want to remove. Additionally, in HFST implementation, it is also required to remove the brackets from the transducers alphabets.

4 Examples

Let us show how the replace rule is compiled on different examples.

Since it would take too much space to show whole transducers, we will show only output of the intermediate results applied to an input string.

The first example shows how to achieve a non-optional replacement. Intermediate results of the replace rule $a \rightarrow x \ || \ a \_ a$ is shown in the Table 2. Since the arrow demands non-optional replacement, the unconstrained bracketed replace, if applied to the input string $a \ a \ a$, contains three possible results. The first result is the input string itself, which would be part of the non-optional replacement. The second result is necessary to filter out the first one. In this example, because of the restricting context, replacement is possible only in the middle, and therefore, it is bracketed with special brackets. Finally, the third result contains the bracketed replace relation.

$a \rightarrow x \ || \ a \_ a$

UBT	T_{MOST+}	T_{LEST}'
$a \ a \ a$ $a \ [\![a]\!] \ a$ $a\langle a{:}x\rangle \ a$	$a\langle a{:}x\rangle \ a$ $a \ [\![a]\!] \ a$	$a\langle a{:}x\rangle \ a$

Table 2: Steps of the non optional replacement

Once when we have the unconstrained bracketed replace transducer, we are ready to apply filters. First filter, T_{MOST+} will filter out all results that contain smaller number of brackets in every position, without making difference to the type of brackets. In this example, it will filter out the first result, the one that does not have any brackets at all.

The second filter, T_{LEST}' will filter out all the results containing B_2 brackets because they don't contain the replace relation. Finally, to get the final result, it is necessary to remove brackets from the relation.

Following examples will be shown on the input string $a \ a \ a \ a$. Table 3 shows steps of building left to right longest match and Table 4 left to right shortest match.

Both longest match and shortest match have the same first two steps. After building Unconstrained Bracketed Replace, we apply T_{LM} filter which finds all the results with left most brackets in every position and filters out all the rest. This contraints characteristic filters out the results without the brackets as well, so the result will be non-optional. In order to get the longest match, we apply another filter (T_{LRLONG}) to the result of the left most filter. This filter finds the longest of the bracketed matches with the same starting position. In the final step, if we apply filter $T_{LRSHORT}$ instead of T_{LRLONG}, we will get the shortest match (Table 4).

$a+ \ @\!\rightarrow x \ || \ a \_ a$

UBT	T_{LM}	T_{LRLONG}
$a \ a \ a \ a$ $a\langle a{:}x\rangle \ a \ a$ $a\langle a{:}x\rangle\langle a{:}x\rangle \ a$ $a\langle a{:}x \ a{:}\varepsilon\rangle \ a$ $a \ a \ \langle a{:}x\rangle \ a$	$a\langle a{:}x\rangle \ a \ a$ $a\langle a{:}x\rangle\langle a{:}x\rangle \ a$ $a\langle a{:}x \ a{:}\varepsilon\rangle \ a$	$a\langle a{:}x \ a{:}\varepsilon\rangle \ a$

Table 3: Left to right longest match

$a+ \ @\!> x \ || \ a \_ a$

UBT	T_{LM}	$T_{LRSHORT}$
$a \ a \ a \ a$ $a\langle a{:}x\rangle \ a \ a$ $a\langle a{:}x\rangle\langle a{:}x\rangle \ a$ $a\langle a{:}x \ a{:}\varepsilon\rangle \ a$ $a \ a \ \langle a{:}x\rangle \ a$	$a\langle a{:}x\rangle \ a \ a$ $a\langle a{:}x\rangle\langle a{:}x\rangle \ a$ $a\langle a{:}x \ a{:}\varepsilon\rangle \ a$	$a\langle a{:}x\rangle\langle a{:}x\rangle \ a$

Table 4: Left to right shortest match

5 Conclusion

The large number of different replace operators makes it quite complicated and error-prone to build a supporting framework for them. However, the *.r-glc.* operator and preference relations allow splitting the algorithm into small reusable units which are easy to maintain and upgrade with new functionalities.

The replace rules are now part of the HFST library and can be used through *hfst-regexp2fst* command line tool, but there is still some work to be done to build an interactive interface. Additionally, we are planning to add support for two level contexts and parallel weighted rules.

Acknowledgments

The research leading to these results has received funding from the European Commission's 7th Framework Program under grant agreement n° 238405 (CLARA).

References

Beesley, K.R., Karttunen, L.: Finite State Morphology. CSLI publications (2003)

Eisner, J.: Directional constraint evaluation in optimality theory. In: 20th COLING 2000, Proceedings of the Conference, Saarbrücken, Germany (2000) 257–263

Gerdemann, D. (2009). Mix and Match Replacement Rules. Proceedings of the Workshop on RANLP 2009 Workshop on Adaptation of Language Resources and Technology to New Domains, Borovets, Bulgaria, 2011, pages 39-47.

Gerdemann, D., van Noord, G.: Approximation and exactness in Finite-State Optimality Theory. In Eisner, J., Karttunen, L., Thériault, A., eds.: SIGPHON 2000, Finite State Phonology. (2000)

Gerdemann, D., van Noord, G.: Transducers from rewrite rules with backreferences. In: 9th EACL 1999, Proceedings of the Conference. (1999) 126–133

Jäger, G.: Gradient constraints in Finite State OT: The unidirectional and the bidirectional case. In: Proceedings of FSMNLP 2001, an ESSLLI Workshop, Helsinki (2001) (35–40)

Karttunen, L.: The replace operator. In: 33th ACL 1995, Proceedings of the Conference, Cambridge, MA, USA (1995) 16–23

Karttunen, L.: Directed replace operator. In Roche, E., Schabes, Y., eds.: Finitestate language processing, Cambridge, Massachusetts, A Bradford Book. The MIT Press (1996) 117–147

Kempe, A., Karttunen, L.: Parallel replacement in finite state calculus. In: 16th COLING 1996, Proc. Conf. Volume 2., Copenhagen, Denmark (1996) 622–627

Lindén, K., Axelson, E., Hardwick, S., Silfverberg, M., Pirinen, T.: HFST - Framework for Compiling and Applying Morphologies, Communications in Computer and Information Science, vol. 100, pp. 67-85. Springer Berlin Heidelberg (2011)

Lindén, K., Silfverberg, M., Pirinen, T.: Hfst tools for morphology - an efficient open-source package for construction of morphological analyzers. In: Mahlow, C., Pietrowski, M. (eds.) State of the Art in Computational Morphology. Communications in Computer and Information Science, vol. 41, pp. 28-47. Springer Berlin Heidelberg (2009)

Yli-Jyrä, A., Koskenniemi, K.: A new method for compiling parallel replacement rules. In Holub, J., Žďárek, J., eds.: Implementation and Application of Automata, 12th International Conference, CIAA 2007, Revised Selected Papers. Volume 4783 of LNCS., Springer (2007) 320–321

Yli-Jyrä, A.: Applications of Diamonded Double Negation. In Finite-state methods and natural language processing. Thomas Hanneforth and Kay-Michael Würtzner. 6th International Workshop, FSMNLP 2007. Potsdam, Germany, September 14-16. Revised Papers. Universitätsverlag Potsdam (2008a) 6-30

Yli-Jyrä, A., Transducers from Parallel Replace Rules and Modes with Generalized Lenient Composition. In Finite-state methods and natural language processing. Thomas Hanneforth and Kay-Michael Würtzner. 6th International Workshop, FSMNLP 2007. Potsdam, Germany, September 14-16. Revised Papers. Universitätsverlag Potsdam (2008b) 197-212

First approaches on Spanish medical record classification using Diagnostic Term to class transduction

A. Casillas[(1)], **A. Díaz de Ilarraza**[(2)], **K. Gojenola**[(2)], **M. Oronoz**[(2)], **A. Pérez**[(2)]
[(1)] Dep. Electricity and Electronics
[(2)] Dep. Computer Languages and Systems
University of the Basque Country (UPV/EHU)
arantza.casillas@ehu.es

Abstract

This paper presents an application of finite-state transducers to the domain of medicine. The objective is to assign disease codes to each Diagnostic Term in the medical records generated by the Basque Health Hospital System. As a starting point, a set of manually coded medical records were collected in order to code new medical records on the basis of this set of positive samples. Since the texts are written in natural language by doctors, the same Diagnostic Term might show alternative forms. Hence, trying to code a new medical record by exact matching the samples in the set is not always feasible due to sparsity of data. In an attempt to increase the coverage of the data, our work centered on applying a set of finite-state transducers that helped the matching process between the positive samples and a set of new entries. That is, these transducers allowed not only exact matching but also approximate matching. While there are related works in languages such as English, this work presents the first results on automatic assignment of disease codes to medical records written in Spanish.

1 Introduction

During the last years an exponential increase in the number of electronic documents in the medical domain has occurred. The automatic processing of these documents allows to retrieve information, helping the health professionals in their work. There are different sort of valuable data that help to exploit medical information. Our framework lays on the classification of Medical Records (MRs) according to a standard. In our context, the MRs produced in a hospital have to be classified with respect to the World Health Organization's 9th Revision of the International Classification of Diseases[1] (ICD-9). ICD-9 is designed for the classification of morbidity and mortality information and for the indexing of hospital records by disease and procedure. The already classified MRs are stored in a database that serves for further classification purposes. Each MR consists of two pieces of information:

Diagnostic Terms (DTs): one or more terms that describe the diseases corresponding to the MR.

Body-text: a description of the patient's details, antecedents, symptoms, adverse effects, methods of administration of medicines etc.

Even though the DTs are within a limited domain, their description is not subject to a standard. Doctors express the DTs in natural language with their own style and different degrees of precision. Usually, a given concept might be expressed by alternative DTs with variations due to modifiers, abbreviations, acronyms, dates, names, misspellings or style. This is a typical problem that arises in natural language processing due to the fact that doctors focus on the patients and not so much on the writing of the MR. On account of this, there is ample variability in the presentation of the DTs. Consequently, it is not a straightforward task to get the corresponding ICD-codes. That is, the task is by far more complex than a standard dictionary lookup.

[1] http://www.cdc.gov/nchs/icd/icd9.htm

Proceedings of the 10th International Workshop on Finite State Methods and Natural Language Processing, pages 60–64, Donostia–San Sebastián, July 23–25, 2012. ©2012 Association for Computational Linguistics

The Basque Health Hospital System is concerned with the automatization of this ICD-code assignment task. So far, the hospital processes the daily produced documents in the following sequence:

1. **Automatic:** exact match of the DTs in a set of manually coded samples.

2. **Semi-automatic:** through semantic match, ranking the DTs by means of machine-learning techniques. This stage requires that experts select amongst the ranked choices.

3. **Manual:** the documents that were not matched in the previous two stages are examined by professional coders assigning the codes manually.

The goal of this paper is to bypass the variability associated to natural language descriptions in an attempt to maximize the proportion of automatically assigned codes, as the Hospital System aims to expand the use of the automatic codification of MRs to more hospitals. According to experts, even an increase of 1% in exact match would represent a significant improvement allowing to gain time and resources.

Related work can be found in the literature. For instance, Pestian et al. (2007) reported on a shared task involving the assignment of ICD-codes to radiology reports written in English from a reduced set of 45 codes. In general it implied the examination of the full MR (including body-text). In our case, the number of ICD-codes is above 1,000, although we restrict ourselves to exact and approximate match over the diagnoses.

Farkas and Szarvas (2008) used machine learning for the automatic assignment of ICD-9 codes. Their results showed that hand-crafted systems could be reproduced by replacing several laborious steps in their construction with machine learning models.

Tsuruoka et al. (2008) presented a system that tried to normalize different variants of the terms contained in a medical dictionary, automatically getting normalizing rules for genes, proteins, chemicals and diseases in English.

The contribution of this work is: i) to collect manually coded MRs in Spanish; ii) to approximate transduction with finite-state (FS) models for automatic MR coding and, iii) to assess the performance of the proposed FS transduction approaches.

2 Approximate transduction

As it was previously mentioned, there are variations regarding the DT descriptions due to style, miss-spells, etc. Table 1 shows several pairs of DT and ICD-codes within the collected samples that illustrate some of those variations.

	DT	ICD
1	*Adenocarcinoma de prostata*	*185*
2	*Adenocarcinomas próstata.*	*185*
3	*Ca. prostata*	*185*
4	*CÁNCER DE PROSTATA*	*185*
5	*adenocarcinoma de pulmon estadio IV*	*1629*
6	*CA pulmón estadio 4*	*1629*
7	*ADENOCARCINOMA PANCREAS*	*1579*

Table 1: Examples of DTs and their ICD-codes.

There are differences in the use of uppercase/lower case; omissions of accents; use of both standard and non-standard abbreviations (e.g. *ca.* for both *cáncer* and *adenocarcinoma*); punctuation marks (incidental use of full-stop as commas, etc.); omission of prepositions (see rows 1 and 2); equivalence between Roman and Arabic numerals (rows 5 and 6). Due to these variations, our problem can be defined as an approximate lookup in a dictionary.

2.1 Finite-state models

Foma toolkit was used to build the FS machines and code the evaluation sets. Foma (Hulden, 2009) is a freely available[2] toolkit that allows to both build and parse FS automata and transducers. Foma offers a versatile layout that supports imports/exports from/to other tools such as: Xerox XFST (Beesley and Karttunen, 2003), AT&T (Mehryar Mohri and Riley, 2003), OpenFST (Riley et al., 2009). There are, as well, outstanding alternatives such as HFST (Lindén et al., 2010). Refer to (Yli-Jyrä et al., 2006) for a thorough inventory on FS resources.

The FS models in Figure 1 perform the conversions necessary to carry out a soft match between the dictionary entries and their variants.

- First, we define the transducer `Accents` that takes into account the correspondences between standard letters and their versions using accent text marks.

[2] `http://code.google.com/p/foma`

```
define  Accents      [a:á|e:é|i:í|o:ó|u:ú|...];
define  Case         [a:A|b:B|c:C|d:D|e:E|f:F|...];
define  Spaces       [..]  (->) " " || [.#.  | "."] _ ,_ .#.;
define  Punctuation  ["."|"-"|" "]:["."|"-"|" "];
define  Plurals      [..]  -> ([s|es]) || _ [.#.  | "." | " "];
define  PluralsI     [s|es] (->) "" || _ [.#.  | "." | ","| " "];
define  Preps        [..]  (->) [de |del |con |por ] || " "_;
define  Disease      [enf|enf.|enfermedad]:[enf|enf.|enfermedad];
define  AltCa        [tumor|ca|ca.|carcinoma|adenocarcinoma|cáncer];
define  TagNormCa    AltCa:AltCa;
define  AltIzq       [izquierdo|izquierda|izq|izq.|izqda|izqda.|
                     izqdo|izqdo.|izda|izda.|izdo|izdo.];
define  TagNormIzq   AltIzq:AltIzq;
```

Figure 1: A simplified version in Foma source code of the regular expressions and transducers used to bypass several sources of distortion within the DTs in order to parse variations of unseen input DTs.

- The expression `Case` matches uppercase and lowercase versions of the DTs.
- There is a set of transducers (`Spaces`, `Punctuation`, `Plurals` and `PluralsI`) that deal with the addition or deletion of spaces and separators (as full-stop, comma, and hyphen) between words or at the end of the DT.
- `Prepositions`. Many DTs can be differentiated by the use or absence of prepositions, although they correspond to the same ICD-code. For that reason, we designed a transducer that inserts or deletes the prepositions from a reduced set that were identified by inspection of the training set. In this way, expressions as "*Adenocarcinoma prostata*" and "*Adenocarcinoma de prostata*" can be mapped to each other.
- `Tag Normalization` of synonyms, variants and abbreviations. The examination of the DTs in the training set revealed that there were several terms used indistinctly, including synonyms and different kinds of variants (masculine and feminine) and abbreviations. For example, the words *adenocarcinoma, adenoca., carcinoma, ca, ca. and cancer* serve to name the same disease. There are also multiple variants of left/right, indicating the location of an illness, that do not affect the assignment of the ICD-code (e.g. *izquierdo, izq., izda.*).

Finally, all the FS transducers were composed into a single machine that served to overcome all the sources of distortion together.

3 Experimental results

To begin with, coded MRs produced in the hospital throughout 12 months were collected summing up a total of 8,020 MRs as described in Table 2. Note that there are ambiguities in our data-set since there are 3,313 different DTs that have resulted in 3,407 (DT, ICD-code) different pairs (as shown in Table 2). That is, the same DT was not always assigned the same ICD-code.

	DT	**ICD-code**
entries	8,020	
different entries	3,407	
different forms	3,313	1,011

Table 2: The data-set of (DT, ICD-code) pairs.

Next, the data-set was shuffled and divided into 3 disjoint sets for training, development and test purposes as shown in Table 3.

	train	**dev**	**test**
entries	6,020	1,000	1,000
different entries	2,825	734	728

Table 3: The data-set shuffled and divided into 3 sets

Using the set of mappings derived from the training set we performed the experiments on the development set. After several rounds of tuning the system, the resulting system was applied to the test set.

		PERCENTAGE OF UNCLASSIFIED DTs					
TRAIN	**EVAL-SET**	**exact-match**	**+ case-ins.**	**+ punct.**	**+ plurals**	**+preps.**	**+ tag-norm.**
train	**dev**	30.6	27.0	25.2	24.4	23.9	23.2
train	**test**	29.8	26.7	25.1	24.8	24.3	23.2
train+dev	**test**	27.7	24.5	23.0	22.9	22.5	21.4

Table 4: Performance of different FS machines in terms of the percentage of unclassified entries. All the classified entries were correctly classified, yielding, as a result, a precision of 100%.

Given a DT, the goal is to find its corresponding ICD-code despite the variations. Different FS approaches (described in Section 2.1) were proposed to bypass particular sources of noise in the DT. Their performance was assessed by means of the percentage of unclassified DTs, as summarized in Table 4. Note that the lower the number of unclassified DTs the better the performance. In each of the three rows of Table 4 the results of different experimental setups are shown: in the first two rows the training set was used to build the models and either the development or the test set was evaluated in their turn; in the third row, both the training and the development sets were used to build the model and the test set was evaluated. The impact of adding progressively the FS machines built to tackle particular sources of noise is shown by columns. Thus, the results of the last column represent the performance of the transducer allowing exact-match search together with case-insensitive search, bypassing punctuation marks, allowing plurals, bypassing prepositions and allowing tag-normalization. The composition of each transducer outperforms the previous result, yielding an improvement on the test of 6 absolute points over the exact-match baseline, from 27.7% to 21.4%. As it can be derived from the first column of Table 4 the test set contributed to the training+development set with %27.7 of new DTs.

Overall, the FSMs progressively improved the results for the three series of experiments carried out in more than 6%. As a result, less and less DTs are left unclassified. In other words, the FS machines tackling different sources of errors contribute to assign ICD-codes to previously unassigned DTs.

A manual inspection over the results associated to the evaluation of the development set (focus on the first row of Table 4) showed that all the DTs were correctly classified according to the training data. Overall, the resulting transducer was unable to classify 232 DTs out of 1,000 (see last column in first row). Among the unclassified DTs, 10 out of 232 were due to misspellings: e.g. *cic atriz* (instead of *cicatriz*), *desprendimineot* (instead of *desprendimiento*). In fact, spelling correction reported improvements in related tasks (Patrick et al., 2010). The remaining DTs showed wider variations in their forms, as unexpected degree of specificity (e.g. named entities), spurious dates or numbers.

4 Conclusions

Medical records in Spanish were collected yielding a data set of 8,020 DT and ICD-code pairs. While there are a number of references dealing with English medical records, there are few for Spanish.

The goal of this work was to build a system that given a DT it would find its corresponding ICD-code as in a standard key-value dictionary. Yet, the DTs are far from being standard since they contain a number of variations. We proposed the use of several FS models to bypass different variants and allow to provide ICD-codes even when the exact DT was not found. Each source of variations was tackled with a specific transducer based on handwritten rules. The composition of each machine improved the performance of the system gradually, leading to an improvement up to 6% in accuracy, from 27.7% unclassified DTs with the exact-match baseline to 21.4% with the tag-normalization transducer.

Future work will focus on the unclassified DTs. Together with FS models, other strategies shall be explored. Machine-learning strategies in the field of information retrieval might help to make the most of the piece of information that was here discarded (i.e. the body-text). All in all, regardless of the approach, the command in this MR classification context is to get an accuracy of 100%, possibly through the interactive inference framework (Toselli et al., 2011).

Acknowledgments

Authors would like to thank the Hospital Galdakao-Usansolo for their contributions and support, in particular to Javier Yetano, responsible of the Clinical Documentation Service.

This research was supported by the Department of Industry of the Basque Government (IT344-10, S-PE11UN114, GIC10/158 IT375-10), the University of the Basque Country (GIU09/19) and the Spanish Ministry of Science and Innovation (MICINN, TIN2010- 20218).

References

[Beesley and Karttunen2003] Kenneth R. Beesley and Lauri Karttunen. 2003. *Finite State Morphology*. CSLI Publications,.

[Farkas and Szarvas2008] Richárd Farkas and György Szarvas. 2008. Automatic construction of rule-based ICD-9-CM coding systems. *BMC Bioinformatics.*, 9 (Suppl 3): S10.

[Hulden2009] Mans Hulden. 2009. Foma: a Finite-State Compiler and Library. In *EACL (Demos)*, pages 29–32. The Association for Computer Linguistics.

[Lindén et al.2010] Krister Lindén, Miikka Silfverberg, and Tommi Pirinen. 2010. HFST tools for morphology – an efficient open-source package for construction of morphological analyzers.

[Mehryar Mohri and Riley2003] Fernando C. N. Pereira Mehryar Mohri and Michael D. Riley. 2003. AT&T FSM LibraryTM – Finite-State Machine Library. www.research.att.com/sw/tools/fsm.

[Patrick et al.2010] Jon Patrick, Mojtaba Sabbagh, Suvir Jain, and Haifeng Zheng. 2010. Spelling correction in clinical notes with emphasis on first suggestion accuracy. In *2nd Workshop on Building and Evaluating Resources for Biomedical Text Mining (BioTxtM2010) LREC*. ELRA.

[Pestian et al.2007] John P. Pestian, Chris Brew, Pawel Matykiewicz, D. J Hovermale, Neil Johnson, K. Bretonnel Cohen, and Wlodzislaw Duch. 2007. A shared task involving multi-label classification of clinical free text. In *Biological, translational, and clinical language processing*, pages 97–104, Prague, Czech Republic, June. Association for Computational Linguistics.

[Riley et al.2009] Michael Riley, Cyril Allauzen, and Martin Jansche. 2009. OpenFST: An open-source, weighted finite-state transducer library and its applications to speech and language. In *Proceedings of Human Language Technologies: The 2009 Annual Conference of the North American Chapter of the Association for Computational Linguistics, Companion Volume: Tutorial Abstracts*, pages 9–10, Boulder, Colorado, May. Association for Computational Linguistics.

[Toselli et al.2011] Alejandro H. Toselli, Enrique Vidal, and Francisco Casacuberta. 2011. *Multimodal Interactive Pattern Recognition and Applications*. Springer.

[Tsuruoka et al.2008] Yoshimasa Tsuruoka, John McNaught, and Sophia Ananiadou. 2008. Normalizing biomedical terms by minimizing ambiguity and variability. *BMC Bioinformatics*, 9(Suppl 3):S2.

[Yli-Jyrä et al.2006] A. Yli-Jyrä, K. Koskenniemi, and K.. Lindén. 2006. Common infrastructure for finite-state based methods and linguistic descriptions. In *Proceedings of International Workshop Towards a Research Infrastructure for Language Resources.*, Genoa, May.

Developing an open-source FST grammar for verb chain transfer in a Spanish-Basque MT System

Aingeru Mayor, Mans Hulden, Gorka Labaka
Ixa Group
University of the Basque Country
aingeru@ehu.es, mhulden@email.arizona.edu, gorka.labaka@ehu.es

Abstract

This paper presents the current status of development of a finite state transducer grammar for the verbal-chain transfer module in *Matxin*, a Rule Based Machine Translation system between Spanish and Basque. Due to the distance between Spanish and Basque, the verbal-chain transfer is a very complex module in the overall system. The grammar is compiled with *foma*, an open-source finite-state toolkit, and yields a translation execution time of 2000 verb chains/second.

1 Introduction

This paper presents the current status of development of an FST (Finite State Transducer) grammar we have developed for *Matxin*, a Machine Translation system between Spanish and Basque.

Basque is a minority language isolate, and it is likely that an early form of this language was already present in Western Europe before the arrival of the Indo-European languages.

Basque is a highly inflected language with free order of sentence constituents. It is an agglutinative language, with a rich flexional morphology.

Basque is also a so-called ergative-absolutive language where the subjects of intransitive verbs appear in the absolutive case (which is unmarked), and where the same case is used for the direct object of a transitive verb. The subject of the transitive verb (that is, the agent) is marked differently, with the ergative case (in Basque by the suffix *-k*). The presence of this morpheme also triggers main and auxiliary verbal agreement. Auxiliary verbs, or 'periphrastic' verbs, which accompany most main verbs, agree not only with the subject, but also with the direct object and the indirect object, if present. Among European languages, this polypersonal system (multiple verb agreement) is rare, and found only in Basque, some Caucasian languages, and Hungarian.

The fact that Basque is both a morphologically rich and less-resourced language makes the use of statistical approaches for Machine Translation difficult and raises the need to develop a rule-based architecture which in the future could be combined with statistical techniques.

The *Matxin es-eu* (Spanish-Basque) MT engine is a classic transfer-based system comprising three main modules: analysis of the Spanish text (based on *FreeLing*, (Atserias et al., 2006)), transfer, and generation of the Basque target text.

In the transfer process, lexical transfer is first carried out using a bilingual dictionary coded in the XML format of Apertium dictionary files (.dix) (Forcada et al., 2009), and compiled, using the FST library implemented in the Apertium project (the *lt-toolbox* library), into a finite-state transducer that can be processed very quickly.

Following this, structural transfer at the sentence level is performed, and some information is transferred from some chunks[1] to others while some chunks may be deleted. Finally, the structural trans-

[1] A chunk is a non-recursive phrase (noun phrase, prepositional phrase, verbal chain, etc.) which expresses a constituent (Abney, 1991; Civit, 2003). In our system, chunks play a crucial part in simplifying the translation process, due to the fact that each module works only at a single level, either inside or between chunks.

Proceedings of the 10th International Workshop on Finite State Methods and Natural Language Processing, pages 65–69,
Donostia–San Sebastián, July 23–25, 2012.

fer at the verb chunk level is carried out. The verbal chunk transfer is a very complex module because of the nature of Spanish and Basque auxiliary verb constructions, and is the main subject of this paper.

This verb chain transfer module is implemented as a series of ordered replacement rules (Beesley and Karttunen, 2003) using the *foma* finite-state toolkit (Hulden, 2009). In total, the system consists of 166 separate replacement rules that together perform the verb chunk translation. In practice, the input is given to the first transducer, after which its output is passed to the second, and so forth, in a cascade. Each rule in the system is unambiguous in its output; that is, for each input in a particular step along the verb chain transfer, the transducers never produce multiple outputs (i.e. the transducers in question are functional). Some of the rules are joined together with composition, yielding a total of 55 separate transducers. In principle, all the rules could be composed together into one monolithic transducer, but in practice the size of the composed transducer is too large to be feasible. The choice to combine some transducers while leaving others separate is largely a memory/translation speed tradeoff.

2 Spanish and Basque verb features and their translation

In the following, we will illustrate some of the main issues in translating Spanish verb chains to Basque. Since both languages make frequent use of auxiliary verb constructions, and since periphrastic verb constructions are frequent in Basque, transfer rules can get quite complex in their design.

For example, in translating the phrase

(Yo)	compro	(una	manzana)
(I)	buy	(an	apple)
[PP1CSN00]	**[VMIP1S0]**	**[DI0FS0]**	**[NCFS000]**

we can translate it using the imperfective participle form (*erosten*) of the verb *erosi (to buy)*, and a transitive auxiliary (*dut*) which itself contains both subject agreement information (*I*: 1st sg.) and number agreement with the object (*an apple*: 3rd sg.): *(nik) (sagar bat) erosten dut*. The participle carries information concerning meaning, aspect and tense, whereas the auxiliaries convey information about argument structure, tense and mood.

Table 1 illustrates the central idea of the verb chunk transfer. In the first four examples the form of the transitive auxiliary changes to express agreement with different ergative arguments (the subject of the clause), absolutive arguments (the direct object) and dative arguments (the indirect object). In the fifth example the future participle is used. The last example shows the translation of a periphrastic construction, in which the the Spanish and the Basque word orders are completely different: this is reflected in the Spanish *tengo que*-construction (have to) which appears before the main verb, whereas in the Basque, the equivalent (*behar*) appears after the main verb (*erosi*).

3 The FST grammar

We carry out the verbal chunk transfer using finite-state transducers (Alegria et al., 2005). The grammar rules take as input the Spanish verbal chunk, perform a number of transformations on the input, and then create and output the verbal chunk for Basque.

To illustrate the functioning of the grammar, let us consider the following example sentence in Spanish: "*Un tribunal ha negado los derechos constitucionales a los presos polticos*" (A court has denied constitutional rights to political prisoners). The correct translation into Basque given by the system for this example is as follows: *Auzitegi batek eskubide konstituzionalak ukatu dizkie preso politikoei*. Figure 1 shows a detailed overview of how the whole transfer of the verbal chunk is performed for this particular example.

First, the input to the grammar is assumed to be a string containing (separated by the '&' symbol) the following information :

- the morphological information (using EAGLES-style tags Leech and Wilson (1996)) for all nodes (separated by '+' symbol) in the Spanish verbal chunk (**haber[VAIP3S0]+negar[VMP00SM]**);
- the morphological information of the subject (**[sub3s]**), the direct object (**[obj3p]**) and the indirect object (**[iobj3p]**);
- the translation of the main verb in Basque (**ukatu**) and information about its transitivity

Spanish sentence	English	Basque translation
(Yo) compro (una manzana)	(I) buy (an apple)	(Nik) (sagar bat) erosten dut
(Yo) compro (manzana**s**)	(I) buy (apple**s**)	(Nik) (sagarra**k**) erosten d**it**ut
(**Tú**) compr**as** (manzanas)	(**You**) buy (apples)	(**Zuk**) (sagarrak) erosten dituz**u**
(Yo) (**te**) compro (una manzana)	(I) buy (**you**) (an apple)	(Nik) (**zuri**) (sagar bat) erosten d**izu**t
(Yo) compr**aré** (una manzana)	(I) **will** buy (an apple)	(Nik) (sagar bat) erosi**ko** dut
(Yo) **tengo que** comprar (manzanas)	(I) **must** buy (apples)	(Nik) (sagarrak) erosi **behar** ditut

Table 1: Examples of translations

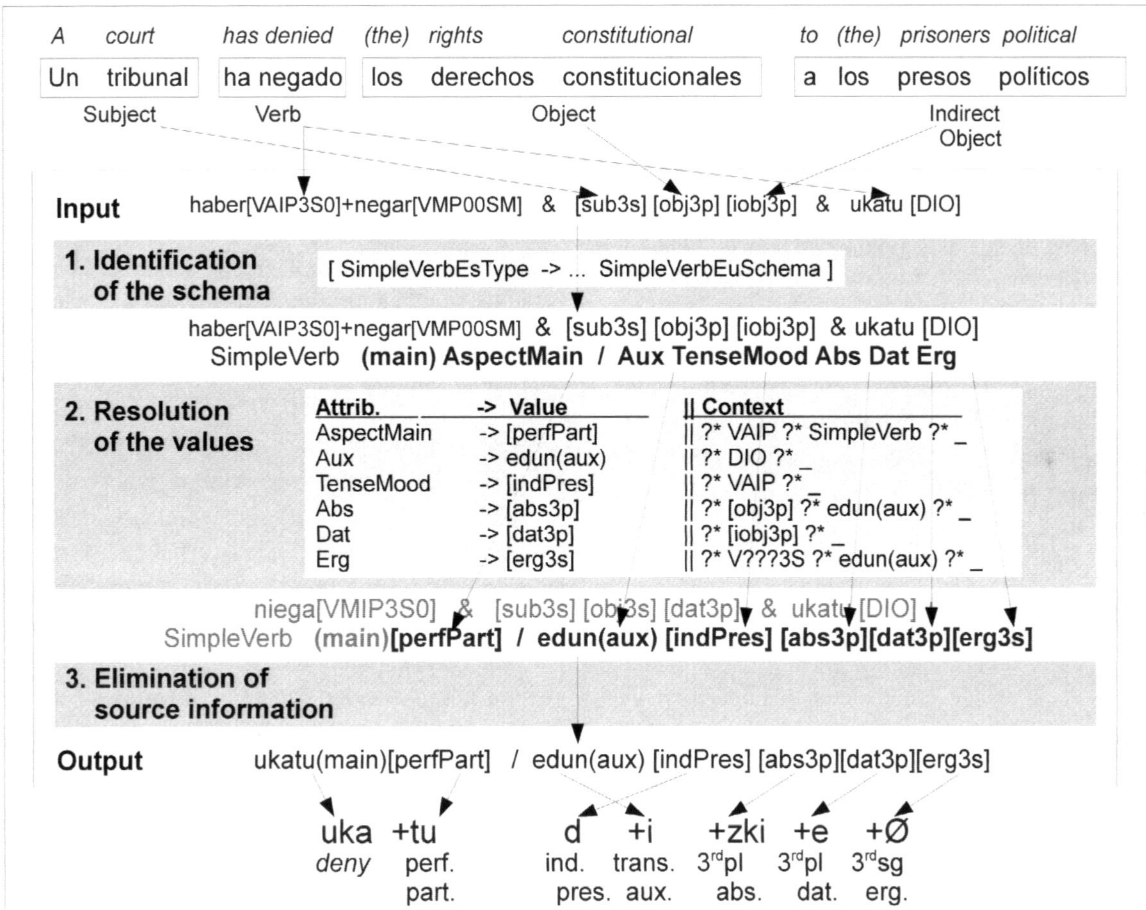

Figure 1: Example of the transfer of a verbal chunk.

([DIO]), indicating a ditransitive construction:

```
haber[VAIP3S0]+negar[VMP00SM] &
[sub3s][obj3p][iobj3p] & ukatu[DIO]
```

The grammatical rules are organized into three groups according to the three main steps defined for translating verbal chunks:

1. Identification of the Basque verbal chunk schema corresponding to the source verbal chunk.

   There are twelve rules which perform this task, each of which corresponds to one of the following verbal chunks in Spanish: non-conjugated verbs, simple non-periphrastic verbs as well as four different groups reserved for the periphrastic verbs.

   The verbal chunk of the example in figure 1 is a simple non-periphrastic one, and the rule that handles this particular case is as follows:

   ```
   [simpleVerbEsType -> ...
   simpleVerbEuSchema]
   ```

   When this rule matches the input string representing a simple non-periphrastic verbal chunk (`simpleVerbEsType`) it adds the corresponding Basque verbal chunk schema (`simpleVerbEuSchema`) to the end of the input string. `simpleVerbEsType` is a complex automaton that has the definition of the Spanish simple verbs. `simpleVerbEuSchema` is the type of the verbal chunk (`SimpleVerb`) and an automaton that contains as strings the pattern of elements (separated by the '/' symbol) that the corresponding Basque verb chunk will need to have (in this case, the main verb and the auxiliary verb):

   ```
   SimpleVerb (main) AspectMain /
   Aux TenseMood Abs Dat Erg
   ```

2. Resolution of the values for the attributes in the Basque schema.

   A total of 150 replacement rules of this type have been written in the grammar. Here are some rules that apply to the above example:

   ```
   [AspectMain -> [perfPart] || ?* VAIP
   ?* SimpleVerb ?* _ ]
   [Aux -> edun(aux) || ?* DIO ?* _ ]
   [Abs -> [abs3p] || ?* [obj3p] ?*
   edun(aux) ?* _ ]
   ```

3. Elimination of source-language information (4 rules in total).

   The output of the grammar for the example is:

   ```
   ukatu(main)[perfPart] /
   edun(aux)[indPres][abs3p][dat3p][erg3s]
   ```

   The first node has the main verb (*ukatu*) with the perfective participle aspect, and the second one contains the auxiliary verb (*edun*) with all its morphological information: indicative present and argument structure.

In the output string, each of the elements contains the information needed by the subsequent syntactic generation and morphological generation phases.

4 Implementation

When the verbal chunk transfer module was first developed, there did not exist any efficient open-source tools for the construction of finite state transducers. At the time, the *XFST*-toolkit (Beesley and Karttunen, 2003) was used to produce the earlier versions of the module: this included 25 separate transducers of moderate size, occupying 2,795 kB in total. The execution speed was roughly 250 verb chains per second. Since *Matxin* was designed to be open source, we built a simple compiler that converted the *XFST* rules into regular expressions that could then be applied without FST technology, at the cost of execution speed. This verbal chunk transfer module read and applied these regular expressions at a speed of 50 verbal chunks per second.

In the work presented here, we have reimplemented and expanded the original rules written for *XFST* with the *foma*[2] toolkit (Hulden, 2009). After adapting the grammar and compiling it, the 55 separate transducers occupy 607 kB and operate at roughly 2,000 complete verb chains per second.[3] Passing the strings from one transducer to the next in the chain of 55 transducers in accomplished by the depth-first-search transducer chaining functionality available in the *foma* API.

[2]http://foma.sourceforge.net

[3]On a 2.8MHz Intel Core 2 Duo.

References

Abney, S. (1991). *Principle-Based Parsing: Computation and Psycholinguistics*, chapter Parsing by Chunks, pages 257–278. Kluwer Academic, Boston.

Alegria, I., Díaz de Ilarraza, A., Labaka, G., Lersundi, M., Mayor, A., and Sarasola, K. (2005). An FST grammar for verb chain transfer in a Spanish–Basque MT system. In *Finite-State Methods and Natural Language Processing*, volume 4002, pages 295–296, Germany. Springer Verlag.

Atserias, J., Casas, B., Comelles, E., González, M., Padró, L., and Padró, M. (2006). Freeling 1.3: Syntactic and semantic services in an open-source NLP library. In *Proceedings of LREC*, volume 6, pages 48–55.

Beesley, K. R. and Karttunen, L. (2003). *Finite State Morphology*. CSLI Publications, Stanford, CA.

Civit, M. (2003). *Criterios de etiquetación y desambiguación morfosintáctica de corpus en Español*. PhD thesis, Universidad de Barcelona.

Forcada, M., Bonev, B. I., Ortiz-Rojas, S., Pérez-Ortiz, J. A., Ramírez-Sanchez, G., Sánchez-Martínez, F., Armentano-Oller, C., Montava, M. A., Tyers, F. M., and Ginestí-Rosell, M. (2009). Documentation of the open-source shallow-transfer machine translation platform Apertium. Technical report, Departament de Llenguatges i Sistemes Informatics. Universitat d'Alacant. Available at http://xixona.dlsi.ua.es/ fran/apertium2-documentation.pdf.

Hulden, M. (2009). Foma: a finite-state compiler and library. In *Proceedings of EACL 2009*, pages 29–32.

Leech, G. and Wilson, A. (1996). EAGLES recommendations for the morphosyntactic annotation of corpora. *Technical report, EAGLES Expert Advisory Group on Language Engineering Standards, Istituto di Linguistica Computazionale, Pisa, Italy*.

Conversion of Procedural Morphologies to Finite-State Morphologies: a Case Study of Arabic

Mans Hulden
University of the Basque Country
IXA Group
IKERBASQUE, Basque Foundation for Science
mhulden@email.arizona.edu

Younes Samih
Heinrich-Heine-Universität Düsseldorf
samih@phil.uni-duesseldorf.de

Abstract

In this paper we describe a conversion of the Buckwalter Morphological Analyzer for Arabic, originally written as a Perl-script, into a pure finite-state morphological analyzer. Representing a morphological analyzer as a finite-state transducer (FST) confers many advantages over running a procedural affix-matching algorithm. Apart from application speed, an FST representation immediately offers various possibilities to flexibly modify a grammar. In the case of Arabic, this is illustrated through the addition of the ability to correctly parse partially vocalized forms without overgeneration, something not possible in the original analyzer, as well as to serve both as an analyzer and a generator.

1 Introduction

Many lexicon-driven morphological analysis systems rely on a general strategy of breaking down input words into constituent parts by consulting customized lexicons and rules designed for a particular language. The constraints imposed by the lexica designed are then implemented as program code that handles co-occurrence restrictions and analysis of possible orthographic variants, finally producing a parse of the input word. Some systems designed along these lines are meant for general use, such as the *hunspell* tool (Halácsy et al., 2004) which allows users to specify lexicons and constraints, while others are language-dependent, such as the Buckwalter Arabic Morphological Analyzer (*BAMA*) (Buckwalter, 2004).

In this paper we examine the possibility of converting such morphological analysis tools to FSTs that perform the same task. As a case study, we have chosen to implement a one-to-one faithful conversion of the Buckwalter Arabic analyzer into a finite-state representation using the *foma* finite state compiler (Hulden, 2009b), while also adding some extensions to the original analyzer. These are useful extensions which are difficult to add to the original Perl-based analyzer because of its procedural nature, but very straightforward to perform in a finite-state environment using standard design techniques.

There are several advantages to representing morphological analyzers as FSTs, as is well noted in the literature. Here, in addition to documenting the conversion, we shall also discuss and give examples of the flexibility, extensibility, and speed of application which results from using a finite-state representation of a morphology.[1]

2 The Buckwalter Analyzer

Without going into an extensive linguistic discussion, we shall briefly describe the widely used Buckwalter morphological analyzer for Arabic. The *BAMA* accepts as input Arabic words, with or without vocalization, and produces as output a breakdown of the affixes participating in the word, the stem, together with information about conjugation classes. For example, for the input word **ktb/كتب**, *BAMA* returns, among others:

```
LOOK-UP WORD: ktb
SOLUTION 1: (kataba) [katab-u_1]
            katab/VERB_PERFECT
            +a/PVSUFF_SUBJ:3MS
 (GLOSS):  + write + he/it <verb>
```

[1]The complete code and analyzer are available at http://buckwalter-fst.googlecode.com/

Proceedings of the 10th International Workshop on Finite State Methods and Natural Language Processing, pages 70–74,
Donostia–San Sebastián, July 23–25, 2012.

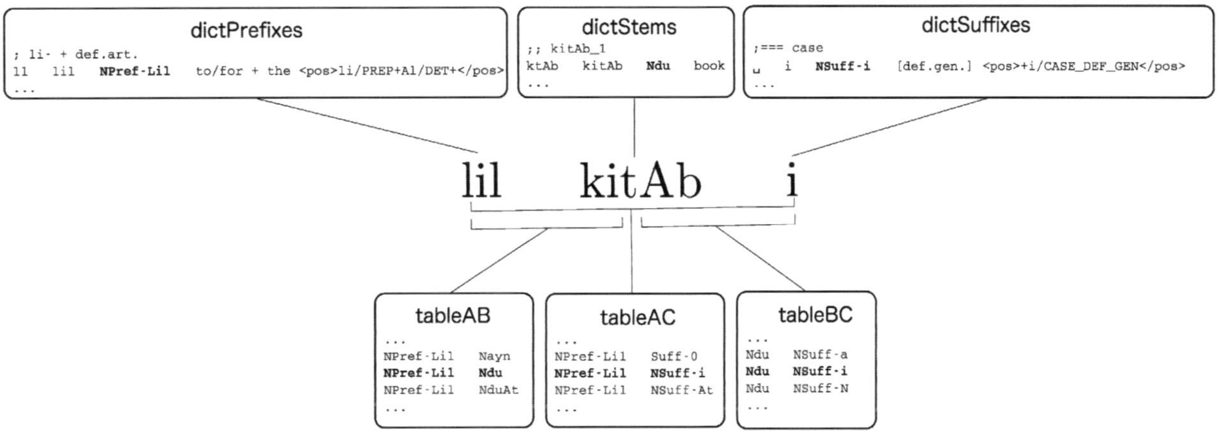

Figure 1: The Buckwalter Arabic Morphological Analyzer's lookup process exemplified for the word **lilkitAbi**.

2.1 *BAMA* lookup

In the *BAMA* system, every Arabic word is assumed to consist of a sometimes optional prefix, an obligatory stem, and a sometimes optional suffix.[2] The system for analysis is performed by a Perl-script that carries out the following tasks:

1. Strips all diacritics (vowels) from the input word (since Arabic words may contain vocalization marks which are not included in the lexicon lookup). Example: `kataba` → `ktb`

2. Factors the input word into all possible combinations of prefix-stem-suffix. Stems may not be empty, while affixes are optional. Example: `ktb` → { <`k,t,b`>,< `kt,b,`∅>, <`k,tb,`∅>, <∅`,k,tb`>, <∅`,kt,b`>, <∅`,ktb,`∅> }.

3. Consults three lexicons (**dictPrefixes**, **dictStems**, **dictSuffixes**) for ruling out impossible divisions. For example, <`kt,b,`∅>, is rejected since **kt** does not appear as a prefix in **dictPrefixes**, while <`k,tb,`∅> is accepted since **k** appears in **dictPrefixes**, **tb** in **dictStems**, and ∅ in **dictSuffixes**.

4. Consults three co-occurrence constraint lists for further ruling out incompatible prefix-stem combinations, stem-suffix combinations, and prefix-suffix combinations. For example, <`k,tb,`∅>, while accepted in the previous step, is now rejected because the file **dictPrefixes** lists **k** as a prefix belonging to class **NPref-Bi**, and the stem **tb** belonging to one of **PV_V**, **IV_V**, **NF**, **PV_C**, or **IV_C**. However, the compatibility file **tableAB** does not permit a combination of prefix class **NPref-Bi** and any of the above-mentioned stem classes.

5. In the event that the lookup fails, the analyzer considers various alternative spellings of the input word, and runs through the same steps using the alternate spellings.

The *BAMA* lookup process is illustrated using a different example in figure 1.

3 Conversion

Our goal in the conversion of the *Perl*-code and the lookup tables is to produce a single transducer that maps input words directly to their morphological analysis, including class and gloss information. In order to do this, we break the process down into three major steps:

(1) We construct a transducer `Lexicon` that accepts on its output side strings consisting of any combinations of fully vocalized prefixes, stems, and suffixes listed in **dictPrefixes**, **dictStems**, and **dictSuffixes**. On the input side, we find a string that represents the class each morpheme on the output side corresponds to, as well as the line number in the correspond-

[2] In reality, these are often conjoined prefixes treated as a single entry within the system.

```
LEXICON Root
                          Prefixes ;

LEXICON Prefixes
[Pref-%0]{P%:34}:0    Stems;
[Pref-Wa]{P%:37}:wa   Stems;
...

LEXICON Stems

[Nprop]{S%:23}:|b     Suffixes;
[Nprop]{S%:27}:%<ib~  Suffixes;
...

LEXICON Suffixes
[Suff-%0]{X%:34}:0    #;
[CVSuff-o]{X%:37}:o   #;
...
```

Figure 2: Skeleton of basic lexicon transducer in LEXC generated from *BAMA* lexicons.

ing file where the morpheme appears. For example, the `Lexicon` transducer would contain the mapping:

```
[Pref-0]{P:34}[PV]{S:102658}[NSuff-a]{X:72}
kataba
```

indicating that for the surface form **kataba/كَتَبَ**, the prefix class is **Pref-0** appearing on line 34 in the file **dictPrefixes**, the stem class is **PV**, appearing on line 102,658 in **dictStems**, and that the suffix class is **NSuff-a**, appearing on line 72 in **dictSuffixes**.

To construct the `Lexicon`, we produced a *Perl*-script that reads the contents of the *BAMA* files and automatically constructs a LEXC-format file (Beesley and Karttunen, 2003), which is compiled with *foma* into a finite transducer (see figure 2).

(2) We construct rule transducers that filter out impossible combinations of prefix classes based on the data in the constraint tables **tableAB**, **tableBC**, and **tableAC**. We then iteratively compose the `Lexicon` transducer with each rule transducer. This is achieved by converting each suffix class mentioned in each of the class files to a constraint rule, which is compiled into a finite automaton. For example, the file **tableBC**, which lists co-occurrence constraints between stems and suffixes contains only the following lines beginning with `Nhy`:

```
Nhy NSuff-h
Nhy NSuff-iy
```

indicating that the `Nhy`-class only combines with `Nsuff-h` or `Nsuff-iy`. These lines are converted by our script into the constraint restriction regular expression:

```
def Rule193 "[Nhy]" => _ ?*
            "[NSuff-h]"|"[NSuff-iy]";
```

This in effect defines the language where each instance `[Nhy]` is always followed sometime later in the string by either `[NSuff-h]`, or `[NSuff-iy]`. By composing this, and the other constraints, with the `Lexicon`-transducer, we can filter out all illegitimate combinations of morphemes as dictated by the original Buckwalter files, by calculating:

```
def Grammar    Lexicon.i .o.
               Rule1     .o.
               ...
               RuleNNN ;
```

In this step, it is crucial to note that one cannot in practice build a separate, single transducer (or automaton) that models the intersection of *all* the lexicon constraints, i.e. `Rule1 .o. Rule2 .o. ... RuleNNN`, and then compose that transducer with the `Lexicon` transducer. The reason for this is that the size of the intersection of all co-occurrence rules grows exponentially with each rule. To avoid this intermediate exponential size, the `Lexicon` transducer must be composed with the first rule, whose composition is then composed with the second rule, etc., as above.

(3) As the previous two steps leave us with a transducer that accepts only legitimate combinations of fully vocalized prefixes, stems, and suffixes, we proceed to optionally remove short vowel diacritics as well as perform optional normalization of the letter Alif (ا) from the

output side of the transducer. This means, for instance, that an intermediate **kataba/كَتَبَ**, would be mapped to the surface forms **kataba**, **katab**, **katba**, **katb**, **ktaba**, **ktab**, **ktba**, and **ktb**. This last step assures that we can parse partially vocalized forms, fully vocalized forms, completely unvocalized forms, and common variants of Alif.

```
def RemoveShortVowels
    [a|u|i|o|%~|%`] (->) 0;

def NormalizeAlif
    ["|"|"<"|">"] (->) A .o.
    "{" (->) [A|"<"] ;

def RemovefatHatAn [F|K|N] -> 0;

def          BAMA    0 <- %{|%} .o.
             Grammar            .o.
             RemoveShortVowels  .o.
             NormalizeAlif      .o.
             RemovefatHatAn;
```

4 Results

Converting the entire *BAMA* grammar as described above produces a final FST of 855,267 states and 1,907,978 arcs, which accepts 14,563,985,397 Arabic surface forms. The transducer occupies 8.5Mb. An optional auxiliary transducer for mapping line numbers to complete long glosses and class names occupies an additional 10.5 Mb. This is slightly more than the original *BAMA* files which occupy 4.0Mb. However, having a FST representation of the grammar provides us with a number of advantages not available in the original *BAMA*, some of which we will briefly discuss.

4.1 Orthographical variants

The original *BAMA* deals with spelling variants and substandard spelling by performing *Perl*-regex replacements to the input string if lookup fails. In the *BAMA* documentation, we find replacements such as:

```
- word final  Y' should be y'
- word final  Y' should be }
- word final  y' should be }
```

In a finite-state system, once the grammar is converted, we can easily build such search heuristics into the FST itself using phonological replacement rules and various composition strategies such as priority union (Kaplan, 1987). We can thus mimic the behavior of the *BAMA*, albeit without incurring any extra lookup time.

4.2 Vocalization

As noted above, by constructing the analyzer from the fully vocalized forms and then optionally removing vowels in surface variants allows us to more accurately parse partially vocalized Arabic forms. We thus rectify one of the drawbacks of the original *BAMA*, which makes no use of vocalization information even when it is provided. For example, given an input word **qabol**, *BAMA* would as a first step strip off all the vocalization marks, producing **qbl**. During the parsing process, *BAMA* could then match **qbl** with, for instance, **qibal**, an entirely different word, even though vowels were indicated. The FST design addresses this problem elegantly: if the input word is **qabol**, it will never match **qibal** because the vocalized morphemes are used throughout the construction of the FST and only optionally removed from the surface forms, whereas *BAMA* used the unvocalized forms to match input. This behavior is in line with other finite-state implementations of Arabic, such as Beesley (1996), where diacritics, if they happen to be present, are taken advantage of in order to disambiguate and rule out illegitimate parses.

This is of practical importance when parsing Arabic as writers often partially disambiguate words depending on context. For example, the word **Hsbt/حسبت**is ambiguous (**Hasabat** = compute, charge; **Hasibat** = regard, consider). One would partially vocalize **Hsbt** as **Hsibt** to denote "she regards", or as **Hsabt** to imply "she computes." The FST-based system correctly narrows down the parses accordingly, while *BAMA* would produce all ambiguities regardless of the vocalization in the input.

4.3 Surface lexicon extraction

Having the *BAMA* represented as a FST also allows us to extract the output projection of the grammar, producing an automaton that only accepts legitimate words in Arabic. This can be then be used in spell checking applications, for example, by integrating the lexicon with weighted transducers reflecting frequency information and error models (Hulden, 2009a; Pirinen et al., 2010).

4.4 Constraint analysis

Interestingly, the *BAMA* itself contains a vast amount of redundant information in the co-occurrence constraints. That is, some suffix-stem-lexicon constraints are entirely subsumed by other constraints and could be removed without affecting the overall system. This can be observed during the chain of composition of the various transducers representing lexicon constraints. If a constraint X fails to remove any words from the lexicon—something that can be ascertained by noting that the number of paths through the new transducer is the same as in the transducer before composition—it is an indication that a previous constraint Y has already subsumed X. In short, the constraint X is redundant.

The original grammar cannot be consistently analyzed for redundancies as it stands. However, redundant constraints can be detected when compiling the `Lexicon` FST together with the set of rules, offering a way to streamline the original grammar.

5 Conclusion

We have shown a method for converting the table-based and producedural constraint-driven Buckwalter Arabic Morphological Analyzer into an equivalent finite-state transducer. By doing so, we can take advantage of established finite-state methods to provide faster and more flexible parsing and also use the finite-state calculus to produce derivative applications that were not possible using the original table-driven Perl parser, such as spell checkers, normalizers, etc. The finite-state transducer implementation also allows us to parse words with any vocalization without sacrificing accuracy.

While the conversion method in this case is specific to the BAMA, the general principle illustrated in this paper can be applied to many other procedural morphologies that rule out morphological parses by first consulting a base lexicon and subsequently applying a batch of serial or parallel constraints over affix occurrence.

References

Attia, M., Pecina, P., Toral, A., Tounsi, L., and van Genabith, J. (2011). An open-source finite state morphological transducer for modern standard Arabic. In *Proceedings of the 9th International Workshop on Finite State Methods and Natural Language Processing*, pages 125–133. Association for Computational Linguistics.

Beesley, K. R. (1996). Arabic finite-state morphological analysis and generation. In *Proceedings of COLING'96—Volume 1*, pages 89–94. Association for Computational Linguistics.

Beesley, K. R. and Karttunen, L. (2003). *Finite State Morphology*. CSLI Publications, Stanford, CA.

Buckwalter, T. (2004). Arabic Morphological Analyzer 2.0. *Linguistics Data Consortium (LDC)*.

Habash, N. (2010). Introduction to Arabic natural language processing. *Synthesis Lectures on Human Language Technologies*.

Halácsy, P., Kornai, A., Németh, L., Rung, A., Szakadát, I., and Trón, V. (2004). Creating open language resources for Hungarian. In *Proceedings of Language Resources and Evaluation Conference (LREC04). European Language Resources Association.*

Hulden, M. (2009a). Fast approximate string matching with finite automata. *Procesamiento del lenguaje natural*, 43:57–64.

Hulden, M. (2009b). Foma: a finite-state compiler and library. In *Proceedings of the 12th conference of the European Chapter of the Association for Computational Linguistics,*, pages 29–32. Association for Computational Linguistics.

Kaplan, R. M. (1987). Three seductions of computational psycholinguistics. In Whitelock, P., Wood, M. M., Somers, H. L., Johnson, R., and Bennett, P., editors, *Linguistic Theory and Computer Applications*, London. Academic Press.

Pirinen, T., Lindén, K., et al. (2010). Finite-state spell-checking with weighted language and error models. In *Proceedings of LREC 2010 Workshop on creation and use of basic lexical resources for less-resourced languages.*

A methodology for obtaining concept graphs from word graphs

Marcos Calvo, Jon Ander Gómez, Lluís-F. Hurtado, Emilio Sanchis
Departament de Sistemes Informàtics i Computació
Universitat Politècnica de València
Camí de Vera s/n, 46022, València, Spain
{mcalvo,jon,lhurtado,esanchis}@dsic.upv.es

Abstract

In this work, we describe a methodology based on the Stochastic Finite State Transducers paradigm for Spoken Language Understanding (SLU) for obtaining concept graphs from word graphs. In the edges of these concept graphs, both semantic and lexical information are represented. This makes these graphs a very useful representation of the information for SLU. The best path in these concept graphs provides the best sequence of concepts.

1 Introduction

The task of SLU can be seen as the process that, given an utterance, computes a semantic interpretation of the information contained in it. This semantic interpretation will be based on a task-dependent set of concepts.

An area where SLU systems are typically applied is the construction of spoken dialog systems. The goal of the SLU subsystem in the context of a dialog system is to process the information given by the Automatic Speech Recognition (ASR) module, and provide the semantic interpretation of it to the Dialog Manager, which will determine the next action of the dialog. Thus, the work of the SLU module can be split into two subtasks, the first of them is the identification of the sequence of concepts and the segments of the original sentence according to them, and the other is the extraction of the relevant information underlying to these labeled segments. In this work we will focus on concept labeling, but we will also consider the other subtask in our evaluation.

We can distinguish between the SLU systems that work with the 1-best transcription and those that take a representation of the n-best (Hakkani-Tür et al., 2006; Tur et al., 2002). The use of a word graph as the input of the SLU module makes this task more difficult, as the search space becomes larger. On the other hand, the advantage of using them is that there is more information that could help to find the correct semantic interpretation, rather than just taking the best sentence given by the ASR.

In the recent literature, a variety of approaches for automatic SLU have been proposed, like those explained in (Hahn et al., 2010; Raymond and Riccardi, 2007; McCallum et al., 2000; Macherey et al., 2001; Léfèvre, 2007; Lafferty et al., 2001). The methodology that we propose in this paper is based on Stochastic Finite State Transducers (SFST). This is a generative approach that composes several transducers containing acoustic, lexical and semantic knowledge. Our method performs this composition on-the-fly, obtaining as a result a *concept graph*, where semantic information is associated with segments of words. To carry out this step, we use a different language model for each concept and also study the use of lexical categorization and lemmas. The best sequence of concepts can be determined by finding the best path in the concept graph, with the help of a language model of sequences of the concepts.

The rest of this paper is structured as follows. In Section 2, the theoretical model for SLU based on SFST is briefly presented. Then, in Section 3 the methodology for converting word graphs into concept graphs is described. A experimentation to eval-

Proceedings of the 10th International Workshop on Finite State Methods and Natural Language Processing, pages 75–79,
Donostia–San Sebastián, July 23–25, 2012. ©2012 Association for Computational Linguistics

uate this methodology for the SLU task is shown in Section 4. Finally, we draw some conclusions and future work.

2 The SFST approach for SLU

The Bayes classifier for the SLU problem can be expressed as stated in equation 1, where C represents a sequence of concepts or semantic labels and A is the utterance that constitutes the input to the system.

$$\hat{C} = \arg\max_{C} p(C|A) \tag{1}$$

Taking into account the underlying sequence of words W, and assuming that the acoustics may depend on W but not on C, this equation can be rewritten as follows.

$$\hat{C} = \arg\max_{C} \max_{W} p(A|W) \cdot p(W, C) \tag{2}$$

To compute the best sequence of concepts $\hat{C}$ expressed as in equation 2, the proposal made by the paradigm based on SFST is to search the best path in a transducer λ_{SLU} result of composing four SFST:

$$\lambda_{SLU} = \lambda_G \circ \lambda_{gen} \circ \lambda_{W2C} \circ \lambda_{SLM} \tag{3}$$

In this equation λ_G is a SFST provided by the ASR module where the acoustic probabilities $p(A|W)$ are represented, λ_{gen} introduces prior information of the task by means of a lexical categorization, λ_{W2C} provides the probability of a sequence of words and labels it with a semantic label and λ_{SLM} modelizes a language model of sequences of concepts.

3 From word graphs to concept graphs

The output of an ASR can be represented as a word graph. This word graph can be enriched with semantic information, obtaining a *concept graph*. This concept graph constitutes a useful representation of the possible semantics, considering the uncertainty expressed in the original word graph. Finally, finding the best path in the concept graph using a language model of sequences of concepts provides as a result the best sequence of concepts $\hat{C}$, the recognized sentence $\tilde{W}$, and its segmentation according to $\hat{C}$.

3.1 Topology and semantics of the word graph

To perform the transformations for obtaining the concept graph, the input graph given by the ASR should represent the information in the following way. First, its nodes will be labeled with timestamps. Also, for every two nodes i, j such that $i < j - 1$, there will be an edge from i to j labeled with w and weight s if the ASR detected w between the instants i and $j - 1$ with an acoustic score s. Finally, there may exist a λ-transition between any pair of adjacent nodes. The score of this edge should be computed by means of a smoothing method.

Defining the word graph in this way allows us to model on it the distribution $p(A|w)$, where A is the sequence of acoustic frames between the initial and final nodes of any edge, and w the word attached to it. This probability distribution is represented in the theoretical model by λ_G.

3.2 Building the concept graph

The concept graph that is obtained has the following features. First, its set of nodes is the same of the word graph, and its meaning is kept. There is at most one edge between every two nodes i and j ($i < j$) labeled with the concept c. Every edge is labeled with a pair (W, c), where W is a sequence of words and c the concept that they represent. The weight of the edge is $\max_W(p(A_i^j|W) \cdot p(W|c))$, where A_i^j are the acoustic frames in the interval $[i, j[$ and W the argument that maximizes the former expression.

In this specification appears the probability distribution $p(W|c)$, which can be estimated by using a language model for each available concept.

This concept graph can be built using a Dynamic Programming algorithm that finds for each concept c and each pair of nodes i, j, with $i < j$, the path from i to j on the word graph that maximizes $p(A_i^j|W) \cdot p(W|c)$. In this case, W is the sequence of words obtained by concatenating the words attached to the edges of the path. Each of the "best paths" computed in this way will become an edge in the resulting concept graph.

Thus, in the concept graph it is represented information about possible sequences of words that might have been uttered by the speaker, along with the concepts each of these sequences expresses. This pair is weighted with a score that is the result of combining the acoustic score expressed in the word graph, and the lexical and syntactic score given by the language model, which is dependent on the current concept. Furthermore, this information is enriched with temporal information, since the initial and final nodes of every edge represent the beginning and ending timestamps of the sequence of words. Consequently, this way of building the concept graph corresponds to the transducer λ_{W2C} of equation 3, since we find sequences of words and attach them to a concept. However, we also take advantage of and keep other information, such as the temporal one.

4 Experiments and results

To evaluate this methodology, we have performed SLU experiments using the concept graphs obtained as explained in Section 3 and then finding the best path in each of them. For this experimentation we have used the DIHANA corpus (Benedí et al., 2006). This is a corpus of telephone spontaneous speech in Spanish composed by 900 dialogs acquired by 225 speakers using the Wizard of Oz technique, with a total of 6,229 user turns. All these dialogs simulate real conversations in an automatic train information phone service. The experiments reported here were performed using the user turns of the dialogs, splitting them into a set of 1,340 utterances (turns) for test and all the remaining 4,889 for training. Some interesting statistics about the DIHANA corpus are given in table 1.

Number of words	47,222
Vocabulary size	811
Average number of words per user turn	7.6
Number of concepts	30

Table 1: Characteristics of the DIHANA corpus.

In the DIHANA corpus, the orthographic transcriptions of the utterances are semi-automatically segmented and labeled in terms of semantic units. This segmentation is used by our methodology as a language model of sequences of words for each concept. All the language models involved in this experimentation are bigram models trained using Witten-Bell smoothing and linear interpolation.

In our experimentation, we have considered three different ways for building the λ_{gen} transducer explained in Section 2. The first way consists of considering a transducer that given a word as its input, outputs that word with probability 1. This means that no generalization is being done.

The second λ_{gen} transducer performs a lexical categorization of some of the nouns of the vocabulary. Some extra words have been added to some lexical categories, in order to make the task more realistic, as the lexical coverage is increased. Nevertheless, it also makes the task harder, as the size of the vocabulary increases. We have used a total of 11 lexical categories.

Finally, the third λ_{gen} transducer we have generated performs the same lexical categorization but it also includes a lemmatization of the verbs. This process is normally needed for real-world systems that work with spontaneous (and maybe telephonic) speech.

We have generated three sets of word graphs to take them as the input for the method. The first of these sets, G_1, is made up by the whole graphs obtained from a word graph builder module that works without using any language model. The *Oracle WER* of these graphs is 4.10. With *Oracle WER* we mean the WER obtained considering the sequence of words $S(G)$ corresponding to the path in the graph G that is the nearest to the reference sentence.

The second set, G_2, is composed by word graphs that only contain the path corresponding to $S(G)$ for each graph $G \in G_1$. These graphs give an idea of the best results we could achieve if we could minimize the confusion due to misrecognized words.

The third set, G_3 is formed by a synthetic word graph for each reference sentence, in which only that sentence is contained. This set of graphs allows us to simulate an experimentation on plain text.

For our evaluation, we have taken two measures. First, we have evaluated the Concept Error Rate (CER) over the best sequence of concepts. The definition of the CER is analogous to that of the WER but taking concepts instead of words. Second, we have also evaluated the slot-level error (SLE). The SLE is similar to the CER but deleting the non-relevant segments (such as courtesies) and substituting the relevant concepts by a canonic value for the sequence of words associated to them.

Tables 2, 3, and 4 show the results obtained using the different λ_{gen} transducers explained before.

Input word graphs	CER	SLE
G_1	31.794	35.392
G_2	11.230	9.104
G_3	9.933	5.321

Table 2: CER and SLE without any categorization.

Input word graphs	CER	SLE
G_1	34.565	38.760
G_2	11.755	8.714
G_3	9.633	4.516

Table 3: CER and SLE with lexical categorization.

From the results of Tables 2, 3, and 4 several facts come to light. First, we can see that, in all the experiments performed with the G_1 set, the CER is lower than the SLE, while with the other sets the CER is larger than the SLE. It is due to the fact that the whole graphs obtained from the word graph builder have more lexical confusion than those from G_2 and G_3, which are based on the reference sentence. This lexical confusion may cause that a well-recognized concept is associated to a misrecognized sequence of words. This would imply that a hit would be considered for the CER calculation, while the value for this slot is missed.

Other interesting fact is that, for the G_1 set, the more complex λ_{gen} transducers give the worse results. This is because in these graphs there is a significant confusion between phonetically similar words, as the graphs were generated without any language model. This phonetic confusion, combined with the generalizations expressed by the lexical categorization and the lemmas, makes the task harder, which leads to worse results. Nevertheless, in a real-world application of this system these generalizations would be needed in order to have a larger coverage of the lexicon of the language. The experiments on G_2 and G_3 show that when the confusion introduced in the graphs due to misrecognized words is minimized, the use of lexical categorization and lemmatization helps to improve the results.

5 Conclusions and future work

In this paper we have described a methodology, based on the SFST paradigm for SLU, for obtaining

Input word graphs	CER	SLE
G_1	36.536	40.640
G_2	11.605	8.445
G_3	9.458	4.064

Table 4: CER and SLE with lemmatization and lexical categorization.

concept graphs from word graphs. The edges of the concept graphs represent information about possible sequences of words that might have been uttered by the speaker, along with the concept each of these sequences expresses. Each of these edges is weighted with a score that combines acoustic, lexical, syntactic and semantic information. Furthermore, this information is enriched with temporal information, as the nodes represent the beginning and ending of the sequence of words. These concepts graphs constitute a very useful representation of the information for SLU.

To evaluate this methodology we have performed an experimental evaluation in which different types of lexical generalization have been considered. The results show that a trade-off between the lexical confusion expressed in the word graphs and the generalizations encoded in the other transducers should be achieved, in order to obtain the best results.

It would be interesting to apply this methodology to word graphs generated with a language model, although this way of generating the graphs would not fit exactly the theoretical model. If a language model is used to generate the graphs, then their lexical confusion could be reduced, so better results could be achieved. Other interesting task in which this methodology could help is in performing SLU experiments on a combination of the output of some different ASR engines. All these interesting applications constitute a line of our future work.

Acknowledgments

This work has been supported by the Spanish Ministerio de Economía y Competitividad, under the project TIN2011-28169-C05-01, by the Vicerrectorat d'Investigació, Desenvolupament i Innovació de la Universitat Politècnica de València, under the project PAID-06-10, and by the Spanish Ministerio de Educación under FPU Grant AP2010-4193.

References

José-Miguel Benedí, Eduardo Lleida, Amparo Varona, María-José Castro, Isabel Galiano, Raquel Justo, Iñigo López de Letona, and Antonio Miguel. 2006. Design and acquisition of a telephone spontaneous speech dialogue corpus in Spanish: DIHANA. In *Proceedings of LREC 2006*, pages 1636–1639, Genoa (Italy).

S. Hahn, M. Dinarelli, C. Raymond, F. Léfèvre, P. Lehnen, R. De Mori, A. Moschitti, H. Ney, and G. Riccardi. 2010. Comparing stochastic approaches to spoken language understanding in multiple languages. *Audio, Speech, and Language Processing, IEEE Transactions on*, 6(99):1569–1583.

D. Hakkani-Tür, F. Béchet, G. Riccardi, and G. Tur. 2006. Beyond ASR 1-best: Using word confusion networks in spoken language understanding. *Computer Speech & Language*, 20(4):495–514.

J. Lafferty, A. McCallum, and F. Pereira. 2001. Conditional random fields: Probabilistic models for segmenting and labeling sequence data. In *International Conference on Machine Learning*, pages 282–289. Citeseer.

F. Léfèvre. 2007. Dynamic bayesian networks and discriminative classifiers for multi-stage semantic interpretation. In *Acoustics, Speech and Signal Processing, 2007. ICASSP 2007. IEEE International Conference on*, volume 4, pages 13–16. IEEE.

K. Macherey, F.J. Och, and H. Ney. 2001. Natural language understanding using statistical machine translation. In *European Conf. on Speech Communication and Technology*, pages 2205–2208. Citeseer.

A. McCallum, D. Freitag, and F. Pereira. 2000. Maximum entropy markov models for information extraction and segmentation. In *Proceedings of the Seventeenth International Conference on Machine Learning*, pages 591–598. Citeseer.

C. Raymond and G. Riccardi. 2007. Generative and discriminative algorithms for spoken language understanding. *Proceedings of Interspeech2007, Antwerp, Belgium*, pages 1605–1608.

G. Tur, J. Wright, A. Gorin, G. Riccardi, and D. Hakkani-Tür. 2002. Improving spoken language understanding using word confusion networks. In *Proceedings of the ICSLP*. Citeseer.

A Finite-State Temporal Ontology and Event-intervals

Tim Fernando
Computer Science Department
Trinity College Dublin
Ireland
tfernand@tcd.ie

Abstract

A finite-state approach to temporal ontology for natural language text is described under which intervals (of the real line) paired with event descriptions are encoded as strings. The approach is applied to an interval temporal logic linked to TimeML, a standard mark-up language for time and events, for which various finite-state mechanisms are proposed.

1 Introduction

A model-theoretic perspective on finite-state methods is provided by an important theorem due to Büchi, Elgot and Trakhtenbrot (Thomas, 1997). Given a finite alphabet Σ, a system MSO_Σ of *monadic second-order logic* is set up with a binary relation symbol (for successor) and a unary relation symbol for each symbol in Σ so that the formulae of MSO_Σ define precisely the regular languages over Σ (minus the null string ϵ). Extensions of this theorem to infinite strings and trees are fundamental to work on formal verification associated with *Model Checking* (Clarke et al., 1999). In that work, a well-defined computational system (of hardware or software) can be taken for granted, against which to evaluate precise specifications. The matter is far more delicate, however, with natural language semantics. It is not clear what models, if any, are appropriate for natural language. Nor is it obvious what logical forms natural language statements translate to. That said, there is a considerable body of work in linguistic semantics that uses model theory, and no shortage of natural language text containing information that cries out for extraction.

A step towards (semi-)automated reasoning about temporal information is taken in TimeML (Pustejovsky et al., 2003), a "mark-up language for temporal and event expressions" (www.timeml.org). The primary aim of the present paper is to show how finite-state methods can push this step further, by building strings, regular languages and regular relations to represent some basic semantic ingredients proposed for TimeML. An instructive example is sentence (1), which is assigned in (Pratt-Hartmann, 2005a; ISO, 2007) the logical form (2).

(1) After his talk with Mary, John drove to Boston.

(2) $p(e) \wedge q(e') \wedge \mathrm{after}(e, e')$

If we read $p(e)$ as "e is an event of John talking with Mary" and $q(e')$ as "e' is an event of John driving to Boston" then (2) says "an event e' of John driving to Boston comes after an event e of John talking with Mary ." Evidently, (1) follows from (3) and (4) below (implicitly quantifying the variables e and e' in (2) existentially).

(3) John talked with Mary from 1pm to 2pm.

(4) John drove to Boston from 2pm to 4pm.

But is (3) not compatible with (5) — and indeed implied by (5)?

(5) John talked with Mary from 1pm to 4pm.

Could we truthfully assert (1), given (4) and (5)? Or if not (1), perhaps (6)?

(6) After talking with Mary for an hour, John drove to Boston.

Proceedings of the 10th International Workshop on Finite State Methods and Natural Language Processing, pages 80–89,
Donostia–San Sebastián, July 23–25, 2012.

The acceptability of (6) suffers, however, if we are told (7).

(7) John drove toward Boston from 1pm to 2pm.

Clearly, individuating events, as (2) does, opens up a can of worms. But since at least (Davidson, 1967), there has been no retreating from events (Parsons, 1990; Kamp and Reyle, 1993; Pratt-Hartmann, 2005). Be that as it may, an appeal to events carries with it an obligation to provide a minimal account of what holds during these events and perhaps even a bit beyond. It is for such an account that finite-state methods are deployed below, viewed through the lens of the Büchi-Elgot-Trakhtenbrot theorem.

That lens gives temporal logic, the formulae of which — hereafter called *fluents* (for brevity) — may or may not hold at a string position, conceived as time and ordered according to succession within the string. For example, we can introduce a fluent p for "John talked with Mary" and a fluent q for "John drove to Boston" to form the string $\boxed{\text{p}}\boxed{\text{q}}$ (of length 2) for "after John talked with Mary, John drove to Boston." The idea is that a string $\alpha_1 \cdots \alpha_n$ of boxes α_i describes a sequence $t_1, \ldots, t_n$ of n times, t_i coming before t_{i+1}, such that every fluent in α_i holds at t_i.[1] To a first approximation, a box α_i is a snapshot at time t_i, making $\alpha_1 \cdots \alpha_n$ a cartoon or filmstrip. But just what is a time t_i: a temporal point or an interval?

For $\boxed{\text{p}}\boxed{\text{q}}$ to apply to (3) and (4), it is natural to regard t_i as an interval, setting up an account of the entailment from (5) to (3) in terms of the so-called *subinterval property* of John-talking-with-Mary (Bennett and Partee, 1972). John-driving-to-Boston, by contrast, does *not* have this property, necessitating the change from *to Boston* in (4) to *toward Boston* in (7). We can bring out this fact by representing individual events as strings, refining, for instance, our picture $\boxed{\text{q}}$ of John's drive to Boston by adding a fluent r for "John in Boston" to form $\boxed{\text{q}}\boxed{\text{q,r}}$. An event of motion is conceptualized as a finite sequence of snapshots in (Tenny, 1987) and elsewhere — a conceptualization resoundingly rejected in (Jackendoff, 1996) because

> it misrepresents the essential continuity of events of motion. For one thing, aside from the beginning and end points, the choice of a finite set of subevents is altogether arbitrary. How many subevents are there, and how is one to choose them? Notice that to stipulate the subevents as equally spaced, for instance one second or 3.5 milliseconds apart, is as arbitrary and unmotivated as any other choice.
>
> Another difficulty with a snapshot conceptualization concerns the representation of nonbounded events (activities) such as John ran along the river (for hours). A finite sequence of subevents necessarily has a specified beginning and ending, so it cannot encode the absence of endpoints. And excluding the specified endpoints simply exposes other specified subevents, which thereby become new endpoints. Thus encoding nonbounded events requires major surgery in the semantic representation. [page 316]

Jackendoff's objections are overcome below by finite-state manipulations that may well be called surgery. Following details supplied in the next section,[2] strings are formed from a finite set X of fluents that is allowed to vary so that

(i) the continuity desired by Jackendoff arises in the inverse limit of a system of projections π_X (defined below; Table 1), and

(ii) the temporal span of any finite string may, on expanding the set X, stretch without bound to the left (past) and/or to the right (future).

Applying π_X, section 2 proceeds to encode a model $\mathcal{A}$ of an interval temporal logic as a string $\mathsf{s}(\mathcal{A})$. Building on that encoding, section 3 develops finite-state methods for interval temporal logic. Section 4 concludes with proposals (drawing on work of the earlier sections) for extending the empirical (linguistic) coverage.

2 From event-intervals to strings

Before equating the set X of fluents with a model interpreting TimeML, let us bring out the intuition

[1] The alphabet Σ from which strings are formed is the family *Pow*(X) of subsets of some set X of fluents. A fluent corresponds to a monadic second-order variable in the Büchi-Elgot-Trakhtenbrot theorem.

[2] The present work extends a line of research most recently reported in (Fernando, 2011, 2011a, 2011b, 2012). That line is related to (Niemi and Koskenniemi, 2009), from which it differs in adopting an alphabet *Pow*(X) that equates sucession in a string with temporal succession.

$$
\begin{aligned}
\rho_X(\alpha_1\cdots\alpha_n) &\overset{\text{def}}{=} (\alpha_1\cap X)\cdots(\alpha_n\cap X)\\
\mathit{bc}(s) &\overset{\text{def}}{=} \begin{cases} \mathit{bc}(\alpha s') & \text{if } s=\alpha\alpha s'\\ \alpha\,\mathit{bc}(\alpha' s') & \text{if } s=\alpha\alpha' s' \text{ and } \alpha\neq\alpha'\\ s & \text{otherwise}\end{cases}\\
\mathit{unpad}(s) &\overset{\text{def}}{=} \begin{cases} \mathit{unpad}(s') & \text{if } s=\boxed{}\,s' \text{ or } s'\boxed{}\\ s & \text{otherwise}\end{cases}
\end{aligned}
$$

Table 1: Behind $\pi_X(s) \overset{\text{def}}{=} \mathit{unpad}(\mathit{bc}(\rho_X(s)))$

underlying the function π_X through a familiar example. We can represent a calendar year by the string

$$s_{mo} \overset{\text{def}}{=} \boxed{\text{Jan}}\boxed{\text{Feb}}\cdots\boxed{\text{Dec}}$$

of length 12 (with a month in each box), or (adding one of 31 days d1, d2,. . ., d31) the string

$$s_{mo,dy} \overset{\text{def}}{=} \boxed{\text{Jan,d1}}\boxed{\text{Jan,d2}}\cdots \boxed{\text{Jan,d31}}\boxed{\text{Feb,d1}}\cdots\boxed{\text{Dec,d31}}$$

of length 365 (a box per day in a non-leap year).[3] Unlike the points in say, the real line $\mathbb{R}$, a box can split if we enlarge the set X of fluents we can put in it, as illustrated by the change from $\boxed{\text{Jan}}$ in s_{mo} to $\boxed{\text{Jan,d1}}\boxed{\text{Jan,d2}}\cdots\boxed{\text{Jan,d31}}$ in $s_{mo,dy}$. Two functions link the strings $s_{mo,dy}$ and s_{mo}

(i) a function ρ_{mo} that keeps only the months in a box so that

$$\rho_{mo}(s_{mo,dy}) = \boxed{\text{Jan}}^{31}\boxed{\text{Feb}}^{28}\cdots\boxed{\text{Dec}}^{31}$$

(ii) *block compression* bc, which compresses consecutive occurrences of a box into one, mapping $\rho_{mo}(s_{mo,dy})$ to

$$\mathit{bc}(\boxed{\text{Jan}}^{31}\boxed{\text{Feb}}^{28}\cdots\boxed{\text{Dec}}^{31}) = s_{mo}$$

so that $\mathit{bc}(\rho_{mo}(s_{mo,dy})) = s_{mo}$. As made precise in Table 1, ρ_X "sees only X" (setting $mo \overset{\text{def}}{=}$ {Jan, Feb, . . . Dec} to make ρ_{mo} an instance of ρ_X), while bc eliminates stutters, hardwiring the view that time passes only if there is change (or rather: we observe time passing only if we observe a change within a box). As this example shows, temporal granularity depends on the set X of observables that may go inside a box. Writing bc_X for the composition mapping s to $\mathit{bc}(\rho_X(s))$, we have

$$
\begin{aligned}
\mathit{bc}_{\{\text{Jan}\}}(s_{mo,dy}) &= \mathit{bc}_{\{\text{Jan}\}}(s_{mo}) = \boxed{\text{Jan}}\boxed{}\\
\mathit{bc}_{\{\text{Feb}\}}(s_{mo,dy}) &= \mathit{bc}_{\{\text{Feb}\}}(s_{mo}) = \boxed{}\boxed{\text{Feb}}\boxed{}\\
\mathit{bc}_{\{\text{d3}\}}(s_{mo,dy}) &= (\boxed{}\boxed{\text{d3}})^{12}\boxed{}.
\end{aligned}
$$

Now, the function π_X is bc_X followed by the deletion *unpad* of any initial or final empty boxes $\boxed{}$ (Table 1).[4] We can then define a fluent x to be an *s-interval* if $\pi_{\{x\}}(s)$ is $\boxed{x}$. Next, let $\mathcal{L}_\pi(X)$ be the language $\pi_X[\bigcap_{x\in X}\pi^{-1}_{\{x\}}\boxed{x}]$ consisting of strings $\pi_X(s)$ for $s \in \mathit{Pow}(X)^*$ such that $\pi_{\{x\}}(s) = \boxed{x}$ for all $x \in X$. Note that $\mathcal{L}_\pi(\{x\}) = \{\boxed{x}\}$ while for $x \neq x'$, $\mathcal{L}_\pi(\{x,x'\})$ consists of 13 strings s_R, one per interval relation R in (Allen, 1983); see columns 1 and 2 of Table 2

$$\mathcal{L}_\pi(\{x,x'\}) = \{s_R \mid R \in \textbf{Allen}\}\,.$$

R ∈**Allen**	$s_R \in \mathcal{L}_\pi(\{x,x'\})$	$\chi_R([a,b],[a',b'])$
$x\ \mathtt{=}\ x'$	$\boxed{x,x'}$	$a=a',\ b=b'$
$x\ \mathtt{s}\ x'$	$\boxed{x,x'}\boxed{x'}$	$a=a',\ b<b'$
$x\ \mathtt{si}\ x'$	$\boxed{x,x'}\boxed{x}$	$a=a',\ b'<b$
$x\ \mathtt{f}\ x'$	$\boxed{x'}\boxed{x,x'}$	$a'<a,\ b=b'$
$x\ \mathtt{fi}\ x'$	$\boxed{x}\boxed{x,x'}$	$a<a',\ b=b'$
$x\ \mathtt{d}\ x'$	$\boxed{x'}\boxed{x,x'}\boxed{x'}$	$a'<a,\ b<b'$
$x\ \mathtt{di}\ x'$	$\boxed{x}\boxed{x,x'}\boxed{x}$	$a<a',\ b'<b$
$x\ \mathtt{o}\ x'$	$\boxed{x}\boxed{x,x'}\boxed{x'}$	$a<a'\leq b<b'$
$x\ \mathtt{oi}\ x'$	$\boxed{x'}\boxed{x,x'}\boxed{x}$	$a'<a\leq b'<b$
$x\ \mathtt{m}\ x'$	$\boxed{x}\boxed{x'}$	--
$x<x'$	$\boxed{x}\boxed{}\boxed{x'}$	$b<a'$
$x\ \mathtt{mi}\ x'$	$\boxed{x'}\boxed{x}$	--
$x>x'$	$\boxed{x'}\boxed{}\boxed{x}$	$b'<a$

Table 2: The Allen relations via $\pi_{\{x,x'\}}$

[3] In (Niemi and Koskenniemi, 2009), s_{mo} is represented as the string

[m Jan]m [m Feb]m [m Mar]m ... [m Dec]m

of length 36 over 14 symbols (the 12 months plus the 2 brackets [m and]m) on which finite-state transducers operate. (See the previous footnote.)

[4] Restricted to a finite alphabet, the maps ρ_X, bc, *unpad* and π_X are computable by finite-state transducers (Fernando, 2011).

For example, in the case of the "*f*inish" relation f∈**Allen**,

$$s \models x\,\mathtt{f}\,x' \iff \pi_{\{x,x'\}}(s) = \boxed{x'}\boxed{x, x'}$$

provided x and x' are s-intervals. The third column of Table 2 characterizes R ∈**Allen** as conditions χ_R on pairs $[a, b]$ and $[a', b']$ of real numbers (in $\mathbb{R}$) denoting closed intervals[5] — e.g.,

$$[a, b]\ \mathtt{f}\ [a', b'] \iff a' < a \text{ and } b = b' \ .$$

This brings us to the semantics of TimeML proposed in (Pratt-Hartmann, 2005a). A system $\mathcal{TPL}$ of *Temporal Preposition Logic* is built from an infinite set E of *event-atoms*, and interpreted relative to the family

$$\mathcal{I} \stackrel{\text{def}}{=} \{[a, b] \mid a, b \in \mathbb{R} \text{ and } a \leq b\}$$

of closed, bounded non-empty intervals in $\mathbb{R}$. A $\mathcal{TPL}$*-model* $\mathcal{A}$ is defined to be a finite subset of $\mathcal{I} \times E$. The intuition is that a pair $\langle I, e\rangle$ in $\mathcal{A}$ represents "an occurrence of an event of type e over the interval" I (Pratt-Hartmann, 2005; page 17), reversing the construal in line (2) above of e as a token. Identifying occurrences with events, we can think of $\mathcal{A}$ as a finite set of events, conceived as "intervals cum description" (van Benthem, 1983; page 113). Treating events as fluents, we have

Proposition 1. *For every $\mathcal{TPL}$-model $\mathcal{A}$, there is a unique string $\mathsf{s}(\mathcal{A}) \in \mathcal{L}_\pi(\mathcal{A})$ such that for all $x, x' \in \mathcal{A}$ with $x = \langle I, e\rangle$ and $x' = \langle I', e'\rangle$,*

$$\pi_{\{x,x'\}}(\mathsf{s}(\mathcal{A})) = s_R \iff \chi_R(I, I')$$

*for R ∈**Allen** and s_R, χ_R specified in Table 2.*

To construct the string $\mathsf{s}(\mathcal{A})$, let *Ends*$(\mathcal{A})$ be the set of endpoints of $\mathcal{A}$

$$\mathit{Ends}(\mathcal{A}) \stackrel{\text{def}}{=} \bigcup_{I \in \mathit{dom}(\mathcal{A})} \mathit{ends}(I)$$

where *dom*$(\mathcal{A})$ is the domain $\{I \mid (\exists e \in E)\ \langle I, e\rangle \in \mathcal{A}\}$ of $\mathcal{A}$, and *ends*$([a, b])$ is the unordered pair $\{a, b\}$. Sorting gives $\mathit{Ends}(\mathcal{A}) = \{r_1, r_2, \ldots, r_n\}$ with $r_1 < r_2 < \cdots < r_n$. Breaking $[r_1, r_n]$ up into $2n - 1$ intervals, let

$$\alpha_i \stackrel{\text{def}}{=} \{\langle I, e\rangle \in \mathcal{A} \mid r_i \in I\} \quad \text{for } 1 \leq i \leq n$$

and

$$\beta_i \stackrel{\text{def}}{=} \{\langle I, e\rangle \in \mathcal{A} \mid [r_i, r_{i+1}] \subseteq I\} \quad \text{for } 1 \leq i < n.$$

Interleaving and block-compressing give

$$\mathsf{s}(\mathcal{A}) \stackrel{\text{def}}{=} bc(\alpha_1\beta_1 \cdots \alpha_{n-1}\beta_{n-1}\alpha_n)$$

(see Table 3 for an example). One may then verify (by induction on the cardinality of the domain of $\mathcal{A}$) that $\mathsf{s}(\mathcal{A})$ is the unique string in $\mathcal{L}_\pi(\mathcal{A})$ satisfying the equivalence in Proposition 1.

$x_1 \stackrel{\text{def}}{=} \langle[1, 5], e\rangle$	$r_1 = 1,\ r_2 = 4$
$x_2 \stackrel{\text{def}}{=} \langle[4, 9], e\rangle$	$r_3 = 5,\ r_4 = 9$
$x_3 \stackrel{\text{def}}{=} \langle[9, 50], e'\rangle$	$r_5 = 50$
$\mathcal{A} \stackrel{\text{def}}{=} \{x_1, x_2, x_3\}$	

Table 3: Example $\mathsf{s}(\mathcal{A}) = \boxed{x_1}\boxed{x_1, x_2}\boxed{x_2}\boxed{x_2, x_3}\boxed{x_3}$

But is encoding $\mathcal{A}$ as a string $\mathsf{s}(\mathcal{A})$ adequate for $\mathcal{TPL}$-satisfaction? Let us introduce $\mathcal{TPL}$-formulae through an English example.

(8) During each of John's drives to Boston, he ate a donut.

(8) translates in $\mathcal{TPL}$ to (9), which is interpreted relative to a $\mathcal{TPL}$-model $\mathcal{A}$ and an interval $I \in \mathcal{I}$ according to (10) and (11), with $[e]\varphi$ abbreviating $\neg\langle e\rangle\neg\varphi$ (as usual), $\top$ a tautology (in that $\mathcal{A} \models_I \top$ always) and $\subset$ as strict (irreflexive) subset.

(9) [John-drive-to-Boston] $\langle$John-eat-a-donut$\rangle\top$

(10) $\mathcal{A} \models_I \langle e\rangle\varphi \stackrel{\text{def}}{\iff} (\exists J \subset I \text{ s.t. } \mathcal{A}(J, e))$ $\mathcal{A} \models_J \varphi$

(11) $\mathcal{A} \models_I \neg\varphi \stackrel{\text{def}}{\iff} \text{not } \mathcal{A} \models_I \varphi$

Clause (10) shows off a crucial feature of $\mathcal{TPL}$: quantification over intervals is bounded by the domain of $\mathcal{A}$; that is, quantification is restricted to intervals that are paired up with an event-atom by the

[5] Over non-empty closed intervals that include points $[a, a]$, the Allen relations m and mi collapse to o and oi, respectively. Alternatively, we can realize m and mi by trading closed intervals for *open* intervals (required to be non-empty); see the Appendix below.

$\mathcal{TPL}$-model (making $\mathcal{TPL}$ "quasi-guarded"; Pratt-Hartmann, 2005; page 5). This is *not* to say that the only intervals I that may appear in forming $\mathcal{A} \models_I \varphi$ are those in the domain of $\mathcal{A}$. Indeed, for $[a, b] \in \mathcal{I}$ and $[a', b'] \in dom(\mathcal{A})$ such that $[a', b'] \subset [a, b]$, $\mathcal{TPL}$ uses intervals

$$\text{init}([a', b'], [a, b]) \stackrel{\text{def}}{=} [a, a']$$
$$\text{fin}([a', b'], [a, b]) \stackrel{\text{def}}{=} [b', b]$$

to interpret $\{e\}_< \varphi$ and $\{e\}_> \varphi$ according to (12).

(12) $$\mathcal{A} \models_I \{e\}_< \varphi \stackrel{\text{def}}{\iff} (\exists! J \subset I \text{ s.t. } \mathcal{A}(J, e))\ \mathcal{A} \models_{\text{init}(J,I)} \varphi$$
$$\mathcal{A} \models_I \{e\}_> \varphi \stackrel{\text{def}}{\iff} (\exists! J \subset I \text{ s.t. } \mathcal{A}(J, e))\ \mathcal{A} \models_{\text{fin}(J,I)} \varphi$$

The bang ! in $\exists! J$ in (12) expresses uniqueness, which means that under the translation of (1) as (13) below, the interval I of evaluation is required to contain a unique event of John talking with Mary.

(1) After $\underbrace{\text{his talk with Mary}}_{\text{p}}$ $\underbrace{\text{John drove to Boston}}_{\text{q}}$.

(13) $\{\mathsf{p}\}_> \langle \mathsf{q} \rangle \top$

For a translation of (1) more faithful to

(2) $p(e) \wedge q(e') \wedge \text{after}(e, e')$

than (13),[6] it suffices to drop ! in (12) for $\langle e \rangle_<$ and $\langle e \rangle_>$ in place of $\{e\}_<$ and $\{e\}_>$ respectively (Fernando, 2011a), and to revise (13) to $\langle \mathsf{p} \rangle_> \langle \mathsf{q} \rangle \top$. Relaxing uniqueness, we can form $[\mathsf{p}]_> \langle \mathsf{q} \rangle \top$ for *after every talk with Mary, John drove to Boston*, as well as $\langle \mathsf{p} \rangle_> \langle \mathsf{p} \rangle \top$ for *after a talk with Mary, John talked with Mary again*. $\mathcal{TPL}$ has further constructs e^f and e^l for the (minimal) first and (minimal) last e-events in an interval.

Returning to the suitability of $\mathsf{s}(\mathcal{A})$ for $\mathcal{TPL}$, consider the question: when do two pairs $\mathcal{A}, I$ and $\mathcal{A}', I'$ of $\mathcal{TPL}$-models $\mathcal{A}, \mathcal{A}'$ and intervals $I, I' \in \mathcal{I}$ satisfy the same $\mathcal{TPL}$-formulae? Some definitions are in order. A bijection $f : A \to B$ between finite sets A and B of real numbers is *order-preserving* if for all $a, a' \in A$,

$$a < a' \iff f(a) < f(a')$$

in which case we write $f : A \cong B$. Given a $\mathcal{TPL}$-model $\mathcal{A}$, and a function $f : \mathit{Ends}(\mathcal{A}) \to \mathbb{R}$, let $\mathcal{A}^f$ be $\mathcal{A}$ with all its intervals renamed by f

$$\mathcal{A}^f \stackrel{\text{def}}{=} \{\langle [f(a), f(b)], e \rangle \mid \langle [a, b], e \rangle \in \mathcal{A}\}.$$

Now, we say $\mathcal{A}$ is *congruent with* $\mathcal{A}'$ and write $\mathcal{A} \cong \mathcal{A}'$ if there is an order-preserving bijection between $\mathit{Ends}(\mathcal{A})$ and $\mathit{Ends}(\mathcal{A}')$ that renames $\mathcal{A}$ to $\mathcal{A}'$

$$\mathcal{A} \cong \mathcal{A}' \stackrel{\text{def}}{\iff} (\exists f : \mathit{Ends}(\mathcal{A}) \cong \mathit{Ends}(\mathcal{A}'))\ \mathcal{A}' = \mathcal{A}^f.$$

Finally, we bring I into the picture by defining the *restriction* $\mathcal{A}_I$ *of* $\mathcal{A}$ *to* I to be the subset

$$\mathcal{A}_I \stackrel{\text{def}}{=} \{\langle J, e \rangle \in \mathcal{A} \mid J \subset I\}$$

of $\mathcal{A}$ with intervals strictly contained in I.

Proposition 2. *For all finite subsets $\mathcal{A}$ and $\mathcal{A}'$ of $\mathcal{I} \times E$ and all intervals $I, I' \in \mathcal{I}$, if $\mathcal{A}_I \cong \mathcal{A}'_{I'}$ then for every $\mathcal{TPL}$-formula φ,*

$$\mathcal{A} \models_I \varphi \iff \mathcal{A}' \models_{I'} \varphi.$$

Proposition 2 suggests normalizing a $\mathcal{TPL}$ model $\mathcal{A}$ with endpoints $r_1 < r_2 < \cdots < r_n$ to $\mathsf{nr}(\mathcal{A})$ with r_i renamed to i

$$\mathsf{nr}(\mathcal{A}) \stackrel{\text{def}}{=} \mathcal{A}^f \quad \text{where } f \stackrel{\text{def}}{=} \{\langle r_1, 1 \rangle, \ldots, \langle r_n, n \rangle\}.$$

Assigning every $\mathcal{TPL}$-formula φ the *truth set*

$$\mathcal{T}(\varphi) \stackrel{\text{def}}{=} \{\mathsf{s}(\mathsf{nr}(\mathcal{A}_I)) \mid \mathcal{A} \text{ is a } \mathcal{TPL}\text{-model}, I \in \mathcal{I} \text{ and } \mathcal{A} \models_I \varphi\}$$

gives

Proposition 3. *For every $\mathcal{TPL}$-formula φ, $\mathcal{TPL}$-model $\mathcal{A}$, and interval $I \in \mathcal{I}$,*

$$\mathcal{A} \models_I \varphi \iff \mathsf{s}(\mathsf{nr}(\mathcal{A}_I)) \in \mathcal{T}(\varphi).$$

To bolster the claim that $\mathcal{T}(\varphi)$ encodes $\mathcal{TPL}$-satisfaction, we may construct $\mathcal{T}(\varphi)$ by induction on φ, mimicking the clauses for $\mathcal{TPL}$-satisfaction, as in (14).

(14) $$\mathcal{T}(\varphi \wedge \varphi') = \mathcal{T}(\varphi) \cap \mathcal{T}(\varphi')$$

Details are provided in the next section, where we consider the finite-state character of the clauses, and may verify Propositions 2 and 3.

[6] Caution: e and e' are tokens in (2), but types in $\mathcal{TPL}$.

3 Regularity and relations behind truth

A consequence of Proposition 3 is that the entailment from φ to φ' given by

$$\varphi \vdash_{\mathcal{I},E} \varphi' \stackrel{\text{def}}{\iff} (\forall \text{ finite } \mathcal{A} \subseteq \mathcal{I} \times E)(\forall I \in \mathcal{I}) \\ \mathcal{A} \models_I \varphi \text{ implies } \mathcal{A} \models_I \varphi'$$

becomes equivalent to the inclusion $\mathcal{T}(\varphi) \subseteq \mathcal{T}(\varphi')$, or to the unsatisfiability of $\varphi \wedge \neg\varphi'$

$$\varphi \vdash_{\mathcal{I},E} \varphi' \iff \mathcal{T}(\varphi \wedge \neg\varphi') = \emptyset$$

assuming classical interpretations (14) and (15) of conjunction $\wedge$ and negation $\neg$.

(15) $\mathcal{T}(\neg\varphi) \;=\; \Sigma^+ - \mathcal{T}(\varphi)$

Finite-state methods are of interest as regular languages are closed under intersection and complementation. (Context-free languages are not; nor is containment between context-free languages decidable.) The alphabet Σ in (15) is, however, infinite; Σ is the set $\mathit{Fin}(\mathcal{J} \times E)$ of finite subsets of $\mathcal{J} \times E$, where $\mathcal{J}$ is the set

$$\mathcal{J} \stackrel{\text{def}}{=} \{[n,m] \in \mathcal{I} \mid n,m \in \mathbb{Z}_+\}$$

of intervals in $\mathcal{I}$ with endpoints in the set $\mathbb{Z}_+$ of positive integers $1, 2, \ldots$ (containing the domain of a normalized $\mathcal{TPL}$-model). As with π_X, regularity demands restricting Σ to a finite subalphabet — or better: subalphabet*s* given by the set $\mathcal{F}$ of pairs $\langle \mathcal{I}', E' \rangle$ of finite subsets $\mathcal{I}'$ and E' of $\mathcal{J}$ and E respectively, for which

$$\Sigma \;=\; \bigcup_{\langle \mathcal{I}', E' \rangle \in \mathcal{F}} \mathit{Pow}(\mathcal{I}' \times E') \,.$$

The basis of the decidability/complexity results in (Pratt-Hartmann, 2005) is a lemma (number 3 in page 20) that, for any $\mathcal{TPL}$-formula φ, bounds the size of a minimal model of φ. We get a computable function mapping a $\mathcal{TPL}$-formula φ to a finite subset $\mathcal{I}_\varphi$ of $\mathcal{J}$ just big enough so that if φ is $\mathcal{TPL}$-satisfiable,

$$(\exists \mathcal{A} \in \mathit{Pow}(\mathcal{I}_\varphi \times E_\varphi))(\exists I \in \mathcal{I}_\varphi)\ \mathcal{A} \models_I \varphi$$

where E_φ is the finite subset of E occurring in φ. To minimize notational clutter, we leave out the choice $\langle \mathcal{I}', E' \rangle \in \mathcal{F}$ of a finite alphabet below.

Next, keeping intersection and complementation in (14) and (15) in mind, let us call an operation *regularity-preserving* (rp) if its output is regular whenever all its inputs are regular. To interpret $\mathcal{TPL}$, we construe operations broadly to allow their inputs and output to range over relations between strings (and not just languages), construing a relation to be *regular* if it is computable by a finite-state transducer. For instance, the modal diamond $\langle e \rangle$ labelled by an event-atom $e \in E$ is interpreted via an accessibility relation $\mathcal{R}(e)$ in the usual Kripke semantics

$$\mathcal{T}(\langle e \rangle \varphi) \;=\; \mathcal{R}(e)^{-1}\mathcal{T}(\varphi)$$

of $\langle e \rangle \varphi$ where $R^{-1}L$ is the set $\{s \in \Sigma^* \mid (\exists s' \in L)\ sRs'\}$ of strings related by R to a string in L. The operation that outputs $R^{-1}L$ on inputs R and L is rp. But what is the accessibility relation $\mathcal{R}(e)$?

Three ingredients go into making $\mathcal{R}(e)$:

(i) a notion of strict containment $\sqsupset$ between strings

(ii) the demarcation $s^\bullet$ of a string s

(iii) a set $\mathcal{D}(e)$ of strings representing full occurrences of e.

We take up each in turn, starting with $\sqsupset$, which combines two ways a string can be part of another. To capture strict inclusion $\subset$ between intervals, we say a string s' is a *proper factor of* a string s, and write s *pfac* s', if s' is s with some prefix u and suffix v deleted, and uv is non-empty

$$s \ \mathit{pfac}\ s' \iff (\exists u, v)\ s = us'v \text{ and } uv \neq \epsilon.$$

(Dropping the requirement $uv \neq \epsilon$ gives *factors* simpliciter.) The second way a string s' may be part of s applies specifically to strings of sets. We say s *subsumes* s', and write $s \unrhd s'$, if they are of the same length, and $\supseteq$ holds componentwise between them

$$\alpha_1 \cdots \alpha_n \unrhd \alpha'_1 \cdots \alpha'_m \stackrel{\text{def}}{\iff} n = m \text{ and} \\ \alpha'_i \subseteq \alpha_i \text{ for } 1 \leq i \leq n.$$

Now, writing $R; R'$ for the *relational composition of* binary relations R and R' in which the output of R is fed as input to R'

$$s\ R; R'\ s' \stackrel{\text{def}}{\iff} (\exists s'')\ sRs'' \text{ and } s''R's' \,,$$

we compose *pfac* with $\trianglerighteq$ for *strict containment* $\sqsupset$

$$\sqsupset \ \stackrel{\text{def}}{=} \ pfac \ ; \trianglerighteq \qquad (= \trianglerighteq \ ; pfac) \ .$$

(It is well-known that relational composition ; is rp.) Next, the idea behind demarcating a string s is to mark the beginning and ending of every interval I mentioned in s, with fresh fluents *bgn-I* and *I-end*. The *demarcation* $(\alpha_1\alpha_2\cdots\alpha_n)^\bullet$ of $\alpha_1\alpha_2\cdots\alpha_n$ adds *bgn-I* to α_i precisely if

> there is some e such that $\langle I, e\rangle \in \alpha_i$ and either $i = 1$ or $\langle I, e\rangle \notin \alpha_{i-1}$

and adds *I-end* to α_i precisely if

> there is some e such that $\langle I, e\rangle \in \alpha_i$ and either $i = n$ or $\langle I, e\rangle \notin \alpha_{i+1}$.[7]

For $s = \mathsf{s}(\mathcal{A})$ given by the example in Table 3,

$$s^\bullet = \boxed{x_1, bgn\text{-}I_1}\boxed{x_1, x_2, I_1\text{-}end, bgn\text{-}I_2}\boxed{x_2}\boxed{x_2, x_3, I_2\text{-}end, bgn\text{-}I_3}\boxed{x_3, I_3\text{-}end}$$

We then form the *denotation* $\mathcal{D}_{\mathcal{I}'}(e)$ *of* e *relative to* a finite subset $\mathcal{I}'$ of $\mathcal{I}$ by demarcating every string in $\bigcup_{I\in\mathcal{I}'}\boxed{\langle I, e\rangle}^+$ as in (16).

$$\text{(16)} \quad \mathcal{D}_{\mathcal{I}'}(e) \ \stackrel{\text{def}}{=} \ \bigcup_{I\in\mathcal{I}'}\{s^\bullet \mid s \in \boxed{\langle I, e\rangle}^+\}$$

To simplify notation, we suppress the subscript $\mathcal{I}'$ on $\mathcal{D}_{\mathcal{I}'}(e)$. Restricting strict containment $\sqsupset$ to $\mathcal{D}(e)$ gives

$$s\, \mathcal{R}_\circ(e)\, s' \ \stackrel{\text{def}}{\iff} \ s \sqsupset s' \text{ and } s' \in \mathcal{D}(e)$$

from which we define $\mathcal{R}(e)$, making adjustments for demarcation

$$s\, \mathcal{R}(e)\, s' \ \stackrel{\text{def}}{\iff} \ s^\bullet\, \mathcal{R}_\circ(e)\, s'^\bullet .$$

That is, $\mathcal{R}(e)$ is the composition $\cdot^\bullet; \mathcal{R}_\circ(e); \cdot_\bullet$ where demarcation $\cdot^\bullet$ is inverted by $\cdot_\bullet$. As $\mathcal{TPL}$'s other constructs are shown in §4.1 of (Fernando, 2011a) to be interpretable by rp operations, we have

Proposition 4. *All $\mathcal{TPL}$-connectives can be interpreted by rp operations.*

Beyond $\mathcal{TPL}$, the interval temporal logic $\mathcal{HS}$ of (Halpern and Shoham, 1991) suggests variants of $\langle e\rangle\varphi$ with strict containment $\sqsupset$ in $\mathcal{R}(e)$ replaced by any of Allen's 13 interval relations R.

$$\text{(17)} \quad \mathcal{A} \models_I \langle e\rangle_R\varphi \ \stackrel{\text{def}}{\iff} \ (\exists J \text{ s.t. } I\ R\ J) \ \mathcal{A}(J, e) \text{ and } \mathcal{A} \models_J \varphi$$

To emulate (17), we need to mark the evaluation interval I in $\mathcal{A}$ by some $r \notin E$, setting

$$\mathcal{A}_r[I] \ \stackrel{\text{def}}{=} \ \mathcal{A} \cup \{\langle I, r\rangle\}$$

rather than simply forming $\mathcal{A}_I$ (which will do if we can always assume the model's full temporal extent is marked). A string $s = \alpha_1\cdots\alpha_n$ *r-marks* I if $\langle I, r\rangle \in \bigcup_{i=1}^n \alpha_i$. If that interval is unique, we say s is *r-marked*, and write $\mathsf{I}(s)$ for the interval it r-marks, and s_- for s with the fluent $\langle \mathsf{I}(s), r\rangle$ deleted (so that $\mathsf{s}(\mathcal{A}_r[I])_- = \mathsf{s}(\mathcal{A})$). For any of the relations R $\in$**Allen**, we let $\approx_R$ hold between r-marked strings that are identical except possibly for the intervals they r-mark, which are related by R

$$s \approx_R s' \ \stackrel{\text{def}}{\iff} \ s_- = s'_- \text{ and } \mathsf{I}(s)\ R\ \mathsf{I}(s').$$

Next, given an event-atom e, we let $\mathcal{R}(e)_R$ be a binary relation that holds between r-marked strings related by $\approx_R$, the latter of which picks out a factor subsuming some string in $\mathcal{D}(e)$

$$s\, \mathcal{R}(e)_R\, s' \ \stackrel{\text{def}}{\iff} \ s \approx_R s' \text{ and } (\exists d \in \mathcal{D}(e))\ s'_r \trianglerighteq d$$

where s'_r is the factor of s' that begins with *bgn*-$\mathsf{I}(s')$ and ends with $\mathsf{I}(s')$-*end*. Replacing $\mathcal{A}_I$ by $\mathcal{A}_r[I]$ in $\mathcal{T}(\varphi)$ for

$$\mathcal{T}_r(\varphi) \ \stackrel{\text{def}}{=} \ \{\mathsf{s}(\mathsf{nr}(\mathcal{A}_r[I])) \mid \mathcal{A} \text{ is a } \mathcal{TPL}\text{-model}, \ I \in \mathcal{I} \text{ and } \mathcal{A} \models_I \varphi\} ,$$

(17) corresponds to

$$\mathcal{T}_r(\langle e\rangle_R\varphi) \ = \ \mathcal{R}(e)_R^{-1}\ \mathcal{T}_r(\varphi).$$

[7] The markers *bgn-I* and *I-end* are analogous to the brackets [g and]g in (Niemi and Koskenniemi, 2009), an essential difference being that a grain (type) g supports multiple occurrences of [g and]g, in contrast to the (token) interval I.

4 Conclusion and future work

The key notion behind the analysis above of time in terms of strings is the map π_X, which for X consisting of interval-event pairs $\langle I, e\rangle$, is applied in Proposition 1 to turn a $\mathcal{TPL}$-model $\mathcal{A}$ into a string $\mathsf{s}(\mathcal{A})$. As far as $\mathcal{TPL}$-satisfaction $\mathcal{A} \models_I \varphi$ is concerned, we can normalize the endpoints of the intervals to an initial segment of the positive integers, after restricting $\mathcal{A}$ to intervals contained in the evaluation interval I (Proposition 3). For a finite-state encoding of $\mathcal{TPL}$-satisfaction, it is useful to demarcate the otherwise homogeneous picture $\boxed{\langle I, e\rangle}^+$ of $\langle I, e\rangle$, and to define a notion $\sqsupset$ of proper containment between strings. We close with further finite-state enhancements.

Demarcation is linguistically significant, bearing directly on telicity and the so-called Aristotle-Ryle-Kenny-Vendler classification (Dowty, 1979), illustrated by the contrasts in (18) and (19).

(18) John was driving $\vdash$ John drove

John was driving to L.A. $\not\vdash$ John drove to L.A.

(19) John drove <u>for</u> an hour

John drove to L.A. <u>in</u> an hour

The difference at work in (18) and (19) is that *John driving to L.A.* has a termination condition, *in(John, L.A.)*, missing from *John driving*. Given a fluent such as *in(John, L.A.)*, we call a language L *φ-telic* if for every $s \in L$, there is an $n \geq 0$ such that $s \trianglerighteq \boxed{\neg\varphi}^n\boxed{\varphi}$ (which is to say: a string in L ends as soon as φ becomes true). L is *telic* if it is φ-telic, for some φ. Now, the contrasts in (18) and (19) can be put down formally to the language for *John driving to L.A.* being telic, but not that for *John driving* (Fernando, 2008).

The demarcation (via φ) just described does not rely on some set $\mathcal{I}'$ of intervals I from which fluents *bgn-I* and *I-end* are formed (as in $s^\bullet$ from section 3). There are at least two reasons for attempting to avoid $\mathcal{I}'$ when demarcating or, for that matter, building the set $\mathcal{D}(e)$ of denotations of e. The first is that under a definition such as (16), the number of e-events (i.e., events of type e) is bounded by the cardinality of $\mathcal{I}'$.

(16) $\mathcal{D}_{\mathcal{I}'}(e) \stackrel{\text{def}}{=} \bigcup_{I\in\mathcal{I}'}\{s^\bullet \mid s \in \boxed{\langle I, e\rangle}^+\}$

The second is that an interval arguably has little to do with an e-event being an e-event. An interval [4,9] does not, in and of itself, make $\langle[4,9], e\rangle$ an e-event; $\langle[4,9], e\rangle$ is an e-event only *in* a $\mathcal{TPL}$-model that says it is. An alternative is to express in strings what holds during an event that makes it an e-event. Consider the event type e of *Pat walking a mile*. Incremental change in an event of that type can be represented through a parametrized fluent $f(r)$ with parameter r ranging over the reals in the unit interval $[0,1]$, such that $f(r)$ says *Pat has walked r·(a mile)*. Let $\mathcal{D}(e)$ be

$$\boxed{f(0)}\boxed{f_\uparrow}^+\boxed{f(1)}$$

where $f_\uparrow$ abbreviates the fluent

$$(\exists r < 1)\ f(r) \wedge \mathsf{Previous}(\neg f(r)).$$

$\mathsf{Previous}$ is a temporal operator that constrains strings $\alpha_1 \cdots \alpha_n$ so that whenever $\mathsf{Previous}(\varphi)$ belongs to α_{i+1}, φ belongs to α_i; that is,

$$\boxed{\ }\boxed{\mathsf{Previous}(\varphi)} \Rightarrow \boxed{\varphi}\boxed{\ }$$

using an rp binary operator $\Rightarrow$ on languages that combines subsumption $\trianglerighteq$ with constraints familiar from finite-state morphology (Beesley and Karttunen, 2003).

The borders and interior of $\langle I, e\rangle$ aside, there is the matter of locating an e-string in a larger string (effected in $\mathcal{TPL}$ through strict inclusion $\supset$, the string-analog of which is proper containment $\sqsupset$). But what larger string? The influential theory of tense and aspect in (Reichenbach, 1947) places e relative not only to the speech S but also to a *reference time* r, differentiating, for instance, the simple past $\boxed{e, r}\boxed{\text{S}}$ from the present perfect $\boxed{e}\boxed{\text{S}, r}$, as required by differences in defeasible entailments $\mid\!\sim$, (20), and acceptability, (21).

(20) Pat has left Paris $\mid\!\sim$ Pat is not in Paris

Pat left Paris $\not\mid\!\sim$ Pat is not in Paris

(21) Pat left Paris. (?Pat has left Paris.)

But Pat is back in Paris.

The placement of r provides a bound on the *inertia* applying to the postcondition of Pat's departure

(Fernando, 2008). The extension $\mathcal{A}_r[I]$ proposed in section 3 to the combination $\mathcal{A}_I$ (adequate for $\mathcal{TPL}$, but not $\mathcal{HS}$) explicitly r-marks the evaluation interval I, facilitating an account more intricate than simply $\sqsupset$ of e's occurrence in the larger string. $\mathcal{TPL}$ goes no further than Ramsey in analyzing *That Caesar died* as an ontological claim that an event of certain sort exists (Parsons, 1990), leading to the view of an event as a truthmaker (Davidson, 1967; Mulligan et al., 1984). The idea of an event (in isolation) as some sort of proof runs into serious difficulties, however, as soon as tense and aspect are brought into the picture; complications such as the *Imperfective Paradox* (Dowty, 1979), illustrated in (22), raise tricky questions about what it means for an event to exist and how to ground it in the world (speaking loosely) in which the utterance is made.

(22) John was drawing a circle when he ran out of ink.

But while the burden of proof may be too heavy to be borne by a single pair $\langle I, e \rangle$ of interval I and event-atom e, the larger picture in which the pair is embedded can be strung out, and a temporal statement φ interpreted as a binary relation $\mathbf{R}_\varphi$ between such strings that goes well beyond $\sqsupset$. The inputs to $\mathbf{R}_\varphi$ serve as indices, with those in the domain of $\mathbf{R}_\varphi$ supporting the truth of φ

$$\varphi \text{ is } \textit{true at } s \quad \stackrel{\text{def}}{\Longleftrightarrow} \quad (\exists s')\ s\ \mathbf{R}_\varphi\ s'$$

(Fernando, 2011, 2012). In witnessing truth at particular inputs, the outputs of $\mathbf{R}_\varphi$ constitute denotations more informative than truth values, from which indices can be built bottom-up, in harmony with a semantic analysis of text from its parts (to which presumably TimeML is committed). An obvious question is how far finite-state methods will take us. Based on the evidence at hand, we have much further to go.

Acknowledgments

My thanks to Daniel Isemann for useful, sustained discussions. The work is supported by EI Grant # CC-2011-2601B:GRCTC.

References

James F. Allen. 1983. Maintaining knowledge about temporal intervals. *Communications of the Association for Computing Machinery* 26(11): 832–843.

James F. Allen and George Ferguson. Actions and events in interval temporal logic. *J. Logic and Computation*, 4(5):531–579, 1994.

Kenneth R. Beesley and Lauri Karttunen. 2003. *Finite State Morphology*. CSLI, Stanford, CA.

Michael Bennett and Barbara Partee. 1972. Toward the logic of tense and aspect in English. Indiana University Linguistics Club, Bloomington, IN.

J.F.A.K. van Benthem. 1983. *The Logic of Time*. Reidel.

Edmund M. Clarke, Jr., Orna Grumberg and Doron A. Peled. 1999. *Model Checking*. MIT Press.

Donald Davidson. 1967. The logical form of action sentences. In *The Logic of Decision and Action*, pages 81–95. University of Pittsburgh Press.

David Dowty. 1979. *Word Meaning and Montague Grammar*. Kluwer.

Tim Fernando. 2008. Branching from inertia worlds. *J. Semantics* 25:321–344.

Tim Fernando. 2011. Regular relations for temporal propositions. *Natural Language Engineering* 17(2): 163–184.

Tim Fernando. 2011a. Strings over intervals. *TextInfer 2011 Workshop on Textual Entailment*, pages 50-58, Edinburgh (ACL Archives).

Tim Fernando. 2011b. Finite-state representations embodying temporal relations. In *9th International Workshop FSMNLP 2011*, Blois, pages 12–20. A revised, extended version is in the author's webpage.

Tim Fernando. 2012. Steedman's temporality proposal and finite automata. In *Amsterdam Colloquium 2011*, Sprnger LNCS 7218, pages 301-310.

Joseph Y. Halpern and Yoav Shoham. 1991. A Propositional Modal Logic of Time Intervals. *J. Association for Computing Machinery* 38(4): 935–962.

ISO. 2007. ISO Draft International Standard 24617-1 *Semantic annotation framework — Part 1: Time and events*. ISO (Geneva).

Ray Jackendoff. 1996. The proper treatment of measuring out, telicity, and perhaps even quantification in English. *Natural Language and Linguistic Theory* 14:305–354.

Hans Kamp and Uwe Reyle. 1993. *From Disocurse to Logic*. Kluwer.

Kevin Mulligan, Peter Simons and Barry Smith. 1984. Truth-makers. *Philosophy and Phenomenological Research* **44**: 287–321.

Jyrki Niemi and Kimmo Koskenniemi. 2009. Representing and combining calendar information by using finite-state transducers. In *7th International Workshop FSMNLP 2008*, pages 122–33. Amsterdam.

Terry Parsons. 1990. *Events in the Semantics of English*. MIT Press.

Ian Pratt-Hartmann. 2005. Temporal prepositions and their logic. *Artificial Intelligence* 166: 1–36.

Ian Pratt-Hartmann. 2005a. From TimeML to TPL*. In *Annotating, Extracting and Reasoning about Time and Events*, Schloss Dagstuhl.

James Pustejovsky, José Castaño, Robert Ingria, Roser Saurí, Robert Gaizauskas, Andrea Setzer and Graham Katz. 2003. TimeML: Robust Specification of Event and Temporal Expressions in Text. In *5th International Workshop on Computational Semantics*, pages 337-353. Tilburg.

Hans Reichenbach. 1947. *Elements of Symbolic Logic*. Macmillan & Co (New York).

Carol Tenny. 1987. Grammaticalizing Aspect and Affectedness. PhD dissertation, Department of Linguistics and Philosophy, MIT.

Wolfgang Thomas. 1997. Languages, automata and logic. In *Handbook of Formal Languages: Beyond Words*, Volume 3, pages 389–455. Springer-Verlag.

Appendix: a case of "less is more"?

Because the set $\mathcal{I}$ of intervals from which a $\mathcal{TPL}$-model $\mathcal{A}$ is constructed includes singleton sets $[a, a] = \{a\}$ (for all real numbers a), there can never be events x and x' in $\mathcal{A}$ such that x meets (or abuts) x', x m x', according to Table 2 above. It is, however, easy enough to throw out sets $[a, a]$ from $\mathcal{I}$, requiring that for $[a, b] \in \mathcal{I}$, a be strictly less than b. (In doing so, we follow (Allen, 1983) and (Pratt-Hartmann, 2005a), but stray from (Pratt-Hartmann, 2005).) The result is that the overlap at b between $[a, b]$ and $[b, c]$ is deeemed un-observable (effectively re-interpreting closed intervals by their interiors, understood to be non-empty). The third column $\chi_R([a, b], [a', b'])$ in Table 2 is modified to a condition $[a, b]\ R^\circ\ [a', b']$ that differs on the cases where R is one of the four Allen relations `o`, `m`, `oi`, `mi`, splitting the disjunction $a' \leq b$ in `o` with `m`, and $a \leq b'$ in `oi` with `mi`.

$R \in$**Allen**	$s_R \in \mathcal{L}_\pi(\{e_1, e_2\})$	$[a, b]\ R^\circ\ [a', b']$
x o x'	$\boxed{x}\boxed{x, x'}\boxed{x'}$	$a < a' < b < b'$
x m x'	$\boxed{x}\boxed{x'}$	$b = a'$
x oi x'	$\boxed{x'}\boxed{x, x'}\boxed{x}$	$a' < a < b' < b$
x mi x'	$\boxed{x'}\boxed{x}$	$b' = a$

All other rows in Table 2 are the same for $[a, b]\ R^\circ\ [a', b']$. The somewhat wasteful encoding $s(\mathcal{A})$ in Proposition 1 then becomes $s^\circ(\mathcal{A})$ in

Proposition 1°. *For every $\mathcal{TPL}$-model $\mathcal{A}$ such that $a < b$ for all $[a, b] \in$ dom$(\mathcal{A})$, there is a unique string $\mathsf{s}^\circ(\mathcal{A}) \in \mathcal{L}_\pi(\mathcal{A})$ such that for all $x, x' \in \mathcal{A}$ with $x = \langle I, e\rangle$ and $x' = \langle I', e'\rangle$, and $R \in$***Allen**

$$\pi_{\{x,x'\}}(\mathsf{s}^\circ(\mathcal{A})) = s_R \iff I\ R^\circ I'.$$

The encoding $\mathsf{s}^\circ(\mathcal{A})$ is formed exactly as $s(\mathcal{A})$ is in section 2 above from the endpoints $r_1 < r_2 < \cdots < r_n$ of *dom*$(\mathcal{A})$, except that the α_i's for the endpoints r_i are dropped (these being un-observable), leaving us with the β_i's for $[r_i, r_{i+1}]$

$$\mathsf{s}^\circ(\mathcal{A}) \stackrel{\text{def}}{=} bc(\beta_1 \cdots \beta_{n-1}).$$

Beyond Proposition 1, the arguments above for $\mathsf{s}(\mathcal{A})$ carry over to $\mathsf{s}^\circ(\mathcal{A})$, with the requirement on a $\mathcal{TPL}$-model $\mathcal{A}$ that $a < b$ for all $[a, b] \in$ *dom*$(\mathcal{A})$. It is noteworthy that (Pratt-Hartmann, 2005a) makes no mention that this requirement is a departure from (Pratt-Hartmann, 2005). Although the restriction $a < b$ rules out $\mathcal{TPL}$-models with points $[a, a]$ in their domain, it also opens $\mathcal{TPL}$ up to strings in which events meet — a trade-off accepted in (Allen and Ferguson, 1994). To properly accommodate points alongside larger intervals, we can introduce a fluent *indiv* marking out boxes corresponding to points $[a, a]$ (as opposed to divisible intervals $[a, b]$ where $a < b$), and re-define π_X to leave boxes with *indiv* in them alone. From this perspective, the restriction $a < b$ is quite compatible with π_X as defined above. But can we justify the notational overhead in introducing *indiv* and complicating π_X? We say no more here.

A finite-state approach to phrase-based statistical machine translation

Jorge González
Departamento de Sistemas Informáticos y Computación
Universitat Politècnica de València
València, Spain
jgonzalez@dsic.upv.es

Abstract

This paper presents a finite-state approach to phrase-based statistical machine translation where a log-linear modelling framework is implemented by means of an on-the-fly composition of weighted finite-state transducers. Moses, a well-known state-of-the-art system, is used as a machine translation reference in order to validate our results by comparison. Experiments on the TED corpus achieve a similar performance to that yielded by Moses.

1 Introduction

Statistical machine translation (SMT) is a pattern recognition approach to machine translation which was defined by Brown et al. (1993) as follows: given a sentence $\mathbf{s}$ from a certain source language, a corresponding sentence $\hat{\mathbf{t}}$ in a given target language that maximises the posterior probability $\Pr(\mathbf{t}|\mathbf{s})$ is to be found. State-of-the-art SMT systems model the translation distribution $\Pr(\mathbf{t}|\mathbf{s})$ via the log-linear approach (Och and Ney, 2002):

$$\hat{\mathbf{t}} = \arg\max_{\mathbf{t}} \Pr(\mathbf{t}|\mathbf{s}) \quad (1)$$

$$\approx \arg\max_{\mathbf{t}} \sum_{m=1}^{M} \lambda_m h_m(\mathbf{s}, \mathbf{t}) \quad (2)$$

where $h_m(\mathbf{s}, \mathbf{t})$ is a logarithmic function representing an important feature for the translation of $\mathbf{s}$ into $\mathbf{t}$, M is the number of features (or models), and λ_m is the weight of h_m in the log-linear combination.

This feature set typically includes several *translation* models so that different relations between a source and a target sentence can be considered. Nowadays, these models are strongly based on phrases, i.e. variable-length n-grams, which means that they are built from some other lower-context models that, in this case, are defined at phrase level. *Phrase-based* (PB) models (Tomas and Casacuberta, 2001; Och and Ney, 2002; Marcu and Wong, 2002; Zens et al., 2002) constitute the core of the current state-of-the-art in SMT. The basic idea of PB-SMT systems is:

1. to segment the source sentence into phrases, then
2. to translate each source phrase into a target phrase, and finally
3. to reorder them in order to compose the final translation in the target language.

In a monotone translation framework however, the third step is omitted as the final translation is just generated by concatenation of the target phrases.

Apart from translation functions, the log-linear approach is also usually composed by means of a target language model and some other additional elements such as word penalties or phrase penalties. The word and phrase penalties allow an SMT system to limit the number of words or target phrases, respectively, that constitute a translation hypothesis.

In this paper, a finite-state approach to a PB-SMT state-of-the-art system, Moses (Koehn et al., 2007), is presented. Experimental results validate our work because they are similar to those yielded by Moses. A related study can be found in Kumar et al. (2006) for the alignment template model (Och et al., 1999).

Proceedings of the 10th International Workshop on Finite State Methods and Natural Language Processing, pages 90–98,
Donostia–San Sebastián, July 23–25, 2012.

2 Log-linear features for monotone SMT

As a first approach to Moses using finite-state models, a monotone PB-SMT framework is adopted. Under this constraint, Moses' log-linear model is usually taking into account the following 7 features:

Translation features

1. Direct PB translation probability
2. Inverse PB translation probability
3. Direct PB lexical weighting
4. Inverse PB lexical weighting

Penalty features

5. PB penalty
6. Word penalty

Language features

7. Target language model

2.1 Translation features

All 4 features related to translation are PB models, that is, their associated feature functions $h_m(\mathbf{s}, \mathbf{t})$, which are in any case defined for full sentences, are modelled from other PB distributions $\eta_m(\tilde{\mathbf{s}}, \tilde{\mathbf{t}})$, which are based on phrases.

Direct PB translation probability

The first feature $h_1(\mathbf{s}, \mathbf{t}) = \log P(\mathbf{t}|\mathbf{s})$ is based on modelling the posterior probability by using the segmentation between s and $\mathbf{t}$ as a hidden variable β_1. In this manner, $\Pr(\mathbf{t}|\mathbf{s}) = \sum_{\beta_1} \Pr(\mathbf{t}|\mathbf{s}, \beta_1)$ is then approximated by $P(\mathbf{t}|\mathbf{s})$ by using maximization instead of summation: $P(\mathbf{t}|\mathbf{s}) = \max_{\beta_1} P(\mathbf{t}|\mathbf{s}, \beta_1)$.

Given a monotone segmentation between s and $\mathbf{t}$, $P(\mathbf{t}|\mathbf{s}, \beta_1)$ is generatively computed as the product of the translation probabilities for each segment pair according to some PB probability distributions:

$$P(\mathbf{t}|\mathbf{s}, \beta_1) = \prod_{k=1}^{|\beta_1|} P(\tilde{\mathbf{t}}_k|\tilde{\mathbf{s}}_k)$$

where $|\beta_1|$ is the number of phrases that s and $\mathbf{t}$ are segmented into, i.e. every $\tilde{\mathbf{s}}_k$ and $\tilde{\mathbf{t}}_k$, respectively, whose dependence on β_1 is omitted for the sake of an easier reading.

Feature 1 is finally formulated as follows:

$$h_1(\mathbf{s}, \mathbf{t}) = \log \max_{\beta_1} \prod_{k=1}^{|\beta_1|} P(\tilde{\mathbf{t}}_k|\tilde{\mathbf{s}}_k) \qquad (3)$$

where $\eta_1(\tilde{\mathbf{s}}, \tilde{\mathbf{t}}) = P(\tilde{\mathbf{t}}|\tilde{\mathbf{s}})$ is a set of PB probability distributions estimated from bilingual training data, once statistically word-aligned (Brown et al., 1993) by means of GIZA++ (Och and Ney, 2003), which Moses relies on as far as training is concerned. This information is organized as a *translation table* where a pool of phrase pairs is previously collected.

Inverse PB translation probability

Similar to what happens with Feature 1, Feature 2 is formulated as follows:

$$h_2(\mathbf{s}, \mathbf{t}) = \log \max_{\beta_2} \prod_{k=1}^{|\beta_2|} P(\tilde{\mathbf{s}}_k|\tilde{\mathbf{t}}_k) \qquad (4)$$

where $\eta_2(\tilde{\mathbf{s}}, \tilde{\mathbf{t}}) = P(\tilde{\mathbf{s}}|\tilde{\mathbf{t}})$ is another set of PB probability distributions, which are simultaneously trained together with the ones for Feature 1, $P(\tilde{\mathbf{t}}|\tilde{\mathbf{s}})$, over the same pool of phrase pairs already extracted.

Direct PB lexical weighting

Given the word-alignments obtained by GIZA++, it is quite straight-forward to estimate a maximum likelihood stochastic dictionary $P(\mathbf{t}_i|\mathbf{s}_j)$, which is used to score a weight $D(\tilde{\mathbf{s}}, \tilde{\mathbf{t}})$ to each phrase pair in the pool. Details about the computation of $D(\tilde{\mathbf{s}}, \tilde{\mathbf{t}})$ are given in Koehn et al. (2007). However, as far as this work is concerned, these details are not relevant.

Feature 3 is then similarly formulated as follows:

$$h_3(\mathbf{s}, \mathbf{t}) = \log \max_{\beta_3} \prod_{k=1}^{|\beta_3|} D(\tilde{\mathbf{s}}_k, \tilde{\mathbf{t}}_k) \qquad (5)$$

where $\eta_3(\tilde{\mathbf{s}}, \tilde{\mathbf{t}}) = D(\tilde{\mathbf{s}}, \tilde{\mathbf{t}})$ is yet another score to use with the pool of phrase pairs aligned during training.

Inverse PB lexical weighting

Similar to what happens with Feature 3, Feature 4 is formulated as follows:

$$h_4(\mathbf{s}, \mathbf{t}) = \log \max_{\beta_4} \prod_{k=1}^{|\beta_4|} I(\tilde{\mathbf{s}}_k, \tilde{\mathbf{t}}_k) \qquad (6)$$

where $\eta_4(\tilde{s}, \tilde{t}) = I(\tilde{s}, \tilde{t})$ is another weight vector, which is computed by using a dictionary $P(\mathbf{s}_j|\mathbf{t}_i)$, with which the translation table is expanded again, thus scoring a new weight per phrase pair in the pool.

2.2 Penalty features

The penalties are not modelled in the same way. The PB penalty is similar to a translation feature, i.e. it is based on a monotone sentence segmentation. The word penalty however is formulated as a whole, being taken into account by Moses at decoding time.

PB penalty

The PB penalty scores $e = 2.718$ per phrase pair, thus modelling somehow the segmentation length. Therefore, Feature 5 is defined as follows:

$$h_5(\mathbf{s}, \mathbf{t}) = \log \max_{\beta_5} \prod_{k=1}^{|\beta_5|} e \tag{7}$$

where $\eta_5(\tilde{s}, \tilde{t}) = e$ extends the PB table once again.

Word penalty

Word penalties are not modelled as PB penalties. In fact, this feature is not defined from PB scores, but it is formulated at sentence level just as follows:

$$h_6(\mathbf{s}, \mathbf{t}) = \log e^{|\mathbf{t}|} \tag{8}$$

where the exponent of e is the number of words in $\mathbf{t}$.

2.3 Language features

Language models approach the a priori probability that a given sentence belongs to a certain language. In SMT, they are usually employed to guarantee that translation hypotheses are built according to the peculiarities of the target language.

Target language model

An n-gram is used as target language model $P(\mathbf{t})$, where a word-based approach is usually considered. Then, $h_7(\mathbf{s}, \mathbf{t}) = \log P(\mathbf{t})$ is based on a model where sentences are generatively built word by word under the influence of the last $n-1$ previous words, with the cutoff derived from the start of the sentence:

$$h_7(\mathbf{s}, \mathbf{t}) = \log \prod_{i=1}^{|\mathbf{t}|} P(\mathbf{t}_i|\mathbf{t}_{i-n+1} \ldots \mathbf{t}_{i-1}) \tag{9}$$

where $P(\mathbf{t}_i|\mathbf{t}_{i-n+1} \ldots \mathbf{t}_{i-1})$ are word-based probability distributions learnt from monolingual corpora.

3 Data structures

This section shows how the features from Section 2 are actually organized into different data structures in order to be efficiently used by the Moses decoder, which implements the search defined by Equation 2 to find out the most likely translation hypothesis $\hat{\mathbf{t}}$ for a given source sentence $\mathbf{s}$.

3.1 PB models

The PB distributions associated to Features 1 to 5 are organized in table form as a translation table for the collection of phrase pairs previously extracted. That builds a PB database similar to that in Table 1

Source	Target	η_1	η_2	η_3	η_4	η_5
barato	low cost	1	0.3	1	0.6	2.718
me gusta	I like	0.6	1	0.9	1	2.718
es decir	that is	0.8	0.5	0.7	0.9	2.718
por favor	please	0.4	0.2	0.1	0.4	2.718
...				...		2.718

Table 1: A Spanish-into-English PB translation table. Each source-target phrase pair is scored by all η models.

where each phrase pair is scored by all five models.

3.2 Word-based models

Whereas PB models are an interesting approach to deal with translation relations between languages, language modelling itself is usually based on words. Feature 6 is a length model of the target sentence, and Feature 7 is a target language model.

Word penalty

Penalties are not models that need to be trained. However, while PB penalties are provided to Moses to take them into account during the search process (see for example the last column of Table 1, η_5), word penalties are internally implemented in Moses as part of the log-linear maximization in Equation 2, and are automatically computed on-the-fly at search.

Target n-gram model

Language models, and n-grams in particular, suffer from a sparseness problem (Rosenfeld, 1996). The n-gram probability distributions are smoothed to be able to deal with the unseen events out of training data, thus aiming for a larger language coverage.

This smoothing is based on the *backoff* method, which introduces some penalties for level downgrading within hierarchical language models. For example, let $\mathcal{M}$ be a trigram language model, which, as regards smoothing, needs both a bigram and a unigram model trained on the same data. Any trigram probability, $P(c|ab)$, is then computed as follows:

$$\begin{array}{lrl} \text{if} & abc \in \mathcal{M}: & P_{\mathcal{M}}(c|ab) \\ \text{elseif} & bc \in \mathcal{M}: & BO_{\mathcal{M}}(ab)P_{\mathcal{M}}(c|b) \\ \text{elseif} & c \in \mathcal{M}: & BO_{\mathcal{M}}(ab)\,BO_{\mathcal{M}}(b)P_{\mathcal{M}}(c) \\ \text{else} & : & BO_{\mathcal{M}}(ab)\,BO_{\mathcal{M}}(b)P_{\mathcal{M}}(unk) \end{array} \quad (10)$$

where $P_{\mathcal{M}}$ is the probability estimated by $\mathcal{M}$ for the corresponding n-gram, $BO_{\mathcal{M}}$ is the backoff weight to deal with the unseen events out of training data, and finally, $P_{\mathcal{M}}(unk)$ is the probability mass reserved for unknown words.

The $P(\mathbf{t}_i|\mathbf{t}_{i-n+1}\ldots\mathbf{t}_{i-1})$ term from Equation 9 is then computed according to that algorithm above, given the model data organized again in table form as a collection of probabilities and backoff weights for the n-grams appearing in the training corpus. This model displays similarly to that in Table 2.

n-gram	P	BO
please	0.02	0.2
low cost	0.05	0.3
I like	0.1	0.7
that is	0.08	0.5
...	...	

Table 2: An English word-based backoff n-gram model. The likelihood and the backoff model score for each n-gram.

4 Weighted finite-state transducers

Weighted finite-state transducers (Mohri et al., 2002) (WFSTs) are defined by means of a tuple $(\Sigma, \Delta, Q, q_0, f, P)$, where Σ is the alphabet of input symbols, Δ is the alphabet of output symbols, Q is a finite set of states, $q_0 \in Q$ is the initial state, $f : Q \to \mathbb{R}$ is a state-based weight distribution to quantify that states may be final states, and finally, the partial function $P : Q \times \Sigma^\star \times \Delta^\star \times Q \to \mathbb{R}$ defines a set of edges between pairs of states in such a way that every edge is labelled with an input string in $\Sigma^\star$, with an output string in $\Delta^\star$, and is assigned a transition weight.

When weights are probabilities, i.e. the range of functions f and P is constrained between 0 and 1, and under certain conditions, a weighted finite-state transducer may define probability distributions. Then, it is called a *stochastic finite-state transducer*.

4.1 WFSTs for SMT models

Here, we show how the SMT models described in Section 3 (that is, the five η scores in the PB translation table, the word penalty, and the n-gram language model) are represented by means of WFSTs.

First of all, the word penalty feature in Equation 8 is equivalently reformulated as another PB score, as in Equations 3 to 7:

$$h_6(\mathbf{s}, \mathbf{t}) = \log e^{|\mathbf{t}|} = \log \max_{\beta_6} \prod_{k=1}^{|\beta_6|} e^{|\tilde{\mathbf{t}}_k|} \quad (11)$$

where the length of $\mathbf{t}$ is split up by summation using the length of each phrase in a segmentation β_6. Actually, this feature is independent of β_6, that is, any segmentation produces the expected value $e^{|\mathbf{t}|}$, and therefore the maximization by β_6 is not needed. However, the main goal is to introduce this feature as another PB score similar to those in Features 1 to 5, and so it is redefined following the same framework. The PB table can be now extended by means of $\eta_6(\tilde{\mathbf{s}}, \tilde{\mathbf{t}}) = e^{|\tilde{\mathbf{t}}|}$, just as Table 3 shows.

Source	Target	η_1	η_2	η_3	η_4	η_5	η_6
barato	low cost			...		e	e^2
me gusta	I like			...		e	e^2
es decir	that is			...		e	e^2
por favor	please			...		e	e
...				...			

Table 3: A word-penalty-extended PB translation table. The exponent of e in η_6 is the number of words in Target.

Now, the translation table including 6 PB scores and the target-language backoff n-gram model can be expressed by means of (some stochastic) WFSTs.

Translation table

Each PB model included in the translation table, i.e. any PB distribution in $\{\eta_1(\tilde{\mathbf{s}}, \tilde{\mathbf{t}}), \ldots, \eta_6(\tilde{\mathbf{s}}, \tilde{\mathbf{t}})\}$, can be represented as a particular case of a WFST. Figure 1 shows a PB score encoded as a WFST, using a different looping transition per table row within a WFST of only one state.

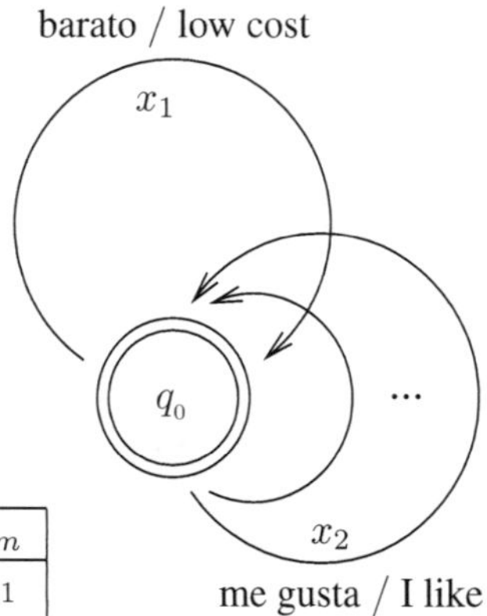

Source	Target	η_m
barato	low cost	x_1
me gusta	I like	x_2
...		...

Figure 1: Equivalent WFST representation of PB scores. Table rows are embedded within as many looping transitions of a WFST which has no topology at all; η-scores are correspondingly stored as transition weights.

It is straight-forward to see that the application of the Viterbi method (Viterbi, 1967) on these WFSTs provides the corresponding feature value $h_m(\mathbf{s}, \mathbf{t})$ for all Features 1 to 6 as defined in Equations 3 to 8.

Language model

It is well known that n-gram models are a subclass of stochastic finite-state automata where backoff can also be adequately incorporated (Llorens, 2000).

Then, they can be equivalently turned into transducers by means of the concept of identity, that is, transducers which map every input label to itself. Figure 2 shows a WFST for a backoff bigram model.

It is also quite straight-forward to see that $h_7(\mathbf{s}, \mathbf{t})$ (as defined in Equation 9 for a target n-gram model where backoff is adopted according to Equation 10) is also computed by means of a parsing algorithm, which is actually a process that is simple to carry out given that these backoff n-gram WFSTs are deterministic.

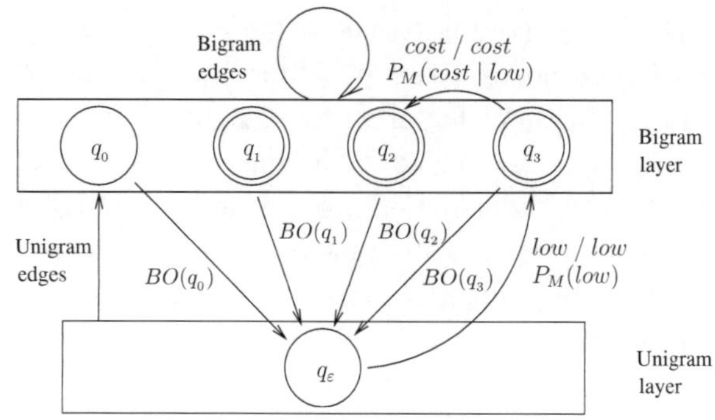

Figure 2: A WFST example for a backoff bigram model. Backoff (BO) is dealt with failure transitions from the bigram layer to the unigram layer. Unigrams go in the other direction and bigrams link states within the bigram layer.

To sum up, our log-linear combination scenario considers 7 (some stochastic) WFSTs, 1 per feature: 6 of them are PB models related to a translation table while the 7th one is a target-language n-gram model.

Next in Section 4.2, we show how these WFSTs are used in conjunction in a homogeneous framework.

4.2 Search

Equation 2 is a general framework for log-linear approaches to SMT. This framework is adopted here in order to combine several features based on WFSTs, which are modelled as their respective Viterbi score.

As already mentioned, the computation of $h_m(\mathbf{s}, \mathbf{t})$ for each PB-WFST, let us say $\mathcal{T}_m$ (with $1 \leq m \leq 6$), provides the most likely segmentation β_m for $\mathbf{s}$ and $\mathbf{t}$ according to $\mathcal{T}_m$. However, a constraint is used here so that all $\mathcal{T}_m$ models define the same segmentation β:

$$|\beta| > 0$$

$$\mathbf{s} = \tilde{\mathbf{s}}_1 \ldots \tilde{\mathbf{s}}_{|\beta|}$$

$$\mathbf{t} = \tilde{\mathbf{t}}_1 \ldots \tilde{\mathbf{t}}_{|\beta|}$$

where the PB scores corresponding to Features 1 to 6 are directly applied on that particular segmentation for each phrase pair $(\tilde{\mathbf{s}}_k, \tilde{\mathbf{t}}_k)$ monotonically aligned. Equations 3 to 7 and 11 can be simplified as follows:

$$\forall m = 1, \ldots, 6$$

$$h_m(\mathbf{s}, \mathbf{t}) = \log \max_{\beta} \prod_{k=1}^{|\beta|} \eta_m(\tilde{\mathbf{s}}_k, \tilde{\mathbf{t}}_k) \qquad (12)$$

Then, Equation 2 can be instanced as follows:

$$\begin{aligned}\hat{\mathbf{t}} &= \arg\max_{\mathbf{t}} \sum_{m=1}^{7} \lambda_m \, h_m(\mathbf{s}, \mathbf{t}) \qquad (13)\\ &= \arg\max_{\mathbf{t}} \left[\sum_{m=1}^{6} \lambda_m \max_{\beta} \sum_{k=1}^{|\beta|} \log \eta_m(\tilde{\mathbf{s}}_k, \tilde{\mathbf{t}}_k) \right] \\ &\quad + \lambda_7 \sum_{i=1}^{|\mathbf{t}|} \log P(\mathbf{t}_i | \mathbf{t}_{i-n+1} \dots \mathbf{t}_{i-1}) \\ &= \arg\max_{\mathbf{t}} \left[\max_{\beta} \sum_{k=1}^{|\beta|} \sum_{m=1}^{6} \lambda_m \log \eta_m(\tilde{\mathbf{s}}_k, \tilde{\mathbf{t}}_k) \right] \\ &\quad + \sum_{i=1}^{|\mathbf{t}|} \lambda_7 \log P(\mathbf{t}_i | \mathbf{t}_{i-n+1} \dots \mathbf{t}_{i-1})\end{aligned}$$

as logarithm rules are applied to Equations 9 and 12.

The square-bracketed expression of Equation 13 is a Viterbi-like score which can be incrementally built through the contribution of all the PB-WFSTs (along with their respective λ_m-weights) over some phrase pair $(\tilde{\mathbf{s}}_k, \tilde{\mathbf{t}}_k)$ that extends a partial hypothesis. As these models share their topology, we implement them jointly including as many scores per transition as needed (González and Casacuberta, 2008). These models can also be merged by means of union once their λ_m-weights are transferred into them. That allows us to model the whole translation table (see Table 3) by means of just 1 WFST structure $\mathcal{T}$. Therefore, the search framework for single models can also be used for their log-linear combination.

As regards the remaining term from Equation 13, i.e. the target n-gram language model for Feature 7, it is seen as a rescoring function (Och et al., 2004) which is applied once the PB-WFST $\mathcal{T}$ is explored. The translation model returns the best hypotheses that are later input to the n-gram language model $\mathcal{L}$, where they are reranked, to finally choose the best $\hat{\mathbf{t}}$.

However, these two steps can be processed at once if both the WFST $\mathcal{T}$ and the WFST $\mathcal{L}$ are merged by means of their composition $\mathcal{T} \circ \mathcal{L}$ (Mohri, 2004). The product of such an operation is another WFST as WFSTs are closed under a composition operation. In practice though, the size of $\mathcal{T} \circ \mathcal{L}$ can be very large so composition is done on-the-fly (Caseiro, 2003), which actually does not build the WFST for $\mathcal{T} \circ \mathcal{L}$ but explores both $\mathcal{T}$ and $\mathcal{L}$ as if they were composed, using the n-gram scores in $\mathcal{L}$ on the target hypotheses from $\mathcal{T}$ as soon as they are partially produced.

Equation 13 represents a Viterbi-based composition framework where all the (weighted) models contribute to the overall score to be maximized, provided that the set of λ_m-weights is instantiated. Using a development corpus, the set of λ_m-weights can be empirically determined by means of running several iterations of this framework, where different values for the λ_m-weights are tried in each iteration.

5 Experiments

Experiments were carried out on the TED corpus, which is described in depth throughout Section 5.1. Automatic evaluation for SMT is often considered and we use the measures enumerated in Section 5.2. Results are shown and also discussed, in Section 5.3.

5.1 Corpora data

The TED corpus is composed of a collection of English-French sentences from audiovisual content whose main statistics are displayed in Table 4.

	Subset	English	French
Train	Sentences	47.5K	
	Running words	747.2K	792.9K
	Vocabulary	24.6K	31.7K
Develop	Sentences	571	
	Running words	9.2K	10.3K
	Vocabulary	1.9K	2.2K
Test	Sentences	641	
	Running words	12.6K	12.8K
	Vocabulary	2.4K	2.7K

Table 4: Main statistics from the TED corpus and its split.

As shown in Table 4, develop and test partitions are statistically comparable. The former is used to train the λ_m-weights in the log-linear approach, in the hope that they can also work well for the latter.

5.2 Evaluation measures

Since its appearance as a translation quality measure, the BLEU metric (Papineni et al., 2002), which stands for *bilingual evaluation understudy*, has become consolidated in the area of automatic evaluation as the most widely used SMT measure. Nevertheless, it was later found that its correlation factor with subjective evaluations (the original reason for its success) is actually not so high as first thought (Callison-Burch et al., 2006). Anyway, it is still the most popular SMT measure in the literature.

However, the *word error rate* (WER) is a very common measure in the area of speech recognition which is also quite usually applied in SMT (Och et al., 1999). Although it is not so widely employed as BLEU, there exists some work that shows a better correlation of WER with human assessments (Paul et al., 2007). Of course, the WER measure has some bad reviews as well (Chen and Goodman, 1996; Wang et al., 2003) and one of the main criticisms that it receives in SMT areas is about the fact that there is only one translation reference to compare with. The MWER measure (Nießen et al., 2000) is an attempt to relax this dependence by means of an average error rate with respect to a set of multiple references of equivalent meaning, provided that they are available.

Another measure also based on the edit distance concept has recently arisen as an evolution of WER towards SMT. It is the *translation edit rate* (TER), and it has become popular because it takes into account the basic post-process operations that professional translators usually do during their daily work. Statistically, it is considered as a measure highly correlated with the result of one or more subjective evaluations (Snover et al., 2006).

The definition of these evaluation measures is as follows:

BLEU: It computes the precision of the unigrams, bigrams, trigrams, and fourgrams that appear in the hypotheses with respect to the n-grams of the same order that occur in the translation reference, with a penalty for too short sentences. Unlike the WER measure, BLEU is not an error rate but an accuracy measure.

WER: This measure computes the minimum number of editions (replacements, insertions or deletions) that are needed to turn the system hypothesis into the corresponding reference.

TER: It is computed similarly to WER, using an additional edit operation. TER allows the movement of phrases, besides replacements, insertions, and deletions.

5.3 Results

The goal of this section is to assess experimentally the finite-state approach to PB-SMT presented here. First, an English-to-French translation is considered, then a French-to-English direction is later evaluated.

On the one hand, our log-linear framework is tuned on the basis of BLEU as the only evaluation measure in order to select the best set of λ_m-weights. That is accomplished by means of development data, however, once the λ_m-weights are estimated, they are extrapolated to test data for the final evaluation. Table 5 shows: a) the BLEU translation results for the development data; and b) the BLEU, WER and TER results for the test data. In both a) and b), the λ_m-weights are trained on the development partition. These results are according to different feature combinations in our log-linear approach to PB-SMT.

As shown in Table 5, the first experimental scenario is not a log-linear framework since only one feature, (a direct PB translation probability model) is considered. The corresponding results are poor and, judging by the remaining results in Table 5, they reflect the need for a log-linear approach.

The following experiments in Table 5 represent a log-linear framework for Features 1 to 6, i.e. the PB translation table encoded as a WFST $\mathcal{T}$, where different PB models are the focus of attention. Only the log-linear combination of Features 1 and 2

Log-linear features	Develop BLEU	Test BLEU	Test WER	Test TER
1 (baseline)	8.5	7.1	102.9	101.5
1+2	4.0	3.0	116.6	115.6
1+2+3	22.7	18.4	66.6	64.4
1+2+3+4	22.8	18.5	66.3	64.2
1+2+3+4+5	22.7	18.8	65.2	63.2
1+2+3+4+5+6	23.1	19.1	65.9	63.8
1+7	24.6	20.5	65.1	62.9
1+2+7	25.5	21.3	63.7	61.6
1+2+3+7	25.9	**22.2**	**62.5**	**60.4**
1+2+3+4+7	26.3	22.0	63.4	61.3
1+2+3+4+5+7	26.4	22.1	63.1	61.0
1+2+3+4+5+6+7	27.0	21.8	64.4	62.2
Moses (1+...+7)	27.1	22.0	64.0	61.8

Table 5: English-to-French results for development and test data according to different log-linear scenarios. The set of λ_m-weights is learnt from development data for every feature combination log-linear scenario defined.

is worse than the baseline, which feeds us back on the fact that the λ_m-weights can be better trained, that is, the log-linear model for Features 1 and 2 can be upgraded until baseline's results with $\lambda_2 = 0$.

This battery of experiments on Features 1 to 6 allows us to see the benefits of a log-linear approach. The baseline results are clearly outperformed now, and we can say that the more features are included, the better are the results.

The next block of experiments in Table 5 always include Feature 7, i.e. the target language model $\mathcal{L}$. Features 1 to 6 are progressively introduced into $\mathcal{T}$. These results confirm that the target language model is still an important feature to take into account, even though PB models are already providing a surrounding context for their translation hypotheses because translation itself is modelled at phrase level. These results are significantly better than the ones where the target language model is not considered. Again, the more translation features are included, the better are the results on the development data. However, an overtraining is presumedly occurring with regard to the optimization of the λ_m-weights, as results on the test partition do not reach their top the same way the ones for the development data do, i.e. when using all 7 features, but when combining Features 1, 2, 3, and 7, instead. These differences are not statistically significant though.

Finally, our finite-state approach to PB-SMT is validated by comparison, as it allows us to achieve similar results to those yielded by Moses itself.

On the other hand, a translation direction where French is translated into English gets now the focus. Their corresponding results are presented in Table 6. A similar behaviour can be observed in Table 6 for the series of French-to-English empirical results.

6 Conclusions and future work

In this paper, a finite-state approach to Moses, which is a PB-SMT state-of-the-art system, is presented. A monotone framework is adopted, where 7 models in log-linear combination are considered: a direct and an inverse PB translation probability model, a direct and an inverse PB lexical weighting model, PB and word penalties, and a target language model.

Five out of these models are based on PB scores which are organized under a PB translation table.

Log-linear features	Develop BLEU	Test BLEU	Test WER	Test TER
1 (baseline)	7.1	7.4	101.6	100.0
1+2	4.1	3.5	117.5	116.0
1+2+3	24.2	21.1	58.9	56.5
1+2+3+4	24.4	20.8	58.0	55.7
1+2+3+4+5	24.9	21.2	56.9	54.8
1+2+3+4+5+6	25.2	21.2	57.1	55.0
1+7	24.7	22.5	60.0	57.7
1+2+7	26.0	23.2	58.8	56.5
1+2+3+7	28.5	23.0	56.1	54.0
1+2+3+4+7	28.4	23.1	56.0	53.8
1+2+3+4+5+7	28.8	23.4	56.0	53.9
1+2+3+4+5+6+7	28.7	**23.8**	**55.8**	**53.7**
Moses (1+...+7)	28.9	23.5	55.8	53.6

Table 6: French-to-English results for development and test data according to different log-linear scenarios.

These models can also be implemented by means of WFSTs on the basis of the Viterbi algorithm. The word penalty can also be equivalently redefined as another PB model, similar to the five others, which allows us to constitute a translation model $\mathcal{T}$ composed of six parallel WFSTs that are constrained to share the same monotonic bilingual segmentation.

A backoff n-gram model for the target language $\mathcal{L}$ can be represented as an identity WFST where $P(\mathbf{t})$ is modelled on the basis of the Viterbi algorithm. The whole log-linear approach to Moses is attained by means of the on-the-fly WFST composition $\mathcal{T} \circ \mathcal{L}$.

Our finite-state log-linear approach to PB-SMT is validated by comparison, as it has allowed us to achieve similar results to those yielded by Moses.

Monotonicity is an evident limitation of this work, as Moses can also feature some limited reordering. However, future work on that line is straight-forward since the framework described in this paper can be easily extended to include a PB reordering model $\mathcal{R}$, by means of the on-the-fly composition $\mathcal{T} \circ \mathcal{R} \circ \mathcal{L}$.

Acknowledgments

The research leading to these results has received funding from the European Union 7th Framework Programme (FP7/2007-2013) under grant agreement no. 287576. Work also supported by the EC (FEDER, FSE), the Spanish government (MICINN, MITyC, "Plan E", grants MIPRCV "Consolider Ingenio 2010" and iTrans2 TIN2009-14511), and the Generalitat Valenciana (grant Prometeo/2009/014).

References

P.F. Brown, S.A. Della Pietra, V.J. Della Pietra, and R.L. Mercer. 1993. The mathematics of machine translation. In *Computational Linguistics*, volume 19, pages 263–311, June.

C. Callison-Burch, M. Osborne, and P. Koehn. 2006. Re-evaluating the Role of Bleu in Machine Translation Research. In *Proceedings of the 11th conference of the European Chapter of the Association for Computational Linguistics*, pages 249–256.

D. Caseiro. 2003. *Finite-State Methods in Automatic Speech Recognition.* PhD Thesis, Instituto Superior Técnico, Universidade Técnica de Lisboa.

S. F. Chen and J. Goodman. 1996. An empirical study of smoothing techniques for language modeling. In *Proceedings of the 34th annual meeting of the Association for Computational Linguistics*, pages 310–318.

J. González and F. Casacuberta. 2008. A finite-state framework for log-linear models in machine translation. In *Proc. of European Association for Machine Translation*, pages 41–46.

P. Koehn, H. Hoang, A. Birch, C. Callison-Burch, M. Federico, N. Bertoldi, B. Cowan, W. Shen, C. Moran, R. Zens, C. Dyer, O. Bojar, A. Constantin, and E. Herbst. 2007. Moses: open source toolkit for statistical machine translation. In *Proc. of Association for Computational Linguistics*, pages 177–180.

S. Kumar, Y. Deng, and W. Byrne. 2006. A weighted finite state transducer translation template model for statistical machine translation. *Natural Language Engineering*, 12(1):35–75.

David Llorens. 2000. *Suavizado de autómatas y traductores finitos estocásticos.* PhD Thesis, Departamento de Sistemas Informáticos y Computación, Universidad Politécnica de Valencia.

D. Marcu and W. Wong. 2002. A phrase-based, joint probability model for statistical machine translation. In *Proc. of Empirical methods in natural language processing*, pages 133–139.

Mehryar Mohri, Fernando Pereira, and Michael Riley. 2002. Weighted finite-state transducers in speech recognition. *Computer Speech and Language*, 16(1):69–88.

Mehryar Mohri. 2004. Weighted finite-state transducer algorithms: An overview. *Formal Languages and Applications*, 148:551–564.

S. Nießen, F. J. Och, G. Leusch, and H. Ney. 2000. An evaluation tool for machine translation: Fast evaluation for MT research. In *Proceedings of the 2nd international Conference on Language Resources and Evaluation*, pages 39–45.

F.J. Och and H. Ney. 2002. Discriminative training and maximum entropy models for statistical machine translation. In *Proc. of Association for Computational Linguistics*, pages 295–302.

F.J. Och and H. Ney. 2003. A systematic comparison of various statistical alignment models. *Computational Linguistics*, 29:19–51, March.

F. J. Och, C. Tillmann, and H. Ney. 1999. Improved alignment models for statistical machine translation. In *Proceedings of the joint conference on Empirical Methods in Natural Language Processing and the 37th annual meeting of the Association for Computational Linguistics*, pages 20–28.

F.J. Och, D. Gildea, S. Khudanpur, A. Sarkar, K. Yamada, A. Fraser, S. Kumar, L. Shen, D. Smith, K. Eng, V. Jain, Z. Jin, and D. Radev. 2004. A smorgasbord of features for statistical machine translation. In D. Marcu S. Dumais and S. Roukos, editors, *HLT-NAACL 2004: Main Proceedings*, pages 161–168, Boston, Massachusetts, USA, May 2 - May 7. Association for Computational Linguistics.

Kishore Papineni, Salim Roukos, Todd Ward, and Wei-Jing Zhu. 2002. Bleu: a method for automatic evaluation of machine translation. In *Proceedings of the 40th annual meeting of the Association for Computational Linguistics*, pages 311–318.

M. Paul, A. Finch, and E. Sumita. 2007. Reducing human assessment of machine translation quality to binary classifiers. In *Proceedings of the conference on Theoretical and Methodological Issues in machine translation*, pages 154–162.

R. Rosenfeld. 1996. A maximum entropy approach to adaptative statistical language modeling. *Computer Speech and Language*, 10:187–228.

Matthew Snover, Bonnie Dorr, Richard Schwartz, Linnea Micciulla, and John Makhoul. 2006. A study of translation edit rate with targeted human annotation. In *Proceedings of the 7th biennial conference of the Association for Machine Translation in the Americas*, pages 223–231.

J. Tomas and F. Casacuberta. 2001. Monotone statistical translation using word groups. In *Proc. of the Machine Translation Summit*, pages 357–361.

A. Viterbi. 1967. Error bounds for convolutional codes and an asymptotically optimum decoding algorithm. *IEEE Transactions on Information Theory*, 13(2):260–269.

Y. Wang, A. Acero, and C. Chelba. 2003. Is word error rate a good indicator for spoken language understanding accuracy. In *Proceedings of the IEEE workshop on Automatic Speech Recognition and Understanding*, pages 577–582.

Richard Zens, Franz Josef Och, and Hermann Ney. 2002. Phrase-based statistical machine translation. In *Proc. of Advances in Artificial Intelligence*, pages 18–32.

Finite-state acoustic and translation model composition in statistical speech translation: empirical assessment

Alicia Pérez[(1)], **M. Inés Torres**[(2)]
[(1)]Dep. Computer Languages and Systems
[(2)]Dep. Electricidad y Electrónica
University of the Basque Country UPV/EHU
Bilbao (Spain)
[(1)]alicia.perez@ehu.es
[(2)]manes.torres@ehu.es

Francisco Casacuberta
Instituto Tecnológico de Informática
Universidad Politécnica de Valencia
Valencia (Spain)
fcn@iti.upv.es

Abstract

Speech translation can be tackled by means of the so-called decoupled approach: a speech recognition system followed by a text translation system. The major drawback of this two-pass decoding approach lies in the fact that the translation system has to cope with the errors derived from the speech recognition system. There is hardly any cooperation between the acoustic and the translation knowledge sources. There is a line of research focusing on alternatives to implement speech translation efficiently: ranging from semi-decoupled to tightly integrated approaches. The goal of integration is to make acoustic and translation models cooperate in the underlying decision problem. That is, the translation is built by virtue of the joint action of both models. As a side-advantage of the integrated approaches, the translation is obtained in a single-pass decoding strategy. The aim of this paper is to assess the quality of the hypotheses explored within different speech translation approaches. Evidence of the performance is given through experimental results on a limited-domain task.

1 Introduction

Statistical speech translation (SST) was typically implemented as a pair of consecutive steps in the so-called *decoupled approach*: with an automatic speech recognition (ASR) system placed before to a text-to-text translation system. This approach involves two independent decision processes: first, getting the most likely string in the source language and next, getting the expected translation into the target language. Since the ASR system is not an ideal device it might make mistakes. Hence, the text translation system would have to manage with the transcription errors. Being the translation models (TMs) trained with positive samples of well-formed source strings, they are very sensitive to ill-formed strings in the source language. Hence, it seems ambitious for TMs to aspire to cope with both well and ill formed sentences in the source language.

1.1 Related work

Regarding the coupling of acoustic and translation models, there are some contributions in the literature that propose the use of semi-decoupled approaches. On the one hand, in (Zhang et al., 2004), SST is carried out by

Proceedings of the 10th International Workshop on Finite State Methods and Natural Language Processing, pages 99–107,
Donostia–San Sebastián, July 23–25, 2012.

an ASR placed before a TM with an additional stage that would re-score the obtained hypotheses within a log-linear framework gathering features from both the ASR system (lexicon and language model) and the TM (eg. distortion, fertility) and also additional features (POS, length etc.).

On the other hand, in (Quan et al., 2005), the N-best hypotheses derived from an ASR system were next translated by a TM, finally, a last stage would re-score the hypotheses and make a choice. Within the list of the N-best hypotheses typically a number of them include some n-grams that are identical, hence, the list results to be an inefficient means of storing data. Alternatively, in (Zhou et al., 2007) the search space extracted from the ASR system, represented as a word-graph (WG), was next explored by a TM following a multilayer search algorithm.

Still, a further approach can be assumed in order to make the graph-decoding computationally cheaper, that is, confusion networks (Bertoldi et al., 2007). Confusion-networks implement a linear approach of the word-graphs, however, as a result, dummy hypotheses might be introduced and probabilities mis-computed. Confusion networks traded off between the accuracy and storage ability of word-graphs for decoding time. Indeed, in (Matusov and Ney, 2011) an efficient means of doing the decoding with confusion networks was presented. Note that these approaches follow a two-pass decoding strategy.

The aforementioned approaches implemented phrase-based TMs within a log-linear framework. In this context, in (Casacuberta et al., 2008) a fully integrated approach was examined. Under this approach, the translation was carried out in a single-pass decoding, involving a single decision process in which acoustic and translations models cooperated. This integration paradigm, was earlier proposed in (Vidal, 1997), showing that a single-pass decoding was enough to carry out SST.

Finally, in (Pérez et al., 2010) several SST decoding approaches including decoupled, N-best lists and integrated were compared. Nevertheless, the paper focused on the potential scope of the approaches, comparing the theoretical upper threshold of their performance.

1.2 Contribution

All the models assessed in this work relay upon exactly the same acoustic and translation models. It is the combination of them on which we are focusing. In brief, the aim of this paper is to compare different approaches to carry out speech translation decoding. The comparison is carried out using exactly the same underlying acoustic and translation models in order to allow to make a fair comparison of the abilities inherent to the decoding strategy. Apart from the decoupled and semi-decoupled strategies we also focus on the fully-integrated approach. While the fully integrated approach allows to provide the most-likely hypothesis, we explored a variant: an integrated architecture with a re-scoring LM that provided alternatives derived from the integrated approach and used re-scoring to make the final decision. Not only an oracle-evaluation is provided as an upper-threshold of the experiments but also an experimental set-up to give empirical evidence.

The paper is arranged as follows: Section 2 introduces the formulation of statistical speech translation (SST); Section 3 describes different approaches to put into practice SST, placing emphasis on the assumptions behind each of them. Section 4 is devoted to assess experimentally the performance of each approach. Finally, in Section 5 the concussions drawn from the experiments are summarized.

2 Statistical speech translation

The goal of speech translation, formulated under the probabilistic framework, is to find the most likely string in the target language ($\widehat{\mathbf{t}}$) given the spoken utterance in the source language. Speech signal in the source language is characterized in terms of an array of acoustic features in the source language, $\mathbf{x}$. The decision problem involved is formulated as follows:

$$\widehat{\mathbf{t}} = \arg\max_{\mathbf{t}} P(\mathbf{t}|\mathbf{x}) \quad (1)$$

In this context, the text transcription in the source language (denoted as $\mathbf{s}$) is introduced as a hidden variable and Bayes' rule applied:

$$\widehat{\mathbf{t}} = \arg\max_{\mathbf{t}} \sum_{\mathbf{s}} P(\mathbf{x}|\mathbf{s},\mathbf{t})P(\mathbf{s},\mathbf{t}) \quad (2)$$

Assuming $P(\mathbf{x}|\mathbf{s},\mathbf{t}) \approx P(\mathbf{x}|\mathbf{s})$, and using the maximum term involved in the sum as an approach to the sum itself for the sake of computational affordability, we yield to:

$$\widehat{\mathbf{t}} \approx \arg\max_{\mathbf{t}} \max_{\mathbf{s}} P(\mathbf{x}|\mathbf{s})P(\mathbf{s},\mathbf{t}) \quad (3)$$

As a result, the expected translation is built relying upon both a translation model ($P(\mathbf{s},\mathbf{t})$) and an acoustic model in the source language ($P(\mathbf{x}|\mathbf{s})$). This approach requires the joint cooperation of both models to implement the decision problem since the maximum over $\mathbf{s}$ concerns both of them.

2.1 Involved models

Being the goal of this paper to compare different techniques to combine acoustic and translation models, it is important to keep constant the underlying models while varying the strategies to combine them. Before to delve into the composition strategies and due to the fact that some combination strategies are based on the finite-state topology of the models, a summary of the relevant features of the underlying models is given in this section.

2.1.1 Translation model

The translation model used in this work to tackle all the approaches consists of a stochastic finite-state transducer (SFST) encompassing phrases in the source and target languages together with a probability of joint occurrence. The SFST ($\mathcal{T}$) is a tuple $\mathcal{T} = \langle \Sigma, \Delta, Q, q_0, R, F, P\rangle$, where:

Σ is a finite set of input symbols;

Δ is a finite set of output symbols;

Q is a finite set of states;

$q_0 \in Q$ is the initial state;

$R \subseteq Q \times \Sigma^+ \times \Delta^* \times Q$ is a set of transitions. $(q, \tilde{s}, \tilde{t}, q') \in R$, represents a transition from the state $q \in Q$ to the state $q' \in Q$, with the source phrase $\tilde{s} \in \Sigma^+$ and producing the substring $\tilde{t} \in \Delta^*$, where $\tilde{t}$ might consist of zero or more target words ($|\tilde{t}| \geq 0$);

$F : Q \rightarrow [0, 1]$ is a final state probability;

$P : R \rightarrow [0, 1]$ is a transition probability;

Subject to the stochastic constraint:

$$\forall q \in Q \quad F(q) + \sum_{\tilde{s},\tilde{t},q'} P(q, \tilde{s}, \tilde{t}, q') = 1 \quad (4)$$

For further reading on formulation and properties of these machines turn to (Vidal et al., 2005).

The SFST can be understood as a statistical bi-language implemented by means of finite-state regular grammar (Casacuberta and Vidal, 2004) (in the same way as a stochastic finite-state automaton can be used to model a single language): $\mathcal{A} = \langle \Gamma, Q, q_0, R, F, P\rangle$, being $\Gamma \subseteq \Sigma^+ \times \Delta^*$ a finite-set of bilingual-phrases. Likewise, bilingual n-gram models can be inferred in practice (Mariño et al., 2006).

2.1.2 Acoustic models

The acoustic model consists of a mapping of text-transcriptions of lexical units in the source language and their acoustic representation. That comprises the composition of: 1) a lexical model consisting of a mapping between the textual representation with their phone-like representation in terms of a left-to-right sequence; and 2) an inventory of phone-like units consists of a typical three-state hidden Markov model (Rabiner, 1989). Thus, acoustic model lays on the composition of two finite-state models (depicted in Figure 1).

(a) Phonetic representation of a text lexical unit

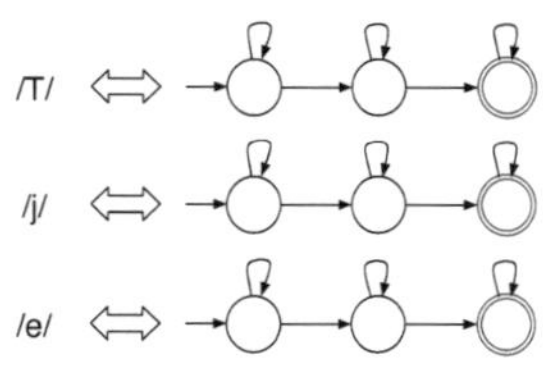

(b) HMM phone-like units

Figure 1: Acoustic model requires composing phone-like units within phonetic representation of lexical units.

3 Decoding strategies

In the previous section the formulation of SST was summarized. Let us now turn into practice and show the different strategies explored to combine acoustic and translation models to tackle SST. The approaches accounted are: decoupled, semi-decoupled and integrated architectures. While the former two are implementable by virtue of alternative TMs, the latter is achieved thanks to the integration allowed by finite-state framework. Thus, in order to compare the combination rather than the TMs themselves, all of the combinations shall be put in practice using the same SFST as TM.

3.1 Decoupled approach

Possibly the most widely used approach to tackle speech translation is the so-called serial, cascade or decoupled approach. It consists of a text-to-text translation system placed after an ASR system. This process is formally stated as:

$$\widehat{\mathbf{t}} \approx \arg\max_{\mathbf{t}} \max_{\mathbf{s}} P(\mathbf{x}|\mathbf{s})P(\mathbf{s})P(\mathbf{t}|\mathbf{s}) \quad (5)$$

In practice, previous expression is implemented in two independent stages as follows:

1st stage: an ASR system would find the most likely transcription ($\hat{\mathbf{s}}$):

$$\hat{\mathbf{s}} \approx \arg\max_{\mathbf{s}} P(\mathbf{x}|\mathbf{s})P(\mathbf{s}) \quad (6)$$

2nd stage next, given the expected string in the source language ($\hat{\mathbf{s}}$), a TM would find the most likely translation:

$$\hat{\mathbf{t}} \approx \arg\max_{\mathbf{t}} P(\mathbf{t}|\hat{\mathbf{s}}) = \arg\max_{\mathbf{t}} P(\hat{\mathbf{s}}, \mathbf{t}) \quad (7)$$

The TM involved in eq.(7) can be based on either posterior or joint-probability as the difference between both of them is a normalization term that does not intervene in the maximization process. The second stage has to cope with expected transcription of speech ($\hat{\mathbf{s}}$) which does not necessarily convey the exact reference source string ($\mathbf{s}$). That is, the ASR might introduce errors in the source string to be translated in the next stage. However, the TMs are typically trained with correct source-target pairs. Thus, transcription errors are seldom foreseen even in models including smoothing (Martin et al., 1999). In addition, TMs are extremely sensitive to the errors in the input, in particular to substitutions (Vilar et al., 2006).

This architecture represents a suboptimal means of contending with SST as referred in eq. (3). This approach barely takes advantage of the involved knowledge sources, namely, acoustic and translation models.

3.2 Semi-Decoupled approach

Occasionally, the most probable translation does not result to be the most accurate one with respect to a given reference. That is, it might happen that hypotheses with a slightly lower probability than that of the expected hypothesis turn to be more similar to the reference than the expected hypothesis. This happens due to several factors, amongst others, due to the sparsity of the data with which the model was trained.

In brief, some sort of disparity between the probability of the hypotheses and their quality might arise in practice. The semi-decoupled approach arose to address this issue. Hence, rather than translating a single transcription hypothesis, a number of them are provided by the ASR to the TM, and it is the latter that makes the decision giving as a result the most likely translation. The decoupled approach is implemented in two steps, and so is it the semi-decoupled approach. Details on the process are as follows:

1st stage: for a given utterance in the source language, an ASR system, laying on source acoustic model and source language model (LM), would provide a search sub-space. This sub-space is traced in the search process for the most likely transcription of speech but without getting rid of other highly probable hypotheses.

For what us concern, this sub-space is represented in terms of a graph of words in the source language ($\mathcal{S}$). The word-graph gathers the hypotheses with a probability within a threshold with respect to the optimal hypothesis at each time-frame as it was formulated in (Ney et al., 1997). The obtained graph is an acyclic directed graph where the nodes are associated with word-prefixes of a variable length, and the edges join the word sequences allowed in the recognition process with an associated recognition probability. The edges consist of the acoustic and language model probabilities as the ASR system handles throughout the trellis.

2nd stage: translating the hypotheses within $\mathcal{S}$ (the graph derived in the 1st stage) allows to take into account alternative translations for the given spoken utterance. The searching space being explored is limited by the source strings conveyed by $\mathcal{S}$. The combination of the recognition probability with the translation probability results in a score that accounts both recognition and translation likelihood:

$$\hat{\mathbf{t}} \approx \arg\max_{\mathbf{t}} \max_{\mathbf{s}\in\mathcal{S}} P(\mathbf{s})P(\mathbf{s},\mathbf{t}) \quad (8)$$

Thus, acoustic and translation models would one re-score the other.

All in all, this semi-decoupled approach results in an extension of the decoupled one. It accounts alternative transcriptions of speech in an attempt to get good quality transcriptions (rather than the most probable transcription as in the case of the decoupled approach). Amongst all the transcriptions, those with high quality are expected to provide the best quality in the target language. That is, by avoiding errors derived from the transcription process, the TM should perform better, and thus get translations of higher quality. Note that finally, a single translation hypothesis is selected. To do so, the highest combined probability is accounted.

3.3 Fully-integrated approach

Finite-state framework (by contrast to other frameworks) makes a tight composition of models possible. In our case, of acoustic and translation finite-state models. The fully-integrated approach, proposed in (Vidal, 1997), encfompassed acoustic and translation models within a single model. To develop the fully-integrated approach a finite-state acoustic model on the source language ($\mathcal{A}$) providing the text transcription of a given acoustic utterance ($\mathcal{A}$:

$X \rightarrow S$) can be composed with a text translation model ($\mathcal{T}$) that provides the translation of a given text in the source language ($\mathcal{T} : S \rightarrow T$) and give as a result a transducer ($\mathcal{Z} = \mathcal{A} \circ \mathcal{T}$) that would render acoustic utterances in the source language to strings in the target language. For the sake of efficiency in terms of spatial cost, the models are integrated on-the-fly in the same manner as it is done in ASR (Caseiro and Trancoso, 2006).

The way in which integrated architecture approaches eq. (3) is looking for the most-likely source-target translation pair as follows:

$$\widehat{(\mathbf{s}, \mathbf{t})} = \arg \max_{(\mathbf{s},\mathbf{t})} P(\mathbf{s}, \mathbf{t}) P(\mathbf{x}|\mathbf{s}) \quad (9)$$

That is, the search is driven by bilingual phrases made up of acoustic elements in the source language integrated within bilingual phrases of words together with target phrases.

Then, the expected translation would simply be approached as the target projection of $\widehat{(\mathbf{s}, \mathbf{t})}$, the expected source-target string (also known as the lower projection); and likewise, the expected transcription is obtained as a side-result by the source projection (aka upper projection).

It is well-worth mentioning that this approach implements fairly the eq. (3) without further assumptions rather than those made in the decoding stage such as Viterbi-like decoding with beam-search. All in all, acoustic and translation models cooperate to find the expected translation. Moreover, it is carried out in a single-pass decoding strategy by contrast to either decoupled or semi-decoupled approaches.

3.4 Integrated WG and re-scoring LM

The fully-integrated approach looks for the single-best hypothesis within the integrated acoustic-and-translation network. Following the reasoning of Section 3.2, the most likely path together with other locally close paths in the integrated searching space can be extracted and arranged in terms of a word graph. While the WG derived in Section 3.2 was in source language, this one would be bilingual.

Given a bilingual WG, the lower-side net ($WG.l$) can be extracted keeping the topology and the associated probability distributions while getting rid of the input string of each transition, this gives as a result the projection of the WG in the target language. Next, a target language model (LM) would help to make the choice for the most likely hypothesis amongst those in the $WG.l$.

$$\hat{\mathbf{t}} \approx \arg \max_{\mathbf{t}} P_{WG.l}(\mathbf{t}) P_{LM}(\mathbf{t}) \quad (10)$$

In other words, while in Section 3.2 the translation model was used to re-score alternative transcriptions of speech whereas in this approach a target language models re-scores alternative translations provided by the bilingual WG. Note that this approach, as well as the semi-decoupled one, entail a two-pass decoding strategy. Both rely upon two models: the former focused on the source language WG, this one focuses on the target language WG.

4 Experiments

The aim of this section is to assess empirically the performance each of the four approaches previously introduced: decoupled, semi-decoupled, fully-integrated and integrated WG with re-scoring LM. The four approaches differ on the decoding strategy implemented to sort out the decision problem, but all of them rely on the very same knowledge sources (that is, the same acoustic and translation model).

The main features of the corpus used to carry out the experimental layout are summarized in Table 1. The training set was used to infer the

TM consisting of an SFST and the test set to assess the SST decoding approaches. The test set consisted of 500 training-independent pairs different each other, each of them was uttered by at least 3 speakers.

		Spanish	Basque
Train	Sentences	15,000	
	Running words	191,000	187,000
	Vocabulary	702	1,135
Test	Sentences	1,800	
	Hours of speech	3.0	3.5

Table 1: Main features of the Meteus corpus.

The performance of each experiment is assessed through well-known evaluation metrics, namely: bilingual evaluation under-study (BLEU) (Papineni et al., 2002), word error-rate (WER), translation edit rate (TER).

4.1 Results

The obtained results are given in Table 2. The performance of the most-likely or single-best translation derived by either decoupled or fully-integrated architectures is shown in the first row of Tables 2a and 2b respectively. The performance of the semi-decoupled and integrated WG with re-scoring LM is shown in the second row. The highest performance achievable by both the semi decoupled approach and the integrated WG with re-scoring LM is given in the third row. To do so, an oracle evaluation of the alternatives was carried out and the score associated to the best choice achievable was given as in (Pérez et al., 2010). Since the oracle evaluation provides an upper threshold of the quality achievable, the scope of each decoupled or integrated approaches can be assessed regardless of the underlying decoding algorithms and approaches. The highest performance achievable is reflected in the last row of Tables 2a and 2b.

4.2 Discussion

While the results with two-pass decoding strategies (either decoupled or semi-decoupled approach) require an ASR engine, integrated approaches have the ability to get both the source string together with its translation. This is why we have make a distinction between ASR-WER in the former and source-WER in the latter. Nevertheless, our aim focuses on translation rather than on recognition.

The results show that semi-decoupled approach outperforms the decoupled one. Similarly, the approach based on the integrated WG with the re-scoring target LM outperforms the integrated approach. As a result, exploring different hypotheses and making the selection with a second model allows to make refined decisions. On the other hand, comparing the first row of the Table 2a with the first row of the Table 2b (or equally the second row of the former with the second row of the latter), we conclude that slightly better performance can be obtained with the integrated approach.

Finally, comparing the third row of both Table 2a and Table 2b, the conclusion is that the eventual quality of the hypotheses within the integrated approach are significantly better than those in the semi-decoupled approaches. That is, what we can learn is that the integrated decoding strategy keeps much better hypotheses than the semi-decoupled one throughout the decoding process. Still, while good quality hypotheses exist within the integrated approach, the re-scoring with a target LM used to select a single hypothesis from the entire network has not resulted in getting the best possible hypothesis. Oracle evaluation shows that the integrated approach offers a leeway to achieve improvements in the quality, yet, alternative strategies have to be explored.

	ASR WER	target BLEU	target WER	target TER
D 1-best	7.9	40.8	50.3	47.7
SD	7.9	42.2	47.6	44.7
SD tgt-oracle	7.5	57.6	36.2	32.8

(a) Decoupled and semi-decoupled

	source WER	target BLEU	target WER	target TER
I 1-best	9.6	40.9	49.6	46.8
I WG + LM	9.3	42.6	46.7	43.9
I tgt-oracle	6.6	64.0	32.2	28.5

(b) Integrated and integrated WG with LM

Table 2: Assessment of SST approaches decoupled (2a) and integrated (2b) respectively.

5 Conclusions

Different approaches to cope with the SST decoding methodology were explored, namely, decoupled approach, semi-decoupled approach, fully-integrated approach and integrated approach with a re-scoring LM. The first two follow a two-pass decoding strategy and focus on exploring alternatives in the source language; while the integrated one follows a single-pass decoding and present tight cooperation between acoustic and translation models.

All the experimental layouts used exactly the same translation and acoustic models differing only on the methodology used to overcome the decision problem. In this way, we can assert that the differences lay on the decoding strategies rather than on the models themselves. Note that implementing all the models in terms of finite-state models allows to build both decoupled and integrated approaches.

Both decoupled and integrated decoding approaches aim at finding the most-likely translation under different assumptions. Occasionally, the most probable translation does not result to be the most accurate one with respect to a given reference. On account of this, we turned to analyzing alternatives and making use of re-scoring techniques on both approaches in an attempt to make the most accurate hypothesis emerge. This resulted in semi-decoupled and integrated-WG with re-scoring target LM approaches.

What we can learn from the experiments is that integrating the models allow to keep good quality hypotheses in the decoding process. Nevertheless, the re-scoring model has not resulted in being able to make the most of the integrated approach. In other words, there are better quality hypotheses within the word-graph rather than that selected by the re-scoring target LM. Hence, further work should be focused on other means of selecting hypotheses from the integrated word-graph.

However, undoubtedly significantly better performance can be reached from the integrated decoding strategy than from the semi-decoupled one. It seems as though knowledge sources modeling the syntactic differences between source and target languages should be tackled in order to improve the performance, particularly in our case, a strategy for further work could go on the line of the recently tackled approach (Durrani et al., 2011).

Acknowledgments

This work was partially funded by the Spanish Ministry of Science and Innovation: through the *Tímpano* (TIN2011-28169-C05-04) and *iTrans2* (TIN2009-14511) projects; also through *MIPRCV* (CSD2007-00018) project within the Consolider-Ingenio 2010 program; by the Basque Government to PR&ST research group (GIC10/158, IT375-10), and by the Generalitat Valenciana under grants *ALMPR* (Prometeo/2009/01) and GV/2010/067.

References

[Bertoldi et al.2007] N. Bertoldi, R. Zens, and M. Federico. 2008. Efficient speech translation by confusion network decoding. *IEEE International Conference on Acoustics, Speech and Signal Processing*, pg. 1696–1705

[Casacuberta and Vidal2004] F. Casacuberta and E. Vidal. 2004. Machine translation with inferred stochastic finite-state transducers. *Computational Linguistics*, 30(2): pg. 205–225.

[Casacuberta et al.2008] F. Casacuberta, M. Federico, H. Ney, and E. Vidal. 2008. Recent efforts in spoken language translation. *IEEE Signal Processing Magazine*, 25(3): pg. 80–88.

[Caseiro and Trancoso2006] D. Caseiro and I. Trancoso. 2006. A specialized on-the-fly algorithm for lexicon and language model composition. *IEEE Transactions on Audio, Speech & Language Processing*, 14(4): pg. 1281–1291.

[Durrani et al.2011] N. Durrani, H. Schmid, and A. Fraser. 2011. A joint sequence translation model with integrated reordering. In *49th Annual Meeting of the Association for Computational Linguistics: Human Language Technologies*, pg. 1045–1054

[Mariño et al.2006] J. B. Mariño, R. E. Banchs, J. M. Crego, A. de Gispert, P. Lambert, J. A. R. Fonollosa, and M. R. Costa-jussà. 2006. N-gram-based machine translation. *Computational Linguistics*, 32(4): pg. 527–549

[Martin et al.1999] S. C. Martin, H. Ney, and J. Zaplo. 1999. Smoothing methods in maximum entropy language modeling. *IEEE International Conference on Acoustics, Speech, and Signal Processing* , vol. 1, pg. 545–548

[Matusov and Ney2011] E. Matusov and H. Ney. 2011. Lattice-based ASR-MT interface for speech translation. *IEEE Transactions on Audio, Speech, and Language Processing*, 19(4): pg. 721 –732

[Ney et al.1997] H. Ney, S. Ortmanns, and I. Lindam. 1997. Extensions to the word graph method for large vocabulary continuous speech recognition. *IEEE International Conference on Acoustics, Speech, and Signal Processing*, vol. 3, pg. 1791 –1794

[Papineni et al.2002] K. Papineni, S. Roukos, T. Ward, and W.-J. Zhu. 2002. Bleu: a method for automatic evaluation of machine translation. *Annual Meeting on Association for Computational Linguistics*, pg. 311–318

[Pérez et al.2010] A. Pérez, M. I. Torres, and F. Casacuberta. 2010. Potential scope of a fully-integrated architecture for speech translation. *Annual Conference of the European Association for Machine Translation*, pg. 1–8

[Quan et al.2005] V. H. Quan, M. Federico, and M. Cettolo. 2005. Integrated n-best re-ranking for spoken language translation. *European Converence on Speech Communication and Technology, Interspeech*, pg. 3181–3184.

[Rabiner1989] L.R. Rabiner. 1989. A tutorial on hidden markov models and selected applications in speech recognition. *Proceedings of the IEEE*, 77(2): pg. 257–286

[Vidal et al.2005] E. Vidal, F. Thollard, C. de la Higuera, F. Casacuberta, and R. C. Carrasco. 2005. Probabilistic finite-state machines - part II. *IEEE Transactions on Pattern Analysis and Machine Intelligence*, 27(7): pg. 1026–1039

[Vidal1997] E. Vidal. 1997. Finite-state speech-to-speech translation. *International Conference on Acoustic, Speech and Signal Processing*, vol. 1, pg. 111–114

[Vilar et al.2006] David Vilar, Jia Xu, Luis Fernando D'Haro, and H. Ney. 2006. Error Analysis of Machine Translation Output. *International Conference on Language Resources and Evaluation*, pg. 697–702

[Zhang et al.2004] R. Zhang, G. Kikui, H. Yamamoto, T. Watanabe, F. Soong, and W. K. Lo. 2004. A unified approach in speech-to-speech translation: integrating features of speech recognition and machine translation. *International Conference on Computational Linguistics*, pg. 1168-1174

[Zhou et al.2007] B. Zhou, L. Besacier, and Y. Gao. 2007. On efficient coupling of ASR and SMT for speech translation. *IEEE International Conference on Acoustics, Speech and Signal Processing*, vol. 4, pg. 101–104

Refining the Design of a Contracting Finite-State Dependency Parser

Anssi Yli-Jyrä and **Jussi Piitulainen** and **Atro Voutilainen**
The Department of Modern Languages
PO Box 3
00014 University of Helsinki
{anssi.yli-jyra, jussi.piitulainen, atro.voutilainen}@helsinki.fi

Abstract

This work complements a parallel paper of a new finite-state dependency parser architecture (Yli-Jyrä, 2012) by a proposal for a linguistically elaborated morphology-syntax interface and its finite-state implementation. The proposed interface *extends* Gaifman's (1965) classical dependency rule formalism by separating lexical word forms and morphological categories from syntactic categories. The separation lets the linguist take advantage of the morphological features in order to reduce the number of dependency rules and to make them lexically selective. In addition, the relative functional specificity of parse trees gives rise to *a measure of parse quality*. By filtering worse parses out from the parse forest using finite-state techniques, the best parses are saved. Finally, we present *a synthesis of strict grammar parsing and robust text parsing* by connecting fragmental parses into trees with additional linear successor links.

1 Introduction

Finite-state dependency parsing aims to combine dependency syntax and finite-state automata into a single elegant system. Deterministic systems such as (Elworthy, 2000) are fast but susceptible to garden-path type errors although some ambiguity is encoded in the output. Some other systems such as (Oflazer, 2003; Yli-Jyrä, 2005) carry out full projective dependency parsing while being much slower, especially if the syntactic ambiguity is high. In the worst case, the size of the minimal finite-state automaton storing the forest is exponentially larger than the sentence: an 80-word sentence has potentially 1.1×10^{62} unrooted unlabeled dependency trees that are stored "compactly" into a finite-state lattice that requires at least 2.4×10^{24} states, see Table 4 in Yli-Jyrä (2012).

A truly compact representation of the parse forest is provided by an interesting new extended finite-state parsing architecture (Yli-Jyrä, 2012) that first recognizes the grammatical sentences in quadratic time and space if the nested dependencies are limited by a constant (in cubic time if the length of the sentence limits the nesting). The new system (Yli-Jyrä, 2012) replaces the additive (Oflazer, 2003) and the intersecting (Yli-Jyrä, 2005) validation of dependency links with reductive validation that gradually contracts the dependencies until the whole tree has been reduced into a trivial one. The idea of the contractions is illustrated in Example 1. In practice, our parser operates on bracketed trees (i.e., strings), but the effect will be similar.

(1) a. b. c.

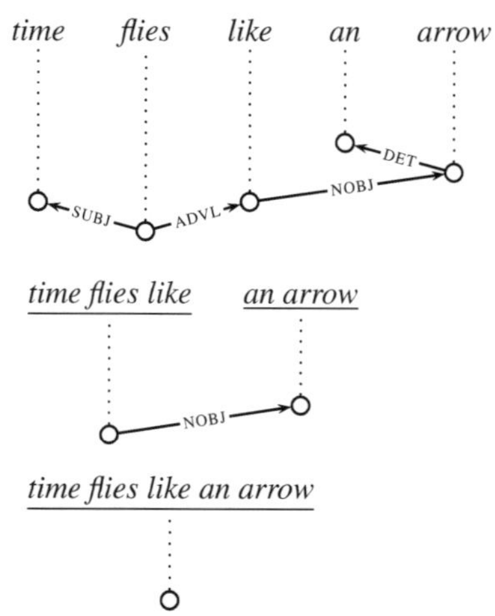

Proceedings of the 10th International Workshop on Finite State Methods and Natural Language Processing, pages 108–115,
Donostia–San Sebastián, July 23–25, 2012.

Despite being non-deterministic and efficient, there are two important requirements that are not fulfilled by the core of the new architecture (Yli-Jyrä, 2012):

1. A mature finite-state dependency parser must be robust. The outputs should not be restricted to complete grammatical parses. For example, Oflazer (2003) builds fragmental parses but later drops those fragmental parses for which there are alternative parses with fewer fragments. However, his approach handles only gap-free bottom-up fragments and optimizes the number of fragments by a counting method whose capacity is limited.

2. Besides robustness, a wide-coverage parser should be able to assign reasonably well-motivated syntactic categories to every word in the input. This amounts to having a morphological guesser and an adequate morphology-syntax interface. Most prior work trivializes the complexity of the interface, being comparable to Gaifman's (1965) legacy formalism that is mathematically elegant but based on word-form lists. A good interface formalism is provided, e.g., by Constraint Grammar parsers (Karlsson et al., 1995) where syntactic rules can refer to morphological features. Oflazer (2003) tests morphological features in complicated regular expressions. The state complexity of the combination of such expressions is, however, a potential problem if many more rules would be added to the system.

This paper makes two main contributions:

1. It adapts Gaifman's elegant formalism to the requirements of morphologically rich languages. With the adapted formalism, grammar writing becomes easier. However, efficient implementation of the rule lookup becomes inherently trickier because testing several morphological conditions in parallel increases the size of the finite-state automata. Fortunately, the new formalism comes with an efficient implementation that keeps the finite-state representation of the rule set as elegant as possible.

2. The paper introduces a linguistically motivated ranking for complete trees. According to it, a tree is better than another tree if a larger proportion of its dependency links is motivated by the linguistic rules. In contrast to Oflazer (2003), our method counts the number of links needed to connect the fragments into a spanning tree. Moreover, since such additional links are indeed included in the parses, the ranking method turns a grammar parser into a robust text parser.

The paper is structured as follows. The next section will give an overview of the new parser architecture. After it, we present the new morphology-syntax interface in Section 3 and the parse ranking method in Section 4. The paper ends with theoretical evaluation and discussion about the proposed formalism in Section 5.

2 The General Design

2.1 The Internal Linguistic Representation

We need to define a string-based representation for the structures that are processed by the parser. For this purpose, we encode the dependency trees and then augment the representation with morphological features.

Dependency brackets encode dependency links *between* pairs of tokens that are separated by an (implicit) token boundary. The four-token string abcd has 12 distinct *undirected unlabeled dependency bracketings* a((()b)c)d, a((b())c)d, a(()b()c)d, a(()bc())d, a(()b)c()d, a(b(()c))d, a(b(c()))d, a(b()c())d, a(b())c()d, a()b(()c)d, a()b(c())d, a()b()c()d.[1]

The basic dependency brackets extend with labels such as in (LBL LBL) and directions such as in <LBL LBL\ and in /LBL LBL>. Directed dependency links designate one of the linked words as the head and another as the dependent. The extended brackets let us encode a full dependency tree in a string format as indicated in (2).[2] The dependent word of each

[1]Dependency bracketing differs clearly from *binary phrase-structure bracketings* that put brackets *around* phrases: the string abcd has only five distinct bracketings ((ab)(cd)), (((ab)c)d), ((a(bc))d), (a((bc)d)), and (a(b(cd))).

[2]The syntactic labels used in this paper are: AG=Agent, by=Preposition 'by' as a phrasal verb complement, D=Determiner, EN=Past Participle, FP=Final Punctuation, P=adjunctive preposition, PC=Preposition Complement, S=Subject, sgS=Singular Subject.

link is indicated in trees with an arrowhead but in bracketing with an angle bracket.

(2)

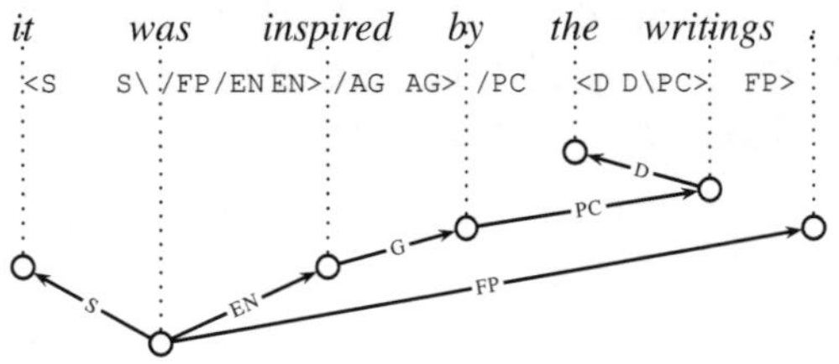

In Table 1, the dependency bracketing is combined with a common textual format for morphological analyses. In this format, the base forms are defined over the alphabet of orthographical symbols Ω whereas the morphological symbols and syntactic categories are multi-character symbols that belong, respectively, to the alphabets Π and Γ. In addition, there is a token boundary symbol #.

Table 1: One morpho-syntactic analysis of a sentence

1	*i t*	PRON NOM SG3	<S	#
2	*b e*	V PAST SG13	S\ /FP /EN	#
3	*i n s p i r e*	EN	EN> /AG	#
4	*b y*	PREP	AG> /PC	#
5	*t h e*	DET SG/PL	<D	#
6	*w r i t i n g*	N NOM PL	D\ PC>	#
7	.	PUNCT	FP>	#

Depending on the type of the languages, one orthographical word can be split into several parts such as the inflectional groups in Turkish (Oflazer, 2003). In this case, a separate word-initial token boundary can be used to separate such parts into lines of their own.

The current dependency bracketing captures projective and weakly non-projective (1-planar) trees only, but an extended encoding for 2-planar and multi-planar dependency trees seems feasible (Yli-Jyrä, 2012):

2.2 The Valid Trees

We are now going to define precisely the semantics of the syntactic grammar component using finite-state relations.

The *finite-state languages* will be defined over a finite alphabet Σ and they include all finite subsets of the universal language Σ^*. The *(binary) finite-state relations* are defined over Σ^* and include all finite subsets of $\Sigma^* \times \Sigma^*$. In addition, they are closed under the operations over finite-state languages L and M and finite-state relations R and S according to Table 2. The language relation $\text{Id}(L)$ restricts the identity relation to a language L. The composition of language relations corresponds to the intersection of their languages.

Table 2: The relevant closure properties

language	relation	meaning
LM	RS	concatenation
L^*	R^*	(Kleene) star
L^+	R^+	(Kleene) plus
$L \cup M$	$R \cup S$	union
	$\text{Id}(L)$	language relation
$\text{Id}^{-1}(R)$		L for $R = \text{Id}(L)$
$L - M$	$\text{Id}(L) - \text{Id}(M)$	set difference
	$L \times M$	cross product
	$R_{\mid L}$	input restriction
	$R \circ S$	composition
	R^{-1}	inverse
	$\text{Proj}_1(R)$	Id(the input side of R)
	$\text{Proj}_2(R)$	Id(the output side of R)

For notational convenience, the empty string is denoted by ϵ. A string x is identified with the singleton set $\{x\}$.

The syntactic component of the grammar defines a set of parse strings where the bracketing is a valid dependency tree. In these parses, there is no morphological information. One way to express the set is to intersect a set of constraints as in (Yli-Jyrä, 2005). However, the contracting dependency parser expresses the Id relation of the set through a composition of simple finite-state relations:

$$\text{Syn}_t = \text{Proj}_1(\text{Abst} \circ \underbrace{R \circ \ldots \circ R}_{t} \circ \text{Root}), \quad (1)$$

$$\text{Root} = \text{Id}(\#). \quad (2)$$

In (1), Abst is a relation that removes all non-syntactic information from the strings,

$$\text{Abst} = (\text{Id}(\Gamma) \cup \text{Id}(\#) \cup \text{Delete})^*, \quad (3)$$

$$\text{Delete} = \{(x, \epsilon) \mid x \in \Omega \cup \Pi\}, \quad (4)$$

and R is a relation that performs one layer of contractions in dependency bracketing.

$$\mathrm{R} = (\mathrm{Id}(\Gamma) \cup \mathrm{Id}(\#) \cup \mathrm{Left} \cup \mathrm{Right})^{*}, \tag{5}$$

$$\mathrm{Left} = \{(<\alpha \; \# \; \alpha\backslash, \epsilon) \mid <\alpha, \alpha\backslash \in \Gamma\}, \tag{6}$$

$$\mathrm{Right} = \{(/\alpha \; \# \; \alpha>, \epsilon) \mid /\alpha, \alpha> \in \Gamma\}. \tag{7}$$

The parameter t determines the maximum number of layers of dependency links in the validated bracketings. The limit of Syn_t as t approaches ∞ is not necessarily a finite-state language, but it remains context-free because only projective trees are assigned to the sentences.

2.3 The Big Picture

We are now ready to embed the contraction based grammar into the bigger picture.

Let $x \in \Omega^*$ be an orthographical string to be parsed. Assume that it is segmented into n tokens. The string x is parsed by composition of four relations: the relation $\{(x, x)\}$, the lexical transducer (Morph), the morphology-syntax interface (Iface), and the syntactic validator Syn_{n-1}.

$$\mathrm{Parses}(x) = \mathrm{Id}(x) \circ \mathrm{Morph} \circ \mathrm{Iface} \circ \mathrm{Syn}_{n-1}. \tag{8}$$

The language relation $\mathrm{Proj}_2(\mathrm{Parses}(x))$ encodes the parse forest of the input x.

In practice, the syntactic validator Syn_{n-1} cannot be compiled into a finite-state transducer due to its large state complexity. However, when each copy of the contracting transducer R in (1) is restricted by its admissible input-side language, a compact representation for the input-side restriction $(\mathrm{Syn}_{n-1})_{|X}$ where $X = \mathrm{Proj}_2(\mathrm{Id}(x) \circ \mathrm{Morph} \circ \mathrm{Iface})$ is computed efficiently as described in (Yli-Jyrä, 2012).

3 The Grammar Formalism

In the parser, the linguistic knowledge is organized into Morph (the morphology) and Iface (the lexicalized morphology-syntax interface), while Syn has mainly a technical role as a tree validator. Implementing the morphology-syntax interface is far from an easy task since it is actually the place that lexicalizes the whole syntax.

3.1 Gaifman's Dependency Rules

Gaifman's legacy notation (Gaifman, 1965; Hays, 1964) for dependency grammars assigns word forms to a finite number of potential *morpho-syntactic* categories that relate word forms to their syntactic functions. The words of particular categories are then related by *dependency rules*:

$$X_0(X_p, \ldots, X_{-1}, \star, X_1, \ldots, X_m). \tag{9}$$

The rule (9) states that a word in category X_0 is the head of dependent words in categories $X_p, \ldots, X_{-1}$ before it and words in categories $X_1, \ldots, X_m$ after it, in the given order. The rule expresses, in a certain sense, the frame or the argument structure of the word. Rule $X(\star)$ indicates that the word in category X can occur without dependents.

In addition, there is a *root rule* $\star(X)$ that states that a word in category X can occur independently, that is, as the root of the sentence.

In the legacy notation, the distinction between complements and adjuncts is not made explicit, as both need to be listed as dependents. To compact the notation, we introduce *optional dependents* that will be indicated by categories $X_p?, \ldots, X_{-1}?$ and categories $X_1?, \ldots, X_m?$. This extension potentially saves a large number of rules in cases where several dependents are actually adjuncts, some kinds of modifiers.[3]

3.2 The Decomposed Categories

In practice, atomic morpho-syntactic categories are often too coarse for morphological description but too refined for convenient description of syntactic frames. A practical description requires a more expressive and flexible formalism.

In our new rule formalism, each morpho-syntactic category X is viewed as a combination of a morphological category M (including the information on the lexical form of the word) and a syntactic category S. The morphological category M is a string of orthographical and morphological feature labels while S is an atomic category label.

The morphological category M_0 and the syntactic category S_0 are specified for the head of each dependency rule. Together, they specify the morpho-syntactic category (M_0, S_0). In contrast, the rule specifies only the syntactic categories $S_p, \ldots, S_{-1}$,

[3] Optional dependents may be a worthwhile extension even in descriptions that treat the modified word as a complement of a modifier.

and $S_1, \ldots, S_m$ of the dependent words and thus delegates the selection of the morphological categories to the respective rules of the dependent words. The categories $S_p, \ldots, S_{-1}$, and $S_1, \ldots, S_m$ may again be marked optional with the question mark.

The rules are separated according to the direction of the head dependency. Rules (10), (11) and (12) attach the head to the right, to the left, and in any direction, respectively. In addition, the syntactic category of the root is specified with a rule of the form (13).

$$\rightarrow S_0(S_p, \ldots, S_{-1}, \star[M_0], S_1, \ldots, S_m), \quad (10)$$
$$\leftarrow S_0(S_p, \ldots, S_{-1}, \star[M_0], S_1, \ldots, S_m), \quad (11)$$
$$S_0(S_p, \ldots, S_{-1}, \star[M_0], S_1, \ldots, S_m), \quad (12)$$
$$\star(S_0). \quad (13)$$

The interpretations of rules (10) - (12) are similar to rule (9), but the rules are lexicalized and directed. The feature string $M_0 \in (\Omega^* \% \Omega^* \cup \Omega^*)\Pi^*$ defines the relevant head word forms using the features provided by Morph. The percent symbol (%) stands for the unspecified part of the lexical base form.

The use of the extended rule formalism is illustrated in Table 3. According to the rules in the table, a phrase headed by preposition *by* has three uses: an adjunctive preposition (P), the complement of a phrasal verb (by), or the agent of a passive verb (AG). Note that the last two uses correspond to a fully lexicalized rule where the morphological category specifies the lexeme. The fourth rule illustrates how morphological features are combined in N NOM SG and then partly propagated to the atomic name of the syntactic category.

Table 3: Extended Gaifman rules

```
P (*[% PREP], PC)                    % prepos.
by (*[b y PREP], PC)                 % phrasal
AG (*[b y PREP], PC)                 % agent
sgS (D?, M?, *[% N NOM SG], M?)      % noun
```

3.3 Making a Gaifman Grammar Robust

Dependency syntax describes complete trees where each node is described by one of the dependency rules. Sometimes, however, no complete tree for an input is induced by the linguistically motivated dependency rules. In these cases, only tree fragments can be motivated by the linguistic knowledge. To glue the fragments together, we interpret the roots of fragments as *linear successors* – thus dependents – for the word that immediately precedes the fragment.

The link to a linear successor is indicated with a special category ++ having a default rule ++($\star$). Since any word can act as a root of a fragment, every word is provided with this potential category. In addition, there is, for every rule (12), an automatic rule ++$(S_p, \ldots, S_{-1}, \star[M], S_1, \ldots, S_m)$ that allows the roots of the fragments to have the corresponding dependents. Similar automatic rules are defined for the directed rules.

The category ++ is used to indicate dependent words that do not have any linguistically motivated syntactic function. The root rule $\star$(++) states that this special category can act as the root of the whole dependency tree. In addition to the root function expressed by that rule, an optional dependent ++? is appended to the end of every dependency rule. This connects fragments to their left contexts.

With the above extensions, all sentences will have at least one complete tree as a parse. A parse with some dependents of the type ++ are linguistically inferior to parses that do not have such dependents or have fewer of them. Removing such inferior analyses from the output of the parser is proposed in Section 4.

3.4 The Formal Semantics of the Interface

Let there be r dependency rules. For each rule i, $i \in \{1, ..., r\}$ of type (10), let

$$F_i = M_0, \quad (14)$$
$$G_i = S_{-1}\backslash \ \ldots S_p\backslash \ S_0{>} \ /S_m .../S_1, \quad (15)$$

where $S_{-1}\backslash, \ldots, S_p\backslash, S_0{>}, /S_m, \ldots, /S_1 \in \Gamma$. For each rule of type (11), $S_0{>}$ in (15) is replaced with ${<}S_0$. Rules with optional dependents are expanded into subrules, and every undirected rule (12) splits into two directed subrules.

In (16), Iface is a finite-state relation that injects dependency brackets to the parses according to the dependency rules.

$$\text{Iface} = \text{Intro} \circ \text{Chk}, \quad (16)$$

$$\text{Intro} = (\text{Id}(\Omega^*\Pi^*)(\epsilon{\times}\Gamma^*)\text{Id}(\#))^*, \quad (17)$$

$$\text{Chk} = \text{Proj}_1(\text{Match} \circ \text{Rules}), \quad (18)$$

$$\text{Rules} = \text{Id}\,(\cup_{i=1}^{r} F_i G_i \#)^*. \quad (19)$$

$$\text{Match} = (\text{Id}(\Omega^*)\ \text{Mid}\ \text{Id}(\Omega^*)\ \text{Tag}^*\ \text{Id}(\#))^* \quad (20)$$

$$\text{Mid} = \text{Id}(\epsilon) \cup (\Omega^* \times \%), \quad (21)$$

$$\text{Tag} = \text{Id}(\Pi) \cup (\Pi{\times}\epsilon). \quad (22)$$

Iface is the composition of relations Intro and Chk. Relation Intro inserts dependency brackets between the morphological analysis of each token and the following token boundary. Relation Chk verifies that the inserted brackets are supported by dependency rules that are represented by relation Rules.

In order to allow generalizations in the specification of morphological categories, the relation Intro does not match dependency rules directly, but through a filter. This filter, Match, optionally replaces the middle part of each lexeme with % and arbitrary morphological feature labels with the empty string.

In addition to the dependency rules, we need to define the semantics of the root rules. Let H be the set of the categories having a root rule. The category of the root word will be indicated in the dependency bracketing as an unmatched bracket. It is checked by relation Root $= \text{Id}(H\#)$ that replaces Root $= \text{Id}(\#)$ in the composition formulas (1) .

3.5 An Efficient Implementation

The definition of Iface gives rise to a naive parser implementation that is based on the formula

$$\text{Parses}(x) = \text{MI}_x \circ \text{Chk} \circ \text{Syn}_{n-1}, \quad (23)$$

$$\text{MI}_x = \text{Id}(x) \circ \text{Morph} \circ \text{Intro}. \quad (24)$$

The naive implementation is inefficient in practice. The main efficiency problem is that the state complexity of relation Chk can be exponential to the number of rules. To avoid this, we replace it with Chk_x, a restriction of Chk. This restriction is computed lazily when the input is known.

$$\text{Parses}(x) = \text{MI}_x \circ \text{Chk}_x \circ \text{Syn}_{n-1}, \quad (25)$$

$$\text{Chk}_x = \text{Proj}_1(\text{Match}_x \circ \text{Rules}) \quad (26)$$

$$\text{Match}_x = \text{Proj}_2(\text{MI}_x) \circ \text{Match}. \quad (27)$$

In this improved method, the application of Iface demands only linear space according to the number of rules. This method is also fast to apply to the input, as far as the morphology-syntax interface is concerned. Meanwhile, one efficient implementation of Syn_{n-1} is already provided in (Yli-Jyrä, 2012).

4 The Most Specific Parse

The parsing method of (Yli-Jyrä, 2012) builds the parse forest efficiently using several transducers, but there is no guarantee that the whole set of parses could be extracted efficiently from the compact representation constructed during the recognition phase. We will now assume, however, that the number of parses is, in practice, substantially smaller than in the theoretically possible worst case. Moreover, it is even more important to assume that the set of parses is compactly packed into a finite automaton. These two assumptions let us proceed by refining the parse forest without using weights such as in (Yli-Jyrä, 2012).

In the following, we restrict the parse forest to those parses that have the smallest number of 'linear successor' dependencies (++). The number of such dependencies is compared with a finite-state relation $\text{Cp} \subseteq (\Gamma \cup \{\#\})^* {\times} (\Gamma \cup \{\#\})^*$ constructed as follows:

$$\Sigma' = \Sigma - \{\text{++>}\}, \quad (28)$$

$$\text{Cp} = \text{Map}_i \circ (\text{Id}(\text{++>}^*)(\epsilon{\times}\text{++>})^+) \circ \text{Map}_i^{-1}, \quad (29)$$

$$\text{Map}_i = (\text{Id}(\text{++>}) \cup (\Sigma'{\times}\epsilon))^*. \quad (30)$$

In practice, the reduction of the parse forest is possible only if the parse forest $\text{Proj}_2(\text{Parses}(x))$ is recognized by a sufficiently small finite-state automaton that can then be operated in Formula (33). The parses that minimize the number of 'linear successor' dependencies are obtained as the output of the relation $\text{Parses}'(x)$.

$$\text{Parses}'(x) = \text{MI}_x \circ \text{Chk}_x \circ T_{x,1}, \quad (31)$$

$$\text{T}_{x,0} = \text{Proj}_2(\text{Parses}(x)), \quad (32)$$

$$\text{T}_{x,1} = \text{T}_{x,0} - \text{Proj}_2(\text{T}_{x,0} \circ \text{Cp} \circ \text{T}_{x,0}). \quad (33)$$

This restriction technique could be repeatedly applied to further levels of specificity. For example, lexically motivated complements could be preferred over adjuncts and other grammatically possible dependents.

5 Evaluation and Discussion

5.1 Elegance

We have retained most of the elegancy in the contracting finite-state dependency parser (Yli-Jyrä, 2012). The changes introduced in this paper are modular and implementable with standard operations on finite-state transducers.

Our refined design for a parser can be implemented largely in similar lines as the general approach (Yli-Jyrä, 2012) up to the point when the parses are extracted from the compact parse forest.

Parsing by arc contractions is closely related to the idea of reductions with restarting automata (Plátek et al., 2003).

5.2 Coverage

The representation of the parses can be extended to handle word-internal token boundaries, which facilitates the adequate treatment of agglutinative languages, cf. (Oflazer, 2003).

The limit for nested brackets is based on the psycholinguistic reality (Miller, 1956; Kornai and Tuza, 1992) and the observed tendency for short dependencies (Lin, 1995; Eisner and Smith, 2005) in natural language.

The same general design can be used to produce non-projective dependency analyses as required by many European languages. The crossing dependencies can be assigned to two or more planes as suggested in (Yli-Jyrä, 2012). 2-planar bracketing already achieves very high recall in practice (Gómez-Rodríguez and Nivre, 2010).

5.3 Ambiguity Management

Oflazer (2003) uses the lenient composition operation to compute the number of bottom-up fragments in incomplete parses. The current solution improves above this by supporting gapped fragments and unrestricted counting of the graph components.

Like in another extended finite-state approach (Oflazer, 2003), the ambiguity in the output of our parsing method can be reduced by removing parses with high total link length and by applying filters that enforce barrier constraints to the dependency links.

5.4 Computational Complexity

Thanks to dynamically applied finite-state operations and the representation of feature combinations as strings rather than regular languages, the dependency rules can be compiled quickly into the transducers used by the parser. For example, the actual specifications of dependency rules are now compiled into a linear-size finite-state transducer, Chk. The proposed implementation for the morphology-syntax interface is, thus, a significant improvement in comparison to the common approach that compiles and combines replacement rules into a single transducer where the morphological conditions of the rules are potentially mixed in a combinatorial manner.

Although we have started to write an experimental grammar, we do not exactly know how many rules a mature grammar will contain. Lexicalization of the rules will increase the number of rules significantly. The number of syntactic categories will increase even more if complements are lexicalized.

5.5 Robustness

In case the grammar does not fully disambiguate or build a complete dependency structure, the parser should be able to build and produce a partial analysis. (In interactive treebanking, it would be useful if an additional knowledge source, e.g. a human, can be used to provide additional information to help the parser carry on the analysis to a complete structure.)

The current grammar system indeed assumes that it can build complete trees for all input sentences. This assumption is typical for all generative grammars, but seems to contradict the requirement of robustness. To support robust parsing, we have now proposed a simple technique where partial analyses are connected into a tree with the "linear successor" links. The designed parser tries its best to avoid these underspecific links, but uses the smallest possible number of them to connect the partial analyses into a tree if more grammatical parses are not available.

5.6 Future Work

Although Oflazer (2003) does not report significant problems with long sentences, it may be difficult to construct a single automaton for the parse forest of a sentence that contains many words. In the future, a more efficient method for finding the most specific parse from the forest can be worked out using weighted finite-state automata. Such a method would combine the approaches of the companion paper (Yli-Jyrä, 2012) and the current paper.

It seems interesting to study further how the specificity reasoning and statistically learned weights could complement each other in order to find the best analyses. Moreover, the parser can be modified in such a way that debugging information is produced. This could be very useful, especially when learning contractions that handle the crossing dependencies of non-projective trees.

A dependency parser should enable the building of multiple types of analyses, e.g. to account for syntactic and semantic dependencies. Also adding more structure to the syntactic categories could be useful.

6 Conclusions

The current theoretical work paves the way for a full parser implementation. The parser should be able to cope with large grammars to enable efficient development, testing and application cycles.

The current work has sketched an expressive and compact formalism and its efficient implementation for the morphology-syntax interface of the contracting dependency parser. In addition, the work has elaborated strategies that help to make the grammar more robust without sacrificing the optimal specificity of the analysis.

Acknowledgments

The research has received funding from the Academy of Finland under the grant agreement # 128536 and the FIN-CLARIN project, and from the European Commission's 7th Framework Program under the grant agreement # 238405 (CLARA).

References

Jason Eisner and Noah A. Smith. 2005. Parsing with soft and hard constraints on dependency length. In *Proceedings of the International Workshop on Parsing Technologies (IWPT)*, pages 30–41, Vancouver, October.

David Elworthy. 2000. A finite state parser with dependency structure output. In *Proceedings of Sixth International Workshop on Parsing Technologies (IWPT 2000*, Trento, Italy, February 23-25. Institute for Scientific and Technological Research.

Haim Gaifman. 1965. Dependency systems and phrase-structure systems. *Information and Control*, 8:304–37.

Carlos Gómez-Rodríguez and Joakim Nivre. 2010. A transition-based parser for 2-planar dependency structures. In *Proceedings of the 48th Annual Meeting of the Association for Computational Linguistics*, pages 1492—-1501, Uppsala, Sweden, 11-16 July.

David G. Hays. 1964. Dependency theory: A formalism and some observations. *Language*, 40:511–525.

Fred Karlsson, Atro Voutilainen, Juha Heikkiä, and Arto Anttila, editors. 1995. *Constraint Grammar: a Language-Independent System for Parsing Unrestricted Text*, volume 4 of *Natural Language Processing*. Mouton de Gruyter, Berlin and New York.

András Kornai and Zsolt Tuza. 1992. Narrowness, pathwidth, and their application in natural language processing. *Discrete Applied Mathematics*, 36:87–92.

Dekang Lin. 1995. A dependency-based method for evaluating broad-coverage parsers. In *Proceedings of the Fourteenth International Joint Conference on Artificial Intelligence, IJCAI 95, Montréal Québec, Canada, August 20-25, 1995*, volume 2, pages 1420–1425.

George A. Miller. 1956. The magical number seven, plus or minus two: Some limits on our capacity for processing information. *Psychological Review*, 63(2):343–355.

Kemal Oflazer. 2003. Dependency parsing with an extended finite-state approach. *Computational Linguistics*, 29(4):515–544.

Martin Plátek, Markéta Lopatková, and Karel Oliva. 2003. Restarting automata: motivations and applications. In M. Holzer, editor, *Workshop 'Petrinetze' and 13. Theorietag 'Formale Sprachen und Automaten'*, pages 90–96, Institut für Informatik, Technische Universität München.

Anssi Yli-Jyrä. 2005. Approximating dependency grammars through intersection of star-free regular languages. *International Journal of Foundations of Computer Science*, 16(3).

Anssi Yli-Jyrä. 2012. On dependency analysis via contractions and weighted FSTs. In Diana Santos, Krister Lindén, and Wanjiku Ng'ang'a, editors, *Shall we Play the Festschrift Game? Essays on the Occasion of Lauri Carlson's 60th Birthday*. Springer-Verlag, Berlin.

Lattice-Based Minimum Error Rate Training using Weighted Finite-State Transducers with Tropical Polynomial Weights

Aurelien Waite[‡] **Graeme Blackwood**[*] **William Byrne**[‡]
[‡] Department of Engineering, University of Cambridge, Trumpington Street, CB2 1PZ, U.K.
{aaw35|wjb31}@cam.ac.uk
[*] IBM T.J. Watson Research, Yorktown Heights, NY-10598
blackwood@us.ibm.com

Abstract

Minimum Error Rate Training (MERT) is a method for training the parameters of a log-linear model. One advantage of this method of training is that it can use the large number of hypotheses encoded in a translation lattice as training data. We demonstrate that the MERT line optimisation can be modelled as computing the shortest distance in a weighted finite-state transducer using a tropical polynomial semiring.

1 Introduction

Minimum Error Rate Training (MERT) (Och, 2003) is an iterative procedure for training a log-linear statistical machine translation (SMT) model (Och and Ney, 2002). MERT optimises model parameters directly against a criterion based on an automated translation quality metric, such as BLEU (Papineni et al., 2002). Koehn (2010) provides a full description of the SMT task and MERT.

MERT uses a line optimisation procedure (Press et al., 2002) to identify a range of points along a line in parameter space that maximise an objective function based on the BLEU score. A key property of the line optimisation is that it can consider a large set of hypotheses encoded as a weighted directed acyclic graph (Macherey et al., 2008), which is called a lattice. The line optimisation procedure can also be applied to a hypergraph representation of the hypotheses (Kumar et al., 2009).

It has been noted that line optimisation over a lattice can be implemented as a semiring of sets of linear functions (Dyer et al., 2010). Sokolov and Yvon (2011) provide a formal description of such a semiring, which they denote the MERT semiring. The difference between the various algorithms derives from the differences in their formulation and implementation, but not in the objective they attempt to optimise.

Instead of an algebra defined in terms of transformations of sets of linear functions, we propose an alternative formulation using the tropical polynomial semiring (Speyer and Sturmfels, 2009). This semiring provides a concise formalism for describing line optimisation, an intuitive explanation of the MERT shortest distance, and draws on techniques in the currently active field of Tropical Geometry (Richter-Gebert et al., 2005) [1].

We begin with a review of the line optimisation procedure, lattice-based MERT, and the weighted finite-state transducer formulation in Section 2. In Section 3, we introduce our novel formulation of lattice-based MERT using tropical polynomial weights. Section 4 compares the performance of our approach with k-best and lattice-based MERT.

2 Minimum Error Rate Training

Following Och and Ney (2002), we assume that we are given a tuning set of parallel sentences $\{(\mathbf{r}_1, \mathbf{f}_1), ..., (\mathbf{r}_S, \mathbf{f}_S)\}$, where $\mathbf{r}_s$ is the reference translation of the source sentence $\mathbf{f}_s$. We also assume that sets of hypotheses $\mathbf{C}_s = \{\mathbf{e}_{s,1}, ..., \mathbf{e}_{s,K}\}$

[*] The work reported in this paper was carried out while the author was at the University of Cambridge.

[1] An associated technical report contains an extended discussion of our approach (Waite et al., 2011)

Proceedings of the 10th International Workshop on Finite State Methods and Natural Language Processing, pages 116–125, Donostia–San Sebastián, July 23–25, 2012.

are available for each source sentence $\mathbf{f}_s$.

Under the log-linear model formulation with feature functions h_1^M and model parameters λ_1^M, the most probable translation in a set $\mathbf{C}_s$ is selected as

$$\hat{\mathbf{e}}(\mathbf{f}_s; \lambda_1^M) = \underset{\mathbf{e} \in \mathbf{C}_s}{\operatorname{argmax}} \left\{ \sum_{m=1}^{M} \lambda_m h_m(\mathbf{e}, \mathbf{f_s}) \right\}. \quad (1)$$

With an error function of the form $E(\mathbf{r}_1^S, \mathbf{e}_1^S) = \sum_{s=1}^{S} E(\mathbf{r}_s, \mathbf{e}_s)$, MERT attempts to find model parameters to minimise the following objective:

$$\hat{\lambda}_1^M = \underset{\lambda_1^M}{\operatorname{argmin}} \left\{ \sum_{s=1}^{S} E(\mathbf{r}_s, \hat{\mathbf{e}}(\mathbf{f}_s; \lambda_1^M)) \right\}. \quad (2)$$

Note that for MERT the hypotheses set $\mathbf{C}_s$ is a k-best list of explicitly enumerated hypotheses, whereas lattice-based MERT uses a larger space.

2.1 Line Optimisation

Although the objective function in Eq. (2) cannot be solved analytically, the line optimisation procedure of Och (2003) can be used to find an approximation of the optimal model parameters. Rather than evaluating the decision rule in Eq. (1) over all possible points in parameter space, the line optimisation considers a subset of points defined by the line $\lambda_1^M + \gamma d_1^M$, where λ_1^M corresponds to an initial point in parameter space and d_1^M is the direction along which to optimise. Eq. (1) can be rewritten as:

$$\begin{aligned}\hat{\mathbf{e}}(\mathbf{f}_s; \gamma) &= \underset{\mathbf{e} \in \mathbf{C}_s}{\operatorname{argmax}} \left\{ (\lambda_1^M + \gamma d_1^M)^T h_1^M(\mathbf{e}, \mathbf{f}_s) \right\} \\ &= \underset{\mathbf{e} \in \mathbf{C}_s}{\operatorname{argmax}} \Big\{ \underbrace{\sum_m \lambda_m h_m(\mathbf{e}, \mathbf{f}_s)}_{a(\mathbf{e}, \mathbf{f}_s)} + \gamma \underbrace{\sum_m d_m h_m(\mathbf{e}, \mathbf{f}_s)}_{b(\mathbf{e}, \mathbf{f}_s)} \Big\} \\ &= \underset{\mathbf{e} \in \mathbf{C}_s}{\operatorname{argmax}} \{ \underbrace{a(\mathbf{e}, \mathbf{f}_s) + \gamma b(\mathbf{e}, \mathbf{f}_s)}_{\ell_{\mathbf{e}}(\gamma)} \} \quad (3)\end{aligned}$$

This decision rule shows that each hypothesis $\mathbf{e} \in \mathbf{C}_s$ is associated with a linear function of γ: $\ell_{\mathbf{e}}(\gamma) = a(\mathbf{e}, \mathbf{f}_s) + \gamma b(\mathbf{e}, \mathbf{f}_s)$, where $a(\mathbf{e}, \mathbf{f}_s)$ is the y-intercept and $b(\mathbf{e}, \mathbf{f}_s)$ is the gradient. The optimisation problem is further simplified by defining a subspace over which optimisation is performed. The subspace is found by considering a form of the function in Eq. (3) defined with a range of real numbers (Macherey et al., 2008; Och, 2003):

$$\operatorname{Env}(\mathbf{f}) = \max_{\mathbf{e} \in \mathbf{C}} \{ \underbrace{a(\mathbf{e}, \mathbf{f}) + \gamma b(\mathbf{e}, \mathbf{f})}_{\ell_{\mathbf{e}}(\gamma)} : \gamma \in \mathbb{R} \} \quad (4)$$

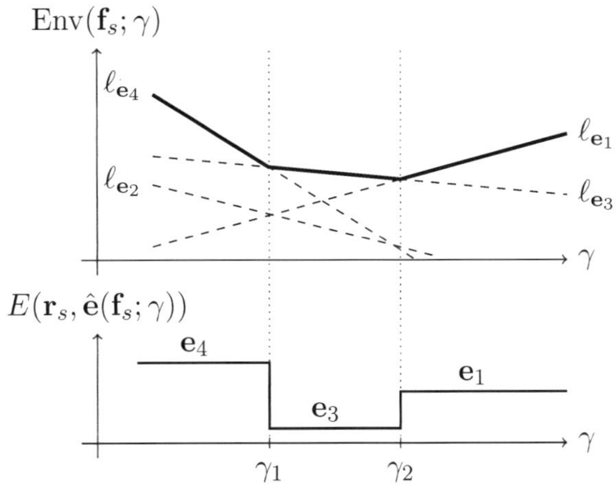

Figure 1: An upper envelope and projected error. Note that the upper envelope is completely defined by hypotheses $\mathbf{e}_4$, $\mathbf{e}_3$, and $\mathbf{e}_1$, together with the intersection points γ_1 and γ_2 (after Macherey et al. (2008), Fig. 1).

For any value of γ the linear functions $\ell_{\mathbf{e}}(\gamma)$ associated with $\mathbf{C}_s$ take (up to) K values. The function in Eq. (4) defines the 'upper envelope' of these values over all γ. The upper envelope has the form of a continuous piecewise linear function in γ. The piecewise linear function can be compactly described by the linear functions which form line segments and the values of γ at which they intersect. The example in the upper part of Figure 1 shows how the upper envelope associated with a set of four hypotheses can be represented by three associated linear functions and two values of γ. The first step of line optimisation is to compute this compact representation of the upper envelope.

Macherey et al. (2008) use methods from computational geometry to compute the upper envelope. The SweepLine algorithm (Bentley and Ottmann, 1979) computes the upper envelope from a set of linear functions with a complexity of $\mathcal{O}(K \log(K))$.

Computing the upper envelope reduces the runtime cost of line optimisation as the error function need only be evaluated for the subset of hypotheses in $\mathbf{C}_s$ that contribute to the upper envelope. These errors are projected onto intervals of γ, as shown in the lower part of Figure 1, so that Eq. (2) can be readily solved.

2.2 Incorporation of Line Optimisation into MERT

The previous algorithm finds the upper envelope along a particular direction in parameter space over a hypothesis set $\mathbf{C_s}$. The line optimisation algorithm is then embedded within a general optimisation procedure. A common approach to MERT is to select the directions using Powell's method (Press et al., 2002). A line optimisation is performed on each coordinate axis. The axis giving the largest decrease in error is replaced with a vector between the initial parameters and the optimised parameters. Powell's method halts when there is no decrease in error.

Instead of using Powell's method, the Downhill Simplex algorithm (Press et al., 2002) can be used to explore the criterion in Eq. (2). This is done by defining a simplex in parameter space. Directions where the error count decreases can be identified by considering the change in error count at the points of the simplex. This has been applied to parameter searching over k-best lists (Zens et al., 2007).

Both Powell's method and the Downhill Simplex algorithms are approaches based on heuristics to select lines $\lambda_1^M + \gamma d_1^M$. It is difficult to find theoretically sound reasons why one approach is superior. Therefore Cer et al. (2008) instead choose the direction vectors d_1^M at random. They report that this method can find parameters that are as good as the parameters produced by more complex algorithms.

2.3 Lattice Line Optimisation

Macherey et al. (2008) describe a procedure for conducting line optimisation directly over a word lattice encoding the hypotheses in $\mathbf{C_s}$. Each lattice edge is labelled with a word e and has a weight defined by the vector of word specific feature function values $h_1^M(e, \mathbf{f})$ so that the weight of a path in the lattice is found by summing over the word specific feature function values on that path. Given a line through parameter space, the goal is to extract from a lattice its upper envelope and the associated hypotheses.

Their algorithm proceeds node by node through the lattice. Suppose that for a state q the upper envelope is known for all the partial hypotheses on all paths leading to q. The upper envelope defines a set of functions $\{\ell_{\tilde{\mathbf{e}}_1}(\gamma), ..., \ell_{\tilde{\mathbf{e}}_N}(\gamma)\}$ over the partial hypotheses $\tilde{\mathbf{e}}_n$. Two operations propagate the upper envelope to other lattice nodes.

We refer to the first operation as the 'extend' operation. Consider a single edge from state q to state q'. This edge defines a linear function associated with a single word $\ell_e(\gamma)$. A path following this edge transforms all the partial hypotheses leading to q by concatenating the word e. The upper envelope associated with the edge from q to q' is changed by adding $\ell_e(\gamma)$ to the set of linear functions. The intersection points are not changed by this operation.

The second operation is a union. Suppose q' has another incoming edge from a state q'' where $q \neq q''$. There are now two upper envelopes representing two sets of linear functions. The first upper envelope is associated with the paths from the initial state to state q' via the state q. Similarly the second upper envelope is associated with paths from the initial state to state q' via the state q''. The upper envelope that is associated with all paths from the initial state to state q' via both q and q'' is the union of the two sets of linear functions. This union is no longer a compact representation of the upper envelope as there may be functions which never achieve a maximum for any value of γ. The SweepLine algorithm (Bentley and Ottmann, 1979) is applied to the union to discard redundant linear functions and their associated hypotheses (Macherey et al., 2008).

The union and extend operations are applied to states in topological order until the final state is reached. The upper envelope computed at the final state compactly encodes all the hypotheses that maximise Eq. (1) along the line $\lambda_1^M + \gamma d_1^M$. Macherey's theorem (Macherey et al., 2008) states that an upper bound for the number of linear functions in the upper envelope at the final state is equal to the number of edges in the lattice.

2.4 Line Optimisation using WFSTs

Formally, a weighted finite-state transducer (WFST) $T = (\Sigma, \Delta, Q, I, F, E, \lambda, \rho)$ over a semiring $(\mathbb{K}, \oplus, \otimes, \bar{0}, \bar{1})$ is defined by an input alphabet Σ, an output alphabet Δ, a set of states Q, a set of initial states $I \subseteq Q$, a set of final states $F \subseteq Q$, a set of weighted transitions E, an initial state weight assignment $\lambda : I \rightarrow \mathbb{K}$, and a final state weight assignment $\rho : F \rightarrow \mathbb{K}$ (Mohri et al., 2008). The weighted transitions of T form the set $E \subseteq Q \times \Sigma \times \Delta \times \mathbb{K} \times Q$, where each transition includes a source state from Q, input symbol from Σ, output symbol from Δ, cost from the weight set $\mathbb{K}$, and target state from Q.

For each state $q \in Q$, let $E[q]$ denote the set of edges leaving state q. For each transition $e \in E[q]$, let $p[e]$ denote its source state, $n[e]$ its target state, and $w[e]$ its weight. Let $\pi = e_1 \cdots e_K$ denote a path in T from state $p[e_1]$ to state $n[e_K]$, so that $n[e_{k-1}] = p[e_k]$ for $k = 2, \ldots, K$. The weight associated by T to path π is the generalised product $\otimes$ of the weights of the individual transitions:

$$w[\pi] = \bigotimes_{k=1}^{K} w[e_k] = w[e_1] \otimes \cdots \otimes w[e_K] \quad (5)$$

If $\mathcal{P}(q)$ denotes the set of all paths in T starting from an initial state in I and ending in state q, then the shortest distance $d[q]$ is defined as the generalised sum $\oplus$ of the weights of all paths leading to q (Mohri, 2002):

$$d[q] = \oplus_{\pi \in \mathcal{P}(q)} w[\pi] \quad (6)$$

For some semirings, such as the tropical semiring, the shortest distance is the weight of the shortest path. For other semirings, the shortest distance is associated with multiple paths (Mohri, 2002); for these semirings there are shortest distances but need not any be shortest paths. That will be the case in what follows. However, the shortest distance algorithms rely only on general properties of semirings, and once the semiring is specified, the general shortest distance algorithms can be directly employed.

Sokolov and Yvon (2011) define the MERT semiring based on operations described in the previous section. The extend operation is used for the generalised product $\otimes$. The union operation followed by an application of the SweepLine algorithm becomes the generalised sum $\oplus$. The word lattice is then transformed for an initial parameter λ_1^M and direction d_1^M. The weight of edge is mapped from a word specific feature function $h_1^M(e, \mathbf{f})$ to a word specific linear function $\ell_e(\gamma)$. The weight of each path is the generalised product $\otimes$ of the word specific feature linear functions. The upper envelope is the shortest distance of all the paths in the WFST.

3 The Tropical Polynomial Semiring

In this section we introduce the tropical polynomial semiring (Speyer and Sturmfels, 2009) as a replacement for the MERT semiring (Sokolov and Yvon, 2011). We then provide a full description and a worked example of our MERT algorithm.

3.1 Tropical Polynomials

A polynomial is a linear combination of a finite number of non-zero monomials. A monomial consists of a real valued coefficient multiplied by one or more variables, and these variables may have exponents that are non-negative integers. In this section we limit ourselves to a description of a polynomial in a single variable. A polynomial function is defined by evaluating a polynomial:

$$f(\gamma) = a_n\gamma^n + a_{n-1}\gamma^{n-1} + \cdots + a_2\gamma^2 + a_1\gamma + a_0$$

A useful property of these polynomials is that they form a ring[2] (Cox et al., 2007) and therefore are candidates for use as weights in WFSTs.

Speyer and Sturmfels (2009) apply the definition of a classical polynomial to the formulation of a tropical polynomial. The tropical semiring uses summation for the generalised product $\otimes$ and a min operation for the generalised sum $\oplus$. In this form, let γ be a variable that represents an element in the tropical semiring weight set $\mathbb{R} \cup \{-\infty, +\infty\}$. We can write a monomial of γ raised to an integer exponent as

$$\gamma^i = \underbrace{\gamma \otimes \cdots \otimes \gamma}_{i}$$

where i is a non-negative integer. The monomial can also have a constant coefficient: $a \otimes \gamma^i$, $a \in \mathbb{R}$. We can define a function that evaluates a tropical monomial for a particular value of γ. For example, the tropical monomial $a \otimes \gamma^i$ is evaluated as:

$$f(\gamma) = a \otimes \gamma^i = a + i\gamma$$

This shows that a tropical monomial is a linear function with the coefficient a as its y-intercept and the integer exponent i as its gradient. A tropical polynomial is the generalised sum of tropical monomials where the generalised sum is evaluated using the min operation. For example:

$$f(\gamma) = (a \otimes \gamma^i) \oplus (b \otimes \gamma^j) = \min(a + i\gamma, b + j\gamma)$$

Evaluating tropical polynomials in classical arithmetic gives the minimum of a finite collection of linear functions.

Tropical polynomials can also be multiplied by a monomial to form another tropical polynomial. For example:

$$\begin{aligned} f(\gamma) &= [(a \otimes \gamma^i) \oplus (b \otimes \gamma^j)] \otimes (c \otimes \gamma^k) \\ &= [(a + c) \otimes \gamma^{i+k}] \oplus [(b + c) \otimes \gamma^{j+k}] \\ &= \min((a + c) + (i + k)\gamma, (b + c) + (j + k)\gamma) \end{aligned}$$

[2] A ring is a semiring that includes negation.

Our re-formulation of Eq. (4) negates the feature function weights and replaces the argmax by an argmin. This allows us to keep the usual formulation of tropical polynomials in terms of the $\min$ operation when converting Eq. (4) to a tropical representation. What remains to be addressed is the role of integer exponents in the tropical polynomial.

3.2 Integer Realisations for Tropical Monomials

In the previous section we noted that the function defined by the upper envelope in Eq. (4) is similar to the function represented by a tropical polynomial. A significant difference is that the formal definition of a polynomial only allows integer exponents, whereas the gradients in Eq. (4) are real numbers. The upper envelope therefore encodes a larger set of model parameters than a tropical polynomial.

To create an equivalence between the upper envelope and tropical polynomials we can approximate the linear functions $\{\ell_{\mathbf{e}}(\gamma) = a(\mathbf{e}, \mathbf{f}_s) + \gamma \cdot b(\mathbf{e}, \mathbf{f}_s)\}$ that compose segments of the upper envelope. We define $\tilde{a}(\mathbf{e}, \mathbf{f}_s) = [a(\mathbf{e}, \mathbf{f}_s) \cdot 10^n]_{\text{int}}$ and $\tilde{b}(\mathbf{e}, \mathbf{f}_s) = [b(\mathbf{e}, \mathbf{f}_s) \cdot 10^n]_{\text{int}}$ where $[x]_{\text{int}}$ denotes the integer part of x. The approximation to $\ell_{\mathbf{e}}(\gamma)$ is:

$$\ell_{\mathbf{e}}(\gamma) \approx \tilde{\ell}_{\mathbf{e}}(\gamma) = \frac{\tilde{a}(\mathbf{e}, \mathbf{f}_s)}{10^n} + \gamma \cdot \frac{\tilde{b}(\mathbf{e}, \mathbf{f}_s)}{10^n} \quad (7)$$

The result of this operation is to approximate the y-intercept and gradient of $\ell_{\mathbf{e}}(\gamma)$ to n decimal places. We can now represent the linear function $\tilde{\ell}_{\mathbf{e}}(\gamma)$ as the tropical monomial $-\tilde{a}(\mathbf{e}, \mathbf{f}_s) \otimes \gamma^{-\tilde{b}(\mathbf{e}, \mathbf{f}_s)}$. Note that $\tilde{a}(\mathbf{e}, \mathbf{f}_s)$ and $\tilde{b}(\mathbf{e}, \mathbf{f}_s)$ are negated since tropical polynomials define the lower envelope as opposed to the upper envelope defined by Eq. (4).

The linear function represented by the tropical monomial is a scaled version of $\ell_{\mathbf{e}}(\gamma)$, but the upper envelope is unchanged (to the accuracy allowed by n). If for a particular value of γ, $\ell_{\mathbf{e}_i}(\gamma) > \ell_{\mathbf{e}_j}(\gamma)$, then $\tilde{\ell}_{\mathbf{e}_i}(\gamma) > \tilde{\ell}_{\mathbf{e}_j}(\gamma)$. Similarly, the boundary points are unchanged: if $\ell_{\mathbf{e}_i}(\gamma) = \ell_{\mathbf{e}_j}(\gamma)$, then $\tilde{\ell}_{\mathbf{e}_i}(\gamma) = \tilde{\ell}_{\mathbf{e}_j}(\gamma)$. Setting n to a very large value removes numerical differences between the upper envelope and the tropical polynomial representation, as shown by the identical results in Table 1.

Using a scaled version of $\ell_{\mathbf{e}}(\gamma)$ as the basis for a tropical monomial may cause negative exponents to be created. Following Speyer and Sturmfels (2009), we widen the definition of a tropical polynomial to allow for these negative exponents.

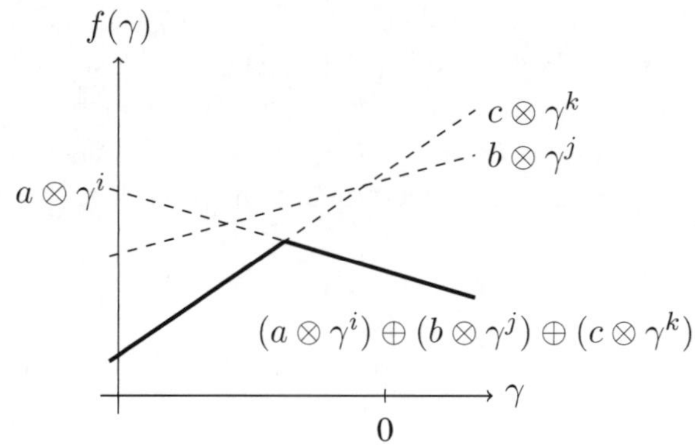

Figure 2: Redundant terms in a tropical polynomial. In this case $(a\otimes\gamma^i)\oplus(b\otimes\gamma^j)\oplus(c\otimes\gamma^k) = (a\otimes\gamma^i)\oplus(c\otimes\gamma^k)$.

3.3 Canonical Form of a Tropical Polynomial

We noted in Section 2.1 that linear functions induced by some hypotheses do not contribute to the upper envelope and can be discarded. Terms in a tropical polynomial can have similar behaviour. Figure 2 plots the lines associated with the three terms of the example polynomial function $f(\gamma) = (a \otimes \gamma^i) \oplus (b \otimes \gamma^j) \oplus (c \otimes \gamma^k)$. We note that the piecewise linear function can also be described with the polynomial $f(\gamma) = (a \otimes \gamma^i) \oplus (c \otimes \gamma^k)$. The latter representation is simpler but equivalent.

Having multiple representations of the same polynomial causes problems when implementing the shortest distance algorithm defined by Mohri (2002). This algorithm performs an equality test between values in the semiring used to weight the WFST. The behaviour of the equality test is ambiguous when there are multiple polynomial representations of the same piecewise linear function. We therefore require a canonical form of a tropical polynomial so that a single polynomial represents a single function. We define the canonical form of a tropical polynomial to be the tropical polynomial that contains only the monomial terms necessary to describe the piecewise linear function it represents.

We remove redundant terms from a tropical polynomial after computing the generalised sum. For a tropical polynomial of one variable we can take advantage of the equivalence with Lattice MERT and compute the canonical form using the SweepLine algorithm (Bentley and Ottmann, 1979). Each term corresponds to a linear function; linear functions that do not contribute to the upper envelope are discarded. Only monomials which correspond to the remaining linear functions are kept in the canonical form. The canonical form of a tropical polynomial thus corresponds to a unique and minimal representation of the upper envelope.

3.4 Relationship to the Tropical Semiring

Tropical monomial weights can be transformed into regular tropical weights by evaluating the tropical monomial for a specific value of γ. For example, a tropical polynomial evaluated at $\gamma = 1$ corresponds to the tropical weight:

$$f(1) = -\tilde{a}(e, \mathbf{f}_s) \otimes 1^{-\tilde{b}(e,\mathbf{f}_s)} = -\tilde{a}(e, \mathbf{f}_s) - \tilde{b}(e, \mathbf{f}_s)$$

Each monomial term in the tropical polynomial shortest distance represents a linear function. The intersection points of these linear functions define intervals of γ (as in Fig. 1). This suggests an alternate explanation for what the shortest distance computed using the tropical polynomial semiring represents. Conceptually, there is a continuum of lattices which have identical edges and vertices but with varying, real-valued edge weights determined by values of $\gamma \in \mathbb{R}$, so that each lattice in the continuum is indexed by γ. The tropical polynomial shortest distance agrees with the shortest distance through each lattice in the continuum.

Our alternate explanation is consistent with the Theorem of Macherey (Section 2.3), as there could never be more paths than edges in the lattice. Therefore the upper bound for the number of monomial terms in the tropical polynomial shortest distance is the number of edges in the input lattice.

We can use the mapping to the tropical semiring to compute the error surface. Let us assume we have $n + 1$ intervals separated by n interval boundaries. We use the midpoint of each interval to transform the lattice of tropical monomial weights into a lattice of tropical weights. The sequence of words that label the shortest path through the transformed lattice is the MAP hypothesis for the interval. The shortest path can be extracted using the WFST shortest path algorithm (Mohri and Riley, 2002). As a technical matter, the midpoints of the first interval $[-\infty, \gamma_1)$ and last interval $[\gamma_n, \infty)$ are not defined. We therefore evaluate the tropical polynomial at $\gamma = \gamma_1 - 1$ and $\gamma = \gamma_n + 1$ to find the MAP hypothesis in the first and last intervals, respectively.

3.5 The TGMERT Algorithm

We now describe an alternative algorithm to Lattice MERT that is formulated using the tropical polynomial shortest distance in one variable. We call the algorithm TGMERT, for Tropical Geometry MERT. As input to this procedure we use a word lattice weighted with word specific feature functions $h_1^M(e, \mathbf{f})$, a starting point λ_1^M, and a direction d_1^M in parameter space.

1. Convert the word specific feature functions $h_1^M(e, \mathbf{f})$ to a linear function $\ell_e(\gamma)$ using λ_1^M and d_1^M, as in Eq. (3).
2. Convert $\ell_e(\gamma)$ to $\tilde{\ell}_e(\gamma)$ by approximating y-intercepts and gradients to n decimal places, as in Eq. (7).
3. Convert $\tilde{\ell}_e(\gamma)$ in Eq. (7) to the tropical monomial $-\tilde{a}(e, \mathbf{f}_s) \otimes \gamma^{-\tilde{b}(e,\mathbf{f}_s)}$.
4. Compute the WFST shortest distance to the exit states (Mohri, 2002) with generalised sum $\oplus$ and generalised product $\otimes$ defined by the tropical polynomial semiring. The resulting tropical polynomial represents the upper envelope of the lattice.
5. Compute the intersection points of the linear functions corresponding to the monomial terms of the tropical polynomial shortest distance. These intersection points define intervals of γ in which the MAP hypothesis does not change.
6. Using the midpoint of each interval convert the tropical monomial $-\tilde{a}(e, \mathbf{f}_s) \otimes \gamma^{-\tilde{b}(e,\mathbf{f}_s)}$ to a regular tropical weight. Find the MAP hypothesis for this interval by extracting the shortest path using the WFST shortest path algorithm (Mohri and Riley, 2002).

3.6 TGMERT Worked Example

This section presents a worked example showing how we can use the TGMERT algorithm to compute the upper envelope of a lattice. We start with a three state lattice with a two dimensional feature vector shown in the upper part of Figure 3.

We want to optimise the parameters along a line in two-dimensional feature space. Suppose the initial parameters are $\lambda_1^2 = [0.7, 0.4]$ and the direction

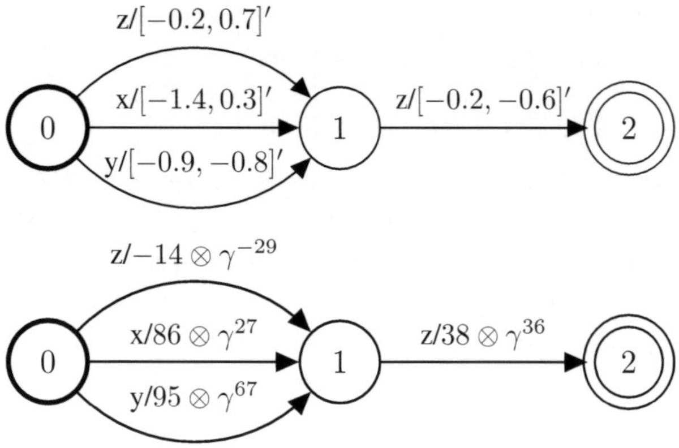

Figure 3: The upper part is a translation lattice with 2-dimensional log feature vector weights $h_1^M(e, \mathbf{f})$ where $M = 2$. The lower part is the lattice from the upper part with weights transformed into tropical monomials.

is $d_1^2 = [0.3, 0.5]$. Step 1 of the TGMERT algorithm (Section 3.5) maps each edge weight to a word specific linear function. For example, the weight of the edge labelled "x" between states 0 and 1 is transformed as follows:

$$\ell_e(\gamma) = \underbrace{\sum_{m=1}^{2} \lambda_m h_1^M(e, \mathbf{f})}_{a(e,\mathbf{f})} + \gamma \underbrace{\sum_{m=1}^{2} d_m h_1^M(e, \mathbf{f_s})}_{b(e,\mathbf{f})}$$

$$= \underbrace{0.7 \cdot -1.4 + 0.4 \cdot 0.3}_{a(e,\mathbf{f})} + \gamma \cdot \underbrace{0.3 \cdot -1.4 + 0.5 \cdot 0.3}_{b(e,\mathbf{f})}$$

$$= -0.86 - 0.27\gamma$$

Step 2 of the TGMERT algorithm converts the word specific linear functions into tropical monomial weights. Since all y-intercepts and gradients have a precision of two decimal places, we scale the linear functions $\ell_\mathbf{e}(\gamma)$ by 10^2 and negate them to create tropical monomials (Step 3). The edge labelled "x" now has the monomial weight of $86 \otimes \gamma^{27}$. The transformed lattice with weights mapped to the tropical polynomial semiring is shown in the lower part of Figure 3.

We can now compute the shortest distance (Mohri, 2002) from the transformed example lattice with tropical monomial weights. There are three unique paths through the lattice corresponding to three distinct hypotheses. The weights associated with these hypotheses are:

$$-14 \otimes \gamma^{-29} \otimes 38 \otimes \gamma^{36} = 24 \otimes \gamma^{7} \qquad \text{z z}$$

$$86 \otimes \gamma^{27} \otimes 38 \otimes \gamma^{36} = 122 \otimes \gamma^{63} \qquad \text{x z}$$

$$95 \otimes \gamma^{67} \otimes 38 \otimes \gamma^{36} = 133 \otimes \gamma^{103} \qquad \text{y z}$$

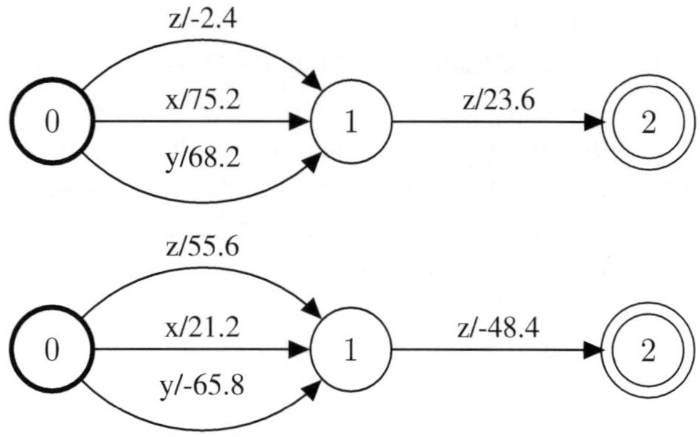

Figure 4: The lattice in the lower part of Figure 3 transformed to regular tropical weights: $\gamma = -0.4$ (top) and $\gamma = -1.4$ (bottom).

The shortest distance from initial to final state is the generalised sum of the path weights: $(24 \otimes \gamma^7) \oplus (133 \otimes \gamma^{103})$. The monomial term $122 \otimes \gamma^{63}$ corresponding to "x z" can be dropped because it is not part of the canonical form of the polynomial (Section 3.3). The shortest distance to the exit state can be represented as the minimum of two linear functions: $\min(24 + 7\gamma, 133 + 103\gamma)$.

We now wish to find the hypotheses that define the error surface by performing Steps 5 and 6 of the TGMERT algorithm. These two linear functions define two intervals of γ. The linear functions intersect at $\gamma \approx -1.4$; at this value of γ the MAP hypothesis changes. Two lattices with regular tropical weights are created using $\gamma = -0.4$ and $\gamma = -2.4$. These are shown in Figure 4. For the lattice shown in the upper part the value for the edge labelled "x" is computed as $86 \otimes -0.4^{27} = 86 + 0.4 \cdot 27 = 75.2$.

When $\gamma = -0.4$ the lattice in the upper part in Figure 4 shows that the shortest path is associated with the hypothesis "z z", which is the MAP hypothesis for the range $\gamma < 1.4$. The lattice in the lower part of Figure 4 shows that when $\gamma = -2.4$ the shortest path is associated with the hypothesis "y z", which is the MAP hypothesis when $\gamma > 1.4$.

3.7 TGMERT Implementation

TGMERT is implemented using the OpenFst Toolkit (Allauzen et al., 2007). A weight class is added for tropical polynomials which maintains them in canonical form. The $\otimes$ and $\oplus$ operations are implemented for piece-wise linear functions, with the SweepLine algorithm included as discussed.

Iteration	Arabic-to-English					
	MERT		LMERT		TGMERT	
	Tune	Test	Tune	Test	Tune	Test
1	36.2		36.2		36.2	
	42.1	40.9	39.7	38.9	39.7	38.9
2	42.0		44.5		44.5	
	45.1	43.2	45.8	44.3	45.8	44.3
3	44.5					
	45.5	44.1				
4	45.6					
	45.7	44.0				

Iteration	Chinese-to-English					
	MERT		LMERT		TGMERT	
	Tune	Test	Tune	Test	Tune	Test
1	19.5		19.5		19.5	
	25.3	16.7	29.3	22.6	29.3	22.6
2	16.4		22.5		22.5	
	18.9	23.9	31.4	32.1	31.4	32.1
3	23.6		31.6		31.6	
	28.2	29.1	32.2	32.5	32.2	32.5
4	29.2		32.2		32.2	
	31.3	31.5	32.2	32.5	32.2	32.5
5	31.3					
	31.8	32.1				
6	32.1					
	32.4	32.3				
7	32.4					
	32.4	32.3				

Table 1: GALE AR→EN and ZH→EN BLEU scores by MERT iteration. BLEU scores at the initial and final points of each iteration are shown for the Tune sets.

4 Experiments

We compare feature weight optimisation using k-best MERT (Och, 2003), lattice MERT (Macherey et al., 2008), and tropical geometry MERT. We refer to these as MERT, LMERT, and TGMERT, resp.

We investigate MERT performance in the context of the Arabic-to-English GALE P4 and Chinese-to-English GALE P3 evaluations[3]. For Arabic-to-English translation, word alignments are generated over around 9M sentences of GALE P4 parallel text. Following de Gispert et al. (2010b), word alignments for Chinese-to-English translation are trained from a subset of 2M sentences of GALE P3 parallel text. Hierarchical rules are extracted from alignments using the constraints described in (Chiang, 2007) with additional count and pattern filters (Iglesias et al., 2009b). We use a hierarchical phrase-based decoder (Iglesias et al., 2009a; de Gispert et al., 2010a) which directly generates word lattices from recursive translation networks without any intermediate hypergraph representation (Iglesias et al., 2011). The LMERT and TGMERT optimisation algorithms are particularly suitable for this realisation of hiero in that the lattice representation avoids the need to use the hypergraph formulation of MERT given by Kumar et al. (2009).

MERT optimises the weights of the following features: target language model, source-to-target and target-to-source translation models, word and rule penalties, number of usages of the glue rule, word deletion scale factor, source-to-target and target-to-source lexical models, and three count-based features that track the frequency of rules in the parallel data (Bender et al., 2007). In both Arabic-to-English and Chinese-to-English experiments all MERT implementations start from a flat feature weight initialization. At each iteration new lattices and k-best lists are generated from the best parameters at the previous iteration, and each subsequent iteration includes 100 hypotheses from the previous iteration. For Arabic-to-English we consider an additional twenty random starting parameters at every iteration. All translation scores are reported for the IBM implementation of BLEU using case-insensitive matching. We report BLEU scores for the Tune set at the start and end of each iteration.

The results for Arabic-to-English and Chinese-to-English are shown in Table 1. Both TGMERT and LMERT converge to a small gain over MERT in fewer iterations, consistent with previous reports (Macherey et al., 2008).

5 Discussion

We have described a lattice-based line optimisation algorithm which can be incorporated into MERT for parameter tuning of SMT systems and systems based on log-linear models. Our approach recasts the optimisation procedure used in MERT in terms of Tropical Geometry; given this formulation implementation is relatively straightforward using standard WFST operations and algorithms.

[3]See http://projects.ldc.upenn.edu/gale/data/catalog.html

References

C. Allauzen, M. Riley, J. Schalkwyk, W. Skut, and M. Mohri. 2007. OpenFst: A general and efficient weighted finite-state transducer library. In *Proceedings of the Ninth International Conference on Implementation and Application of Automata*, pages 11–23.

O. Bender, E. Matusov, S. Hahn, S. Hasan, S. Khadivi, and H. Ney. 2007. The RWTH Arabic-to-English spoken language translation system. In *Automatic Speech Recognition Understanding*, pages 396 –401.

J.L. Bentley and T.A. Ottmann. 1979. Algorithms for reporting and counting geometric intersections. *Computers, IEEE Transactions on*, C-28(9):643 –647.

Daniel Cer, Daniel Jurafsky, and Christopher D. Manning. 2008. Regularization and search for minimum error rate training. In *Proceedings of the Third Workshop on Statistical Machine Translation*, pages 26–34.

David Chiang. 2007. Hierarchical phrase-based translation. *Computational Linguistics*, 33.

David A. Cox, John Little, and Donal O'Shea. 2007. *Ideals, Varieties, and Algorithms: An Introduction to Computational Algebraic Geometry and Commutative Algebra, 3/e (Undergraduate Texts in Mathematics)*.

Adrià de Gispert, Gonzalo Iglesias, Graeme Blackwood, Eduardo R. Banga, and William Byrne. 2010a. Hierarchical phrase-based translation with weighted finite-state transducers and shallow-n grammars. *Computational Linguistics*, 36(3):505–533.

Adrià de Gispert, Juan Pino, and William Byrne. 2010b. Hierarchical phrase-based translation grammars extracted from alignment posterior probabilities. In *Proceedings of the 2010 Conference on Empirical Methods in Natural Language Processing*, pages 545–554.

Chris Dyer, Adam Lopez, Juri Ganitkevitch, Jonathan Weese, Ferhan Ture, Phil Blunsom, Hendra Setiawan, Vladimir Eidelman, and Philip Resnik. 2010. cdec: A decoder, alignment, and learning framework for finite-state and context-free translation models. In *Proceedings of the ACL 2010 System Demonstrations*, pages 7–12, July.

Gonzalo Iglesias, Adrià de Gispert, Eduardo R. Banga, and William Byrne. 2009a. Hierarchical phrase-based translation with weighted finite state transducers. In *Proceedings of HLT: The 2009 Annual Conference of the North American Chapter of the Association for Computational Linguistics*, pages 433–441.

Gonzalo Iglesias, Adrià de Gispert, Eduardo R. Banga, and William Byrne. 2009b. Rule filtering by pattern for efficient hierarchical translation. In *Proceedings of the 12th Conference of the European Chapter of the Association for Computational Linguistics*, pages 380–388.

Gonzalo Iglesias, Cyril Allauzen, William Byrne, Adrià de Gispert, and Michael Riley. 2011. Hierarchical phrase-based translation representations. In *Proceedings of the 2011 Conference on Empirical Methods in Natural Language Processing*, pages 1373–1383. Association for Computational Linguistics.

Philipp Koehn. 2010. *Statistical Machine Translation*. Cambridge University Press.

Shankar Kumar, Wolfgang Macherey, Chris Dyer, and Franz Och. 2009. Efficient minimum error rate training and minimum bayes-risk decoding for translation hypergraphs and lattices. In *Proceedings of the Joint Conference of the 47th Annual Meeting of the ACL and the 4th International Joint Conference on Natural Language Processing of the AFNLP*, pages 163–171.

Wolfgang Macherey, Franz Och, Ignacio Thayer, and Jakob Uszkoreit. 2008. Lattice-based minimum error rate training for statistical machine translation. In *Proceedings of the 2008 Conference on Empirical Methods in Natural Language Processing*, pages 725–734.

Mehryar Mohri and Michael Riley. 2002. An efficient algorithm for the n-best-strings problem. In *Proceedings of the International Conference on Spoken Language Processing 2002*.

Mehryar Mohri, Fernando C. N. Pereira, and Michael Riley. 2008. Speech recognition with weighted finite-state transducers. *Handbook on Speech Processing and Speech Communication*.

Mehryar Mohri. 2002. Semiring frameworks and algorithms for shortest-distance problems. *J. Autom. Lang. Comb.*, 7(3):321–350.

Franz Josef Och and Hermann Ney. 2002. Discriminative training and maximum entropy models for statistical machine translation. In *Proceedings of the 40th Annual Meeting on Association for Computational Linguistics*, pages 295–302.

Franz Josef Och. 2003. Minimum error rate training in statistical machine translation. In *Proceedings of the 41st Annual Meeting on Association for Computational Linguistics*, pages 160–167.

K. A. Papineni, S. Roukos, T. Ward, and W. Zhu. 2002. BLEU: a method for automatic evaluation of machine translation. In *Proceedings of the 40th Annual Meeting on Association for Computational Linguistics*, pages 311–318.

W. H. Press, W. T. Vetterling, S. A. Teukolsky, and B. P. Flannery. 2002. *Numerical Recipes in C++: the art of scientific computing*. Cambridge University Press.

J. Richter-Gebert, B. Sturmfels, and T. Theobald. 2005. First steps in tropical geometry. In *Idempotent mathematics and mathematical physics*.

Artem Sokolov and François Yvon. 2011. Minimum error rate training semiring. In *Proceedings of the European Association for Machine Translation*.

David Speyer and Bernd Sturmfels. 2009. Tropical mathematics. *Mathematics Magazine*.

Aurelien Waite, Graeme Blackwood, and William Byrne. 2011. Lattice-based minimum error rate training using weighted finite-state transducers with tropical polynomial weights. Technical report, Department of Engineering, University of Cambridge.

Richard Zens, Sasa Hasan, and Hermann Ney. 2007. A systematic comparison of training criteria for statistical machine translation. In *Proceedings of the 2007 Joint Conference on Empirical Methods in Natural Language Processing and Computational Natural Language Learning*, pages 524–532.

Author Index

Association for Computational Linguistics
209 N. Eighth Street
Stroudsburg, Pennsylvania 18360

CURRAN ASSOCIATES INC
proceedings.com

4th International Workshop on Semantic Evaluations 2007

(SemEval 2007)

Held in conjunction with ACL 2007

Prague, Czech Republic
23-24 June 2007

ISBN: 978-1-61738-517-9